"America's greatest cartoonist."
—*Connoisseur*

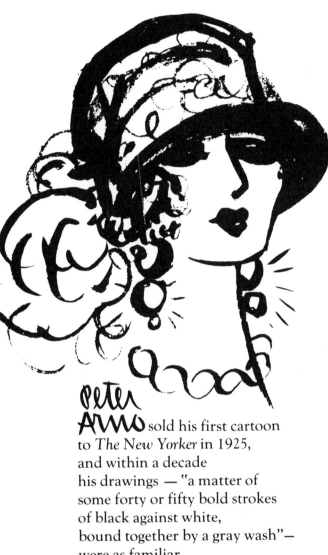

Peter Arno sold his first cartoon
to *The New Yorker* in 1925,
and within a decade
his drawings — "a matter of
some forty or fifty bold strokes
of black against white,
bound together by a gray wash"—
were as familiar
to most Americans as
Henry Ford's cars.
Over the next forty-three years,
until his death in 1968,
the *New Yorker* magazine
would publish hundreds of Arnos;
and the flamboyant young man
who sold his first drawing
to them for $35
would become one of the world's
most successful artists.

Peter Arno

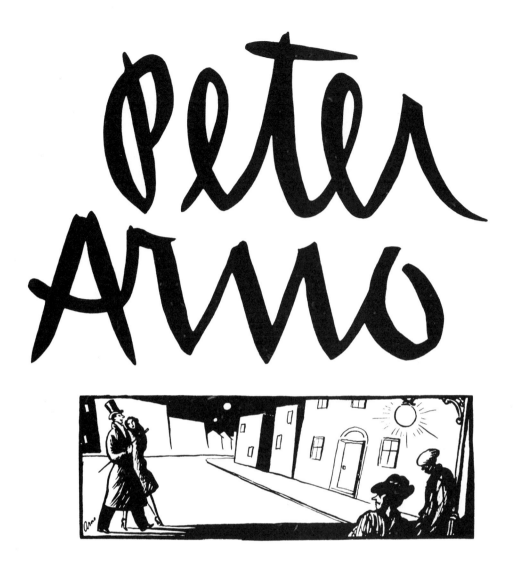

With an Introduction by Charles Saxon

BEAUFORT BOOKS PUBLISHERS
A PETER WEED BOOK
New York

The small drawing on this book's title page was published
by *The New Yorker* on June 20, 1925, and was the first
of Peter Arno's to appear in that magazine.

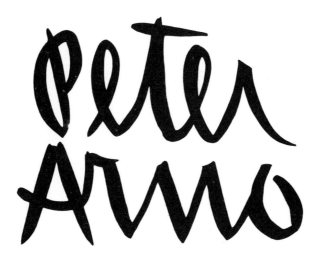

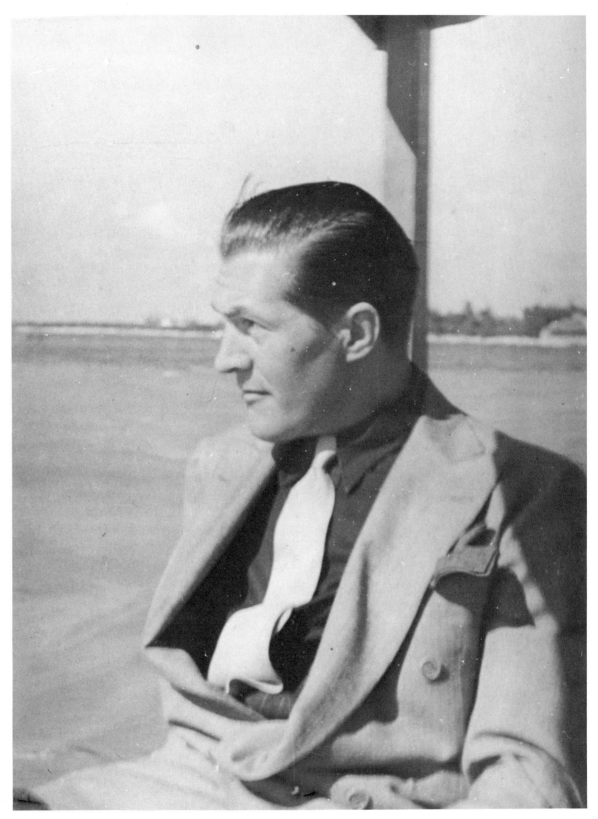

PETER ARNO
1904–1968

Introduction

The New Yorker magazine is nearly fifty-five years old and a new generation of editors, writers, and artists has taken the place of the grand old giants. Looking back, anyone will immediately recognize that much of the best literature produced in America over the last half century either appeared first in *The New Yorker* or was written by people closely associated with the magazine, from E. B. White to Isaac Bashevis Singer, from James Thurber to John Updike. And John O'Hara, Wolcott Gibbs, Janet Flanner, Edmund Wilson, Rachel Carson, and on and on. *The New Yorker*, quite simply, has been the standard for excellence in publishing.

The names of the artists whose work appeared side by side with the text are not as easy to recall. Although, collectively, the cartoons and cover paintings are remembered with warm enthusiasm, many of the earlier names have faded into limbo—a company that includes such serious artists as Reginald Marsh, Miguel Covarrubias, Ludwig Bemelmans, and Peter Arno.

And Peter Arno. In 1929, when Arno's first collection of drawings appeared in anthology, William Bolitho's preface perceived his growing stature, comparing Arno to the great comic artists Daumier, Leech, Rowlandson, and Cruikshank. Bolitho wrote, "Peter Arno will live. Preserve this volume and your grandchildren will bless your name." Arno hardly subsided into obscurity; he continued to draw for *The New Yorker* for forty-three years and produced drawings that were increasingly more forceful, more glowing until his death in 1968. Unlike the current giant Saul Steinberg, Arno remained throughout his life almost completely identified with *The New Yorker* and nearly all the drawings reproduced in this collection are reprinted from its pages.

But today, although much of Arno's original work was purchased by private collectors as he became an instant celebrity, Bolitho's prediction is yet to be fulfilled. No exhibition of Arno's cartoons and paintings has been hung in a major museum, nor has any art critic published a considered appreciation of his work, even at the time of his death.

We live in a strange period of art history, a time when any experimentation, however bizarre, is eagerly embraced and cultivated by critics and galleries. Hanging a curtain ten miles long across a valley is hailed as a creative breakthrough. Replicas of Campbell soup cans are endowed with deep insight into the human condition and are proudly displayed by rich connoisseurs. Some paint targets or American flags, or drip house paint on enormous canvases. No one would deny these artists their talent and the attention they get—experimentation is the lifeblood of creativity. What is disturbing is the tacit concord among experts that excludes from serious consideration any work they define as commercial—that is, produced for money on assignment. Cartoons, though the category includes Hogarth's engravings and the bitter sketches of George Grosz, are generally treated with "benign neglect." Steinberg's recent overwhelming show at the Whitney led to speculation among critics as to precisely when, during Steinberg's growth, he stopped being a cartoonist and became an artist.

I have no intention of trying to resolve this delicate distinction. I come to praise Peter Arno, not to battle the tastemakers. Let us rejoice that, within the phenomenon of *The New Yorker*'s birth, an artist of Arno's brilliance emerged and found in the rather strictly proscribed format of a magazine full scope to develop into one of the most fluent graphic artists of our time. As James Geraghty (his editor and friend for over thirty years) points out, Arno did not adapt to the character of *The New Yorker*; rather, he was one of the most important factors in forming it.

In looking over the many hundreds of cartoons that make up the totality of Arno's output, it becomes obvious that as jokes (that's what Harold Ross called them, "the jokes") they are not equally funny. Some ideas have become dated, some were forced humor to start with. Don't be shocked; one finds the same inconsistency in Beerbohm or Rowlandson or, indeed, in any artist or writer working toward deadlines. Remember that a publication rolling off the presses week after week, fifty-two times a year, must make concessions to necessity. This is not an apology, it's a recognition of reality. The marvelous thing is that so many of the cartoons remain fresh, charming, and pertinent. *The New Yorker* holds a remarkably high average for memorable cartoon ideas. Some have even become part of the language: "I say it's spinach and the hell with it." "Take me to your leader." "Well, back to the old drawing board." The last, of course, was Arno's.

Even the weaker ideas that Arno illustrated offer the opportunity to admire the power and uniqueness of his unmistakably personal style. The cartoon form, at its best, is a perfect union of idea and visual conception—one meaningless without the other and, together, a satiric insight into our social or political foibles. Arno was on target most of the time and, as with all great cartoonists, his drawings can be studied on several other levels: the grace of his line, the subtlety of his composition, the wonderful caricatures of his people, and above all the incisive reportage of his milieu. Like John Held, Jr., Arno has left to social historians a rich legacy of the mores of his time.

Arno was very much a part of the society he satirized. Born Curtis Arnoux Peters (he juggled his name to avoid embarrassing the family), he was the son of a prosperous judge, sent to Hotchkiss and Yale. He left college to form a jazz band (classmate Rudy Vallee was his vocalist). At the start of the 1920s, Arno was the prototype of his era—handsome, rich, breezy and multi-talented—and when in open shirt and tennis shoes he brought his first batch of drawings to Katharine White at *The New Yorker*, he was accepted almost immediately. The wonder is that, given this heritage, Arno was driven to the self-discipline of his art.

Perhaps the greatest influence in his early work was his admiration for Daumier, whose lithographic pencil and bold forms were echoed in Arno's work until the development of the even bolder lines and simplified halftones

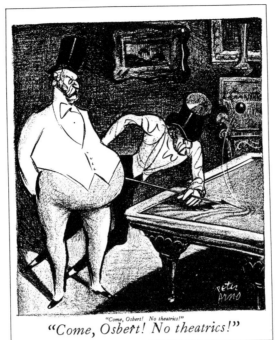

"Come, Osbert! No theatrics!"

"Come, Osbert! No theatrics!"

that identify his mature style. It is no surprise that the only pictures Arno ever bought and hung were by Rouault.

There was a dark side to Peter Arno's character, as there is in many men of genius. Why did his two marriages end in failure? Why did he become pathologically miserly? Why did he alienate himself from all his friends? It would take a book and much more knowledge than I have to attempt an explanation. We know he moved from his Park Avenue duplex to a farmhouse in Harrison, New York, alone with his music, his guns, his sport cars, and his drawings. For years, a daily phone call to Geraghty was his only touch with the magazine and the outside world.

Some critics submit as a distinction between true art and commercial art the idea that the first is inner directed and the other mere artisanship, products on order. Anyone who had the opportunity to watch Arno at work (as very few ever had) would know the intensity of his search for truth. During these later years, when the dashing young man-about-town had become a haunted recluse, work was all. His style had now matured from almost flamboyant facility to uncompromising simplicity. He sometimes stayed in his studio for forty hours at a stretch, the walls lined with dozens of versions of the same drawing, as still he pressed for a purer expression of the essence of the concept.

Peter Arno died alone, aged beyond his sixty-four years from the effects of emphysema and cancer. At his funeral only a small group came to the church and, after the service, his daughter Pat showed those attending a fairly recent photograph of her father. Except for herself, Geraghty, and Arno's devoted nurse-companion, no one had actually seen him for years.

Arno's last cartoon appeared in *The New Yorker* the week he died. It was a picture of a nymph reclining in the forest who says to a fawn prancing by, "Oh, grow up?" It was Arno at his blithe best, and a beautiful drawing.

CHARLES SAXON

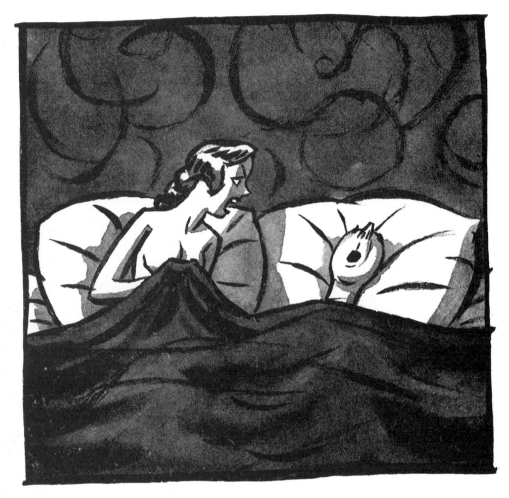

"Wake up, you mutt! We're getting married today."

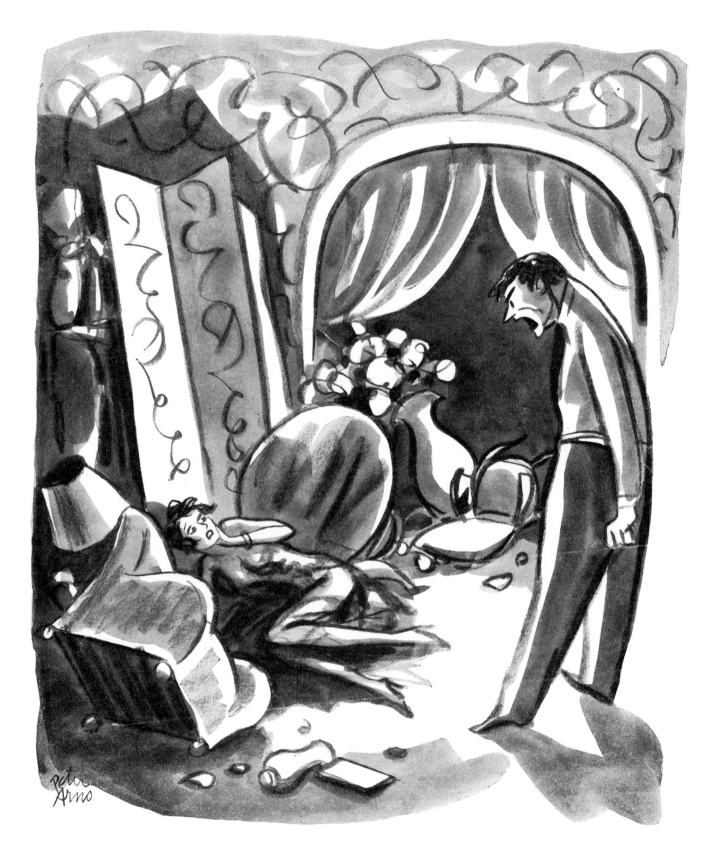

"What the hell d'yuh mean, I'm disagreeable?"

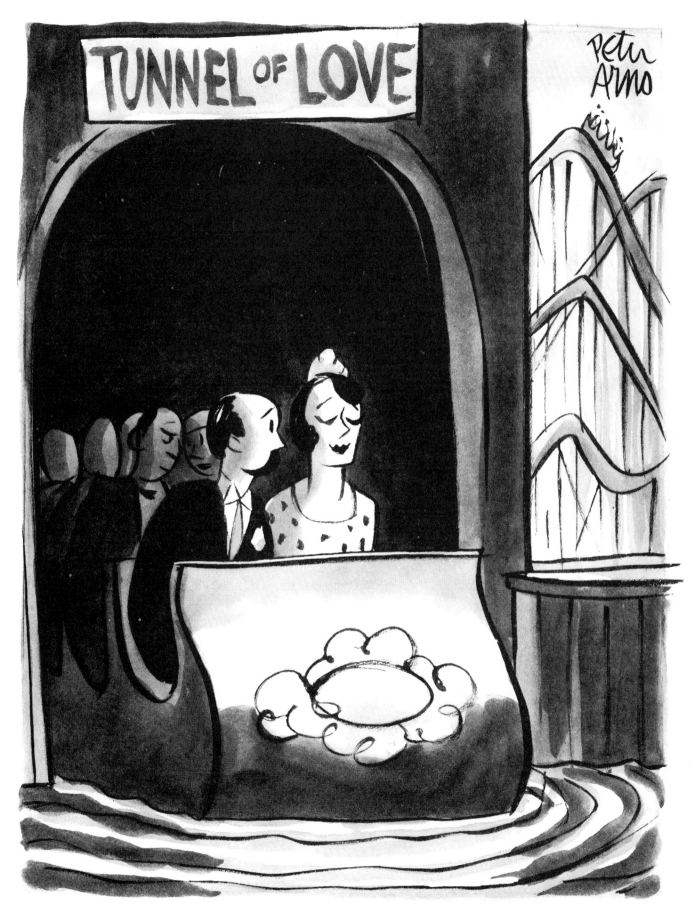

"Ella, I want you to be my wife."

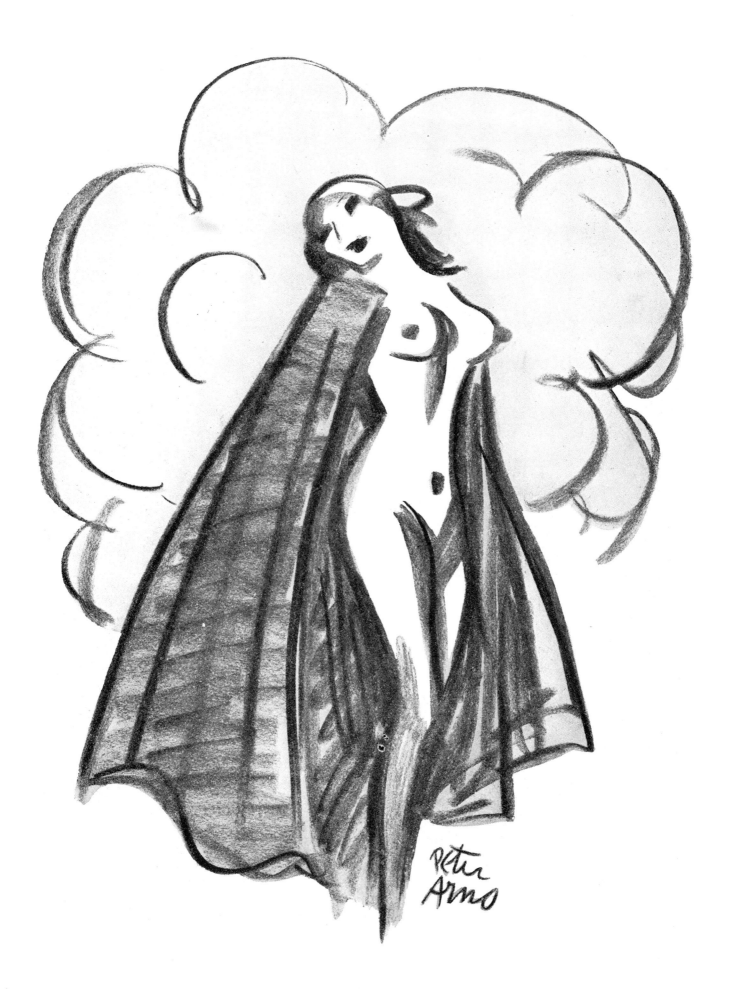

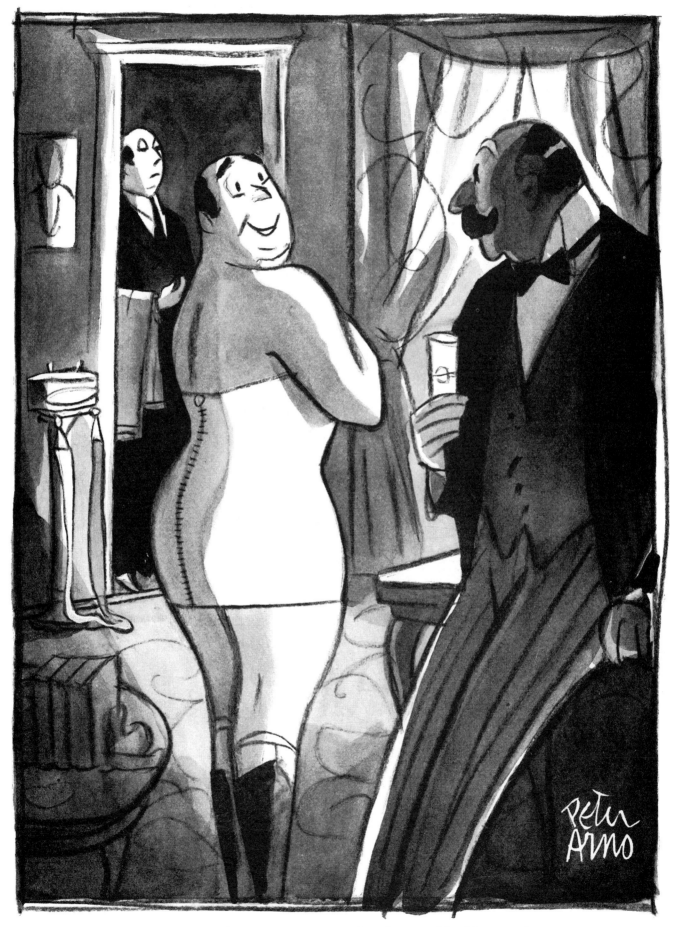

"*Oh, I just send my measurements to London—and back it comes.*"

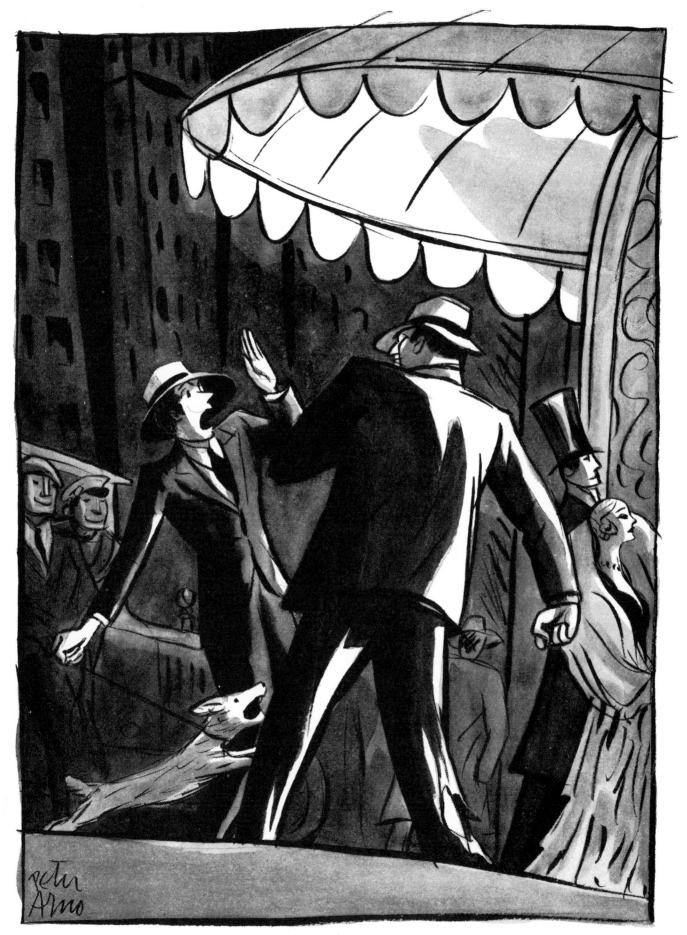

"Now stop and think a minute—did_I bite you?"

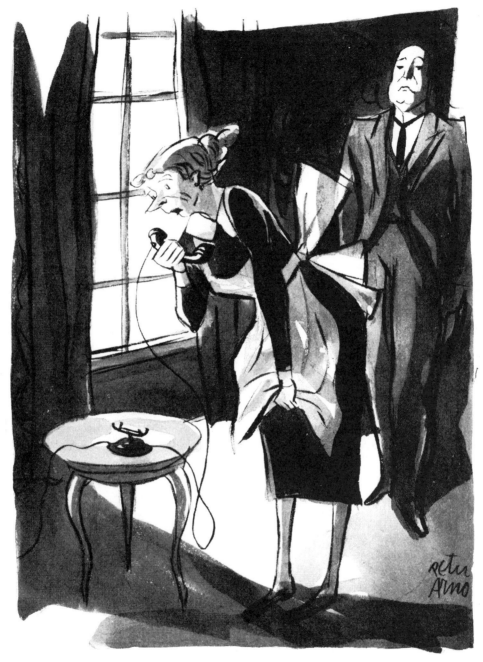

"Wait, I call de butler. He knows more den I do."

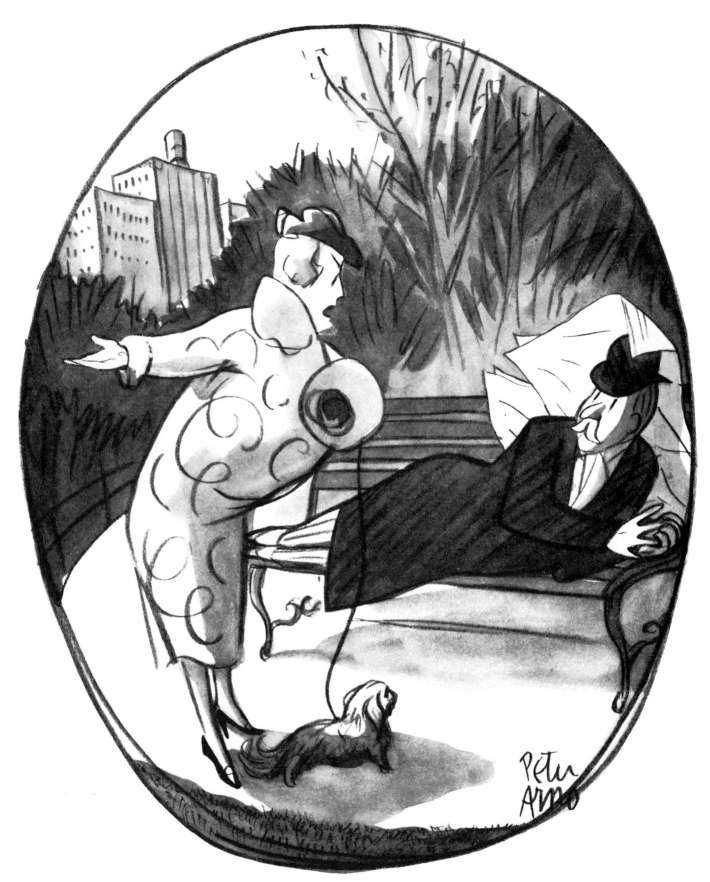

"*The idea, Mr. Schuyler! You could perfectly well have stayed at our house.*"

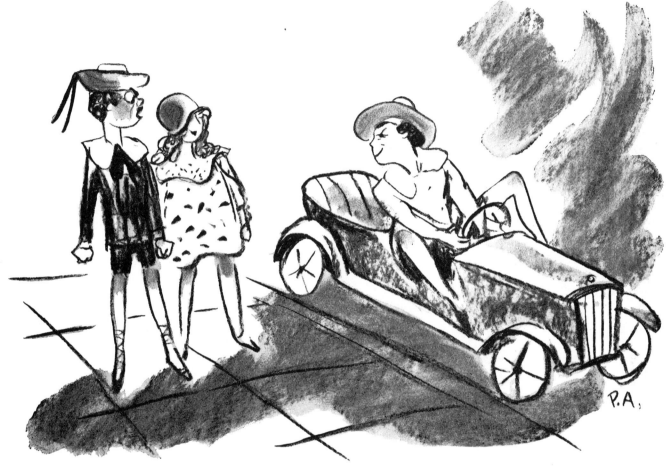

"Don't be a rotter, Farnsworth!"

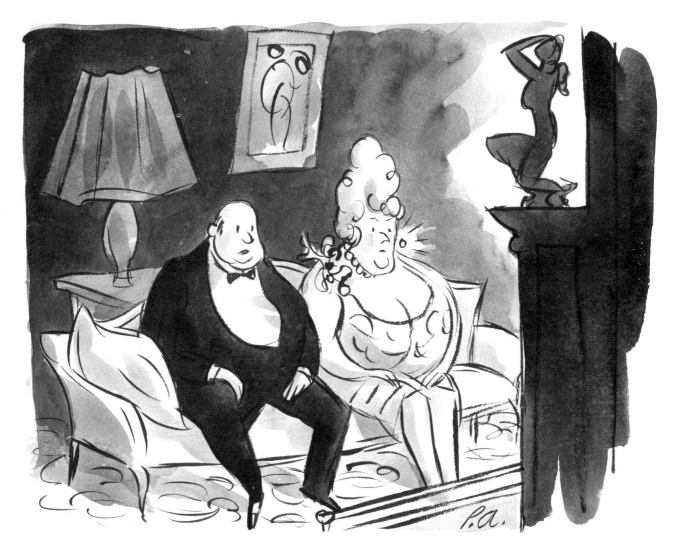

"*Do you remember the night of the hay ride, when you wore that little white muslin dress?*"

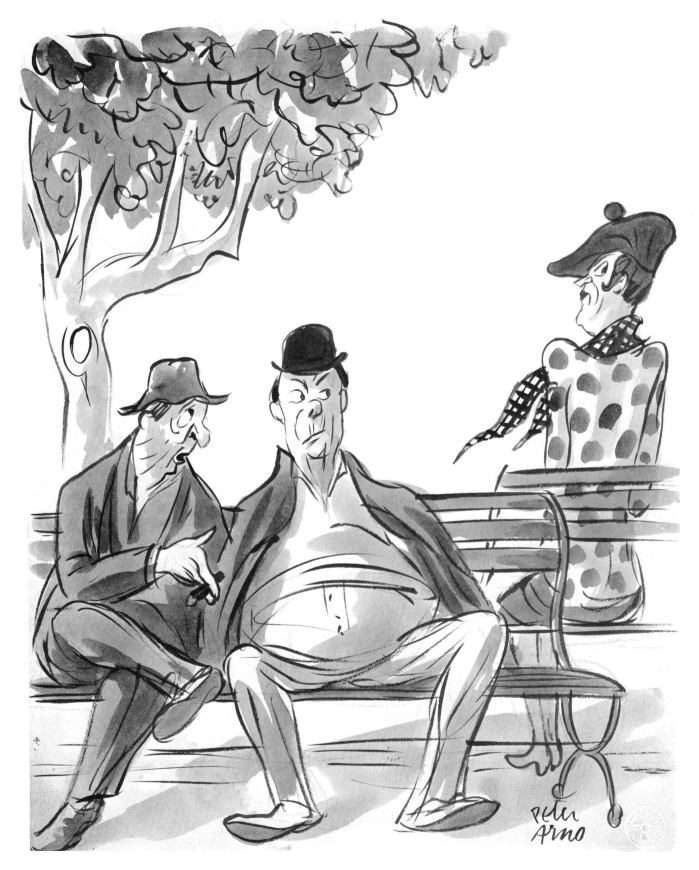

"Demi-monde, ain't she?"

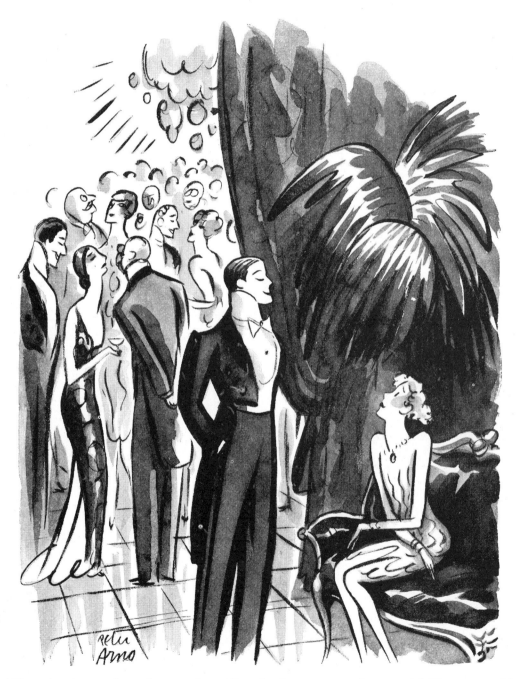

"You do give such perfect parties, Alice. Is there anyone here you'd like to meet?"

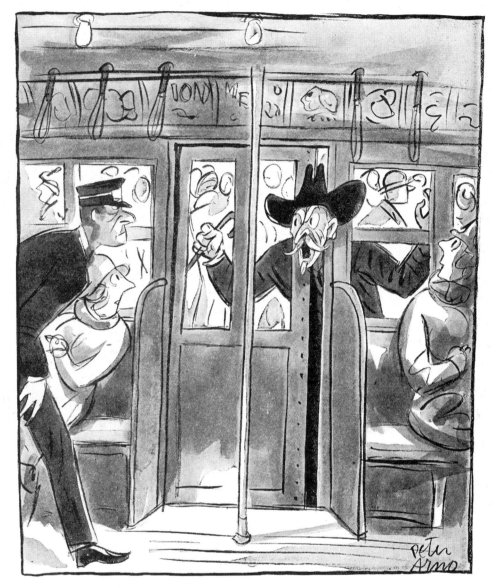

"By God, Suh—Ah won't fohget this insult!"

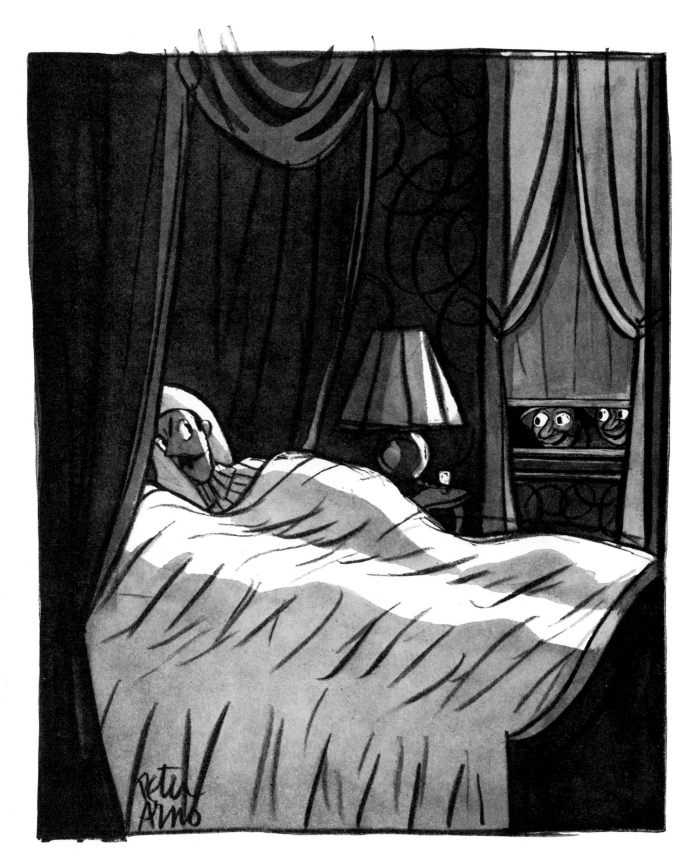

"Pretend you don't notice them."

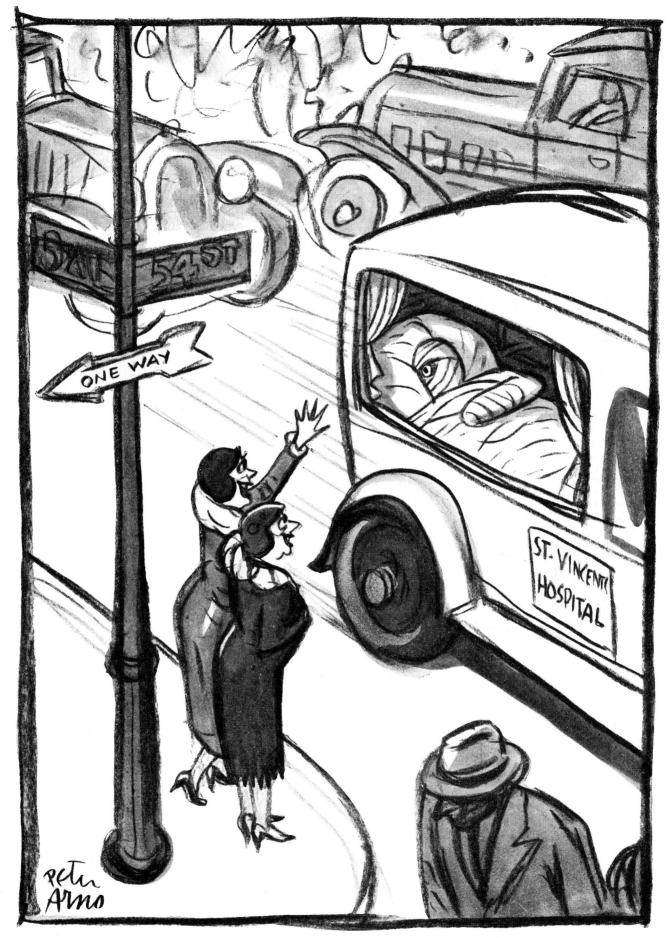

"Isn't that Mr. Moglethoid? Hi there, Mr. Moglethoid!"

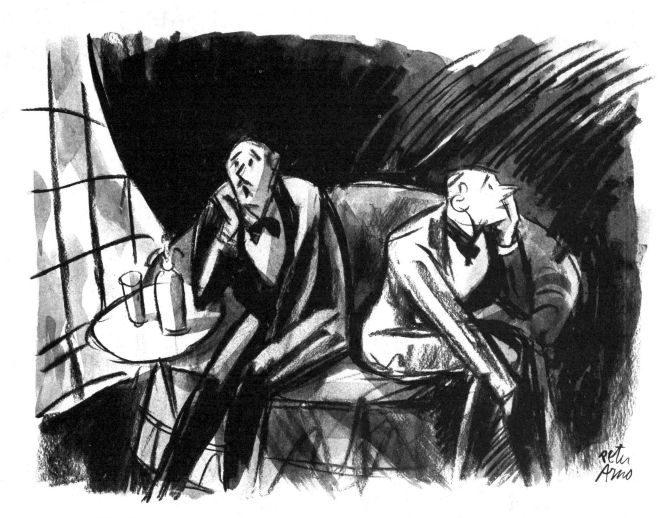

"I'm lost, Farnsworth, without a pretty woman, or a little animal of some kind."

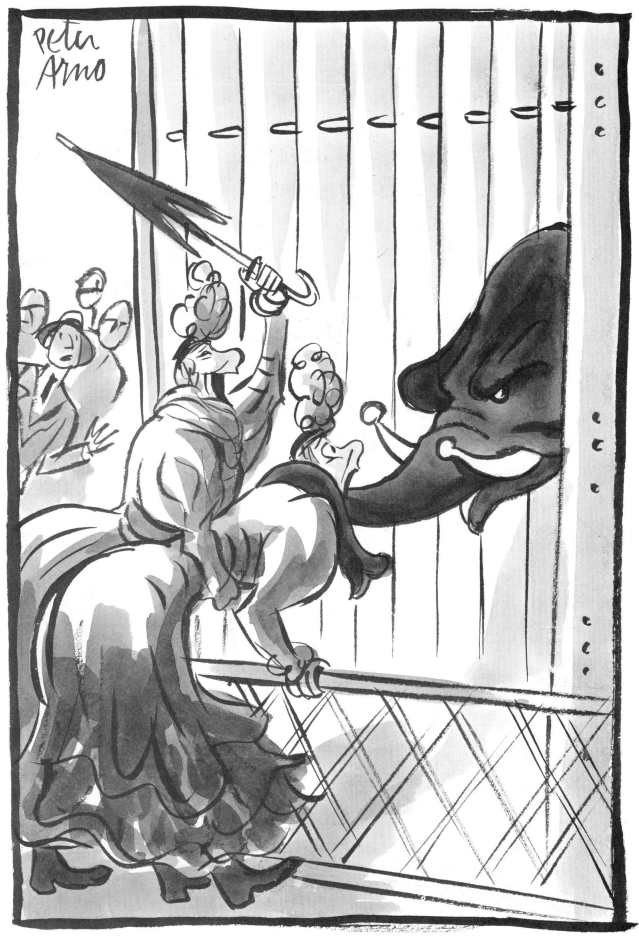

"Whoops! I told y' not t' tempt 'im!"

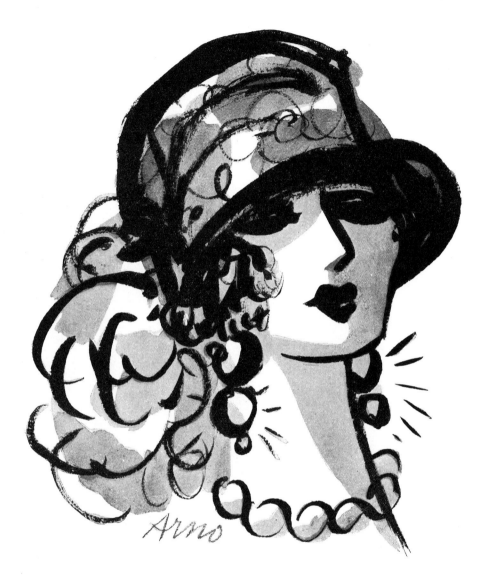

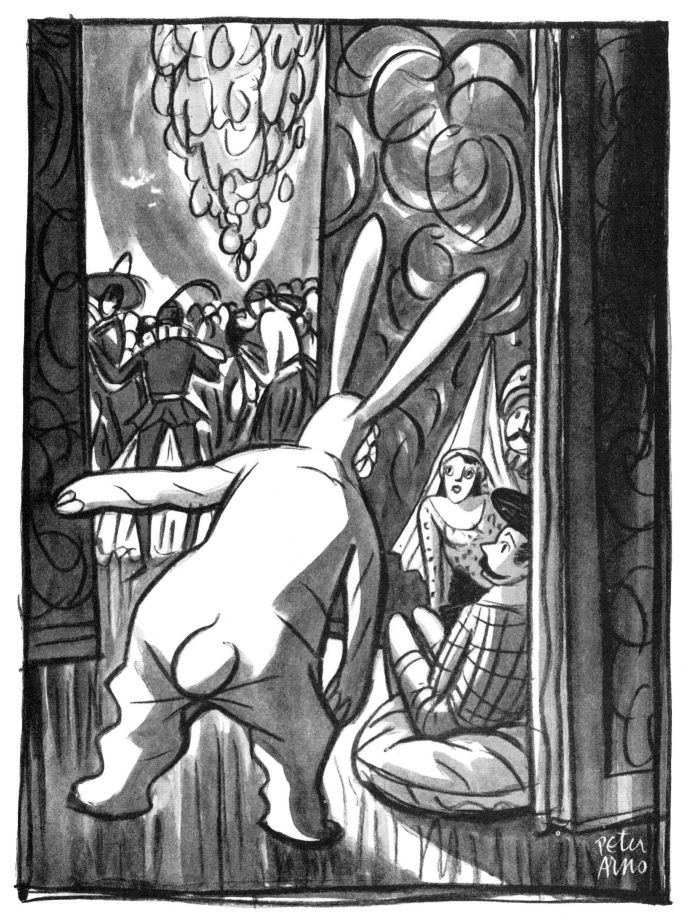

"This is going too far, Remson! Someone's purloined my Burberry!"

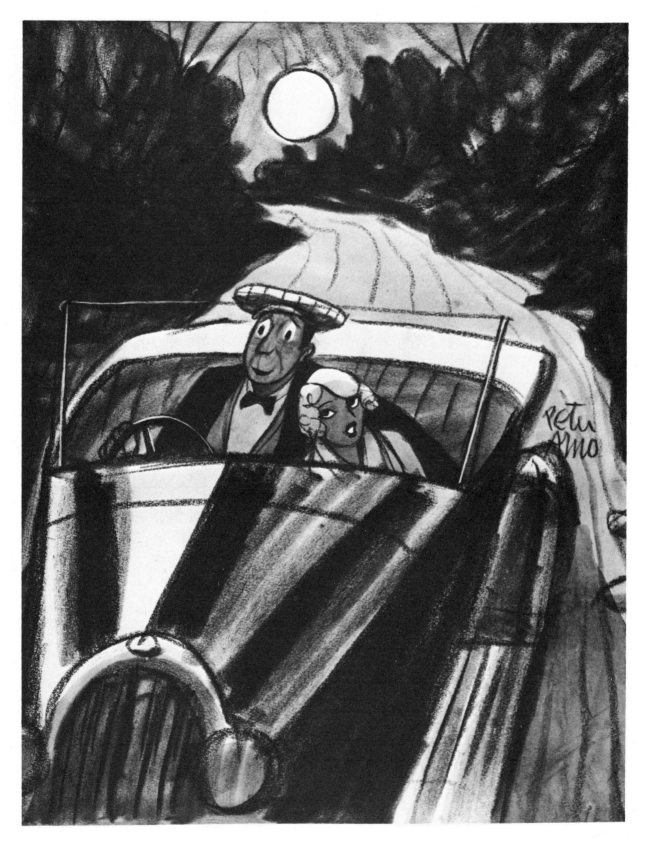

"I adore driving at night, but once I got my foot caught in a bear trap."

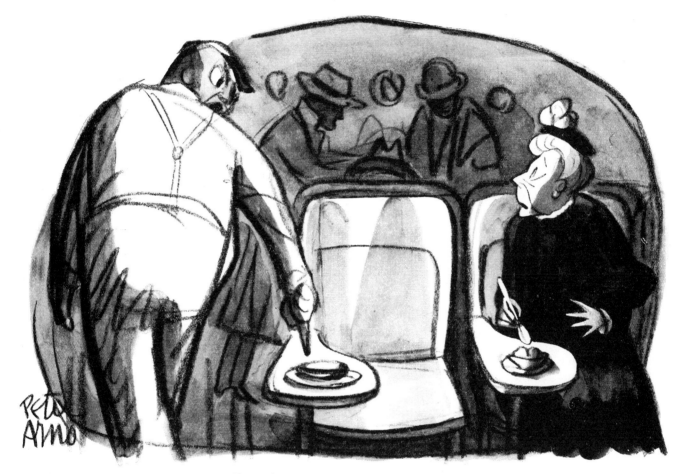

"*Will yuh keep an eye on my hamboigh, sister?*"

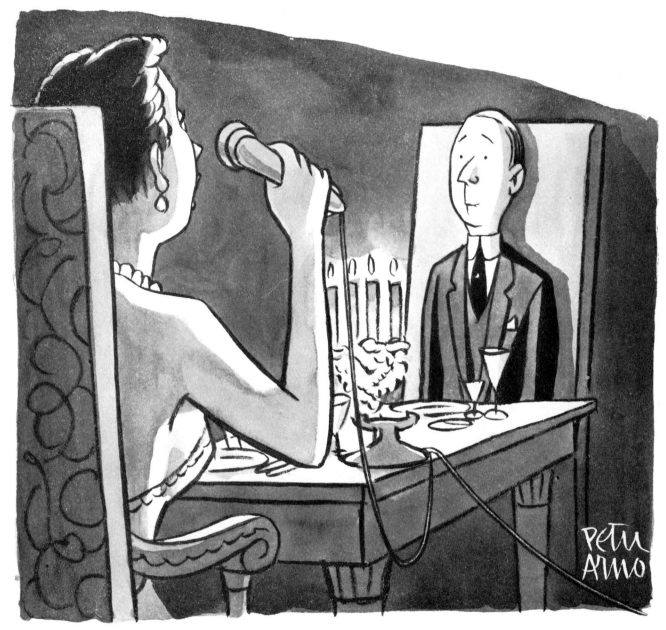

"There's someone answers your description at the Morgue. Shall I say it isn't you?"

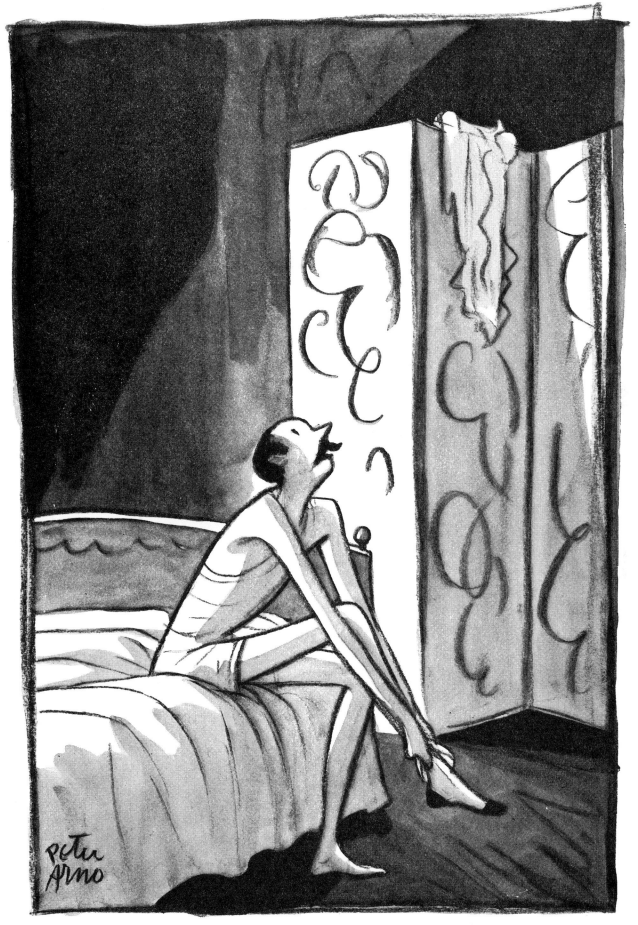

"See, darling, I told you we couldn't have a Platonic friendship."

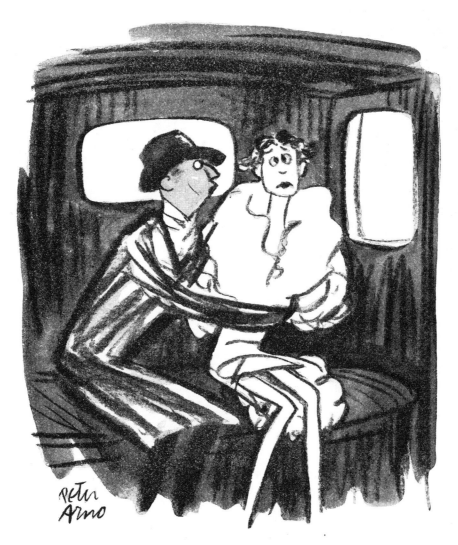

"*Just one little kiss—to remember you by.*"

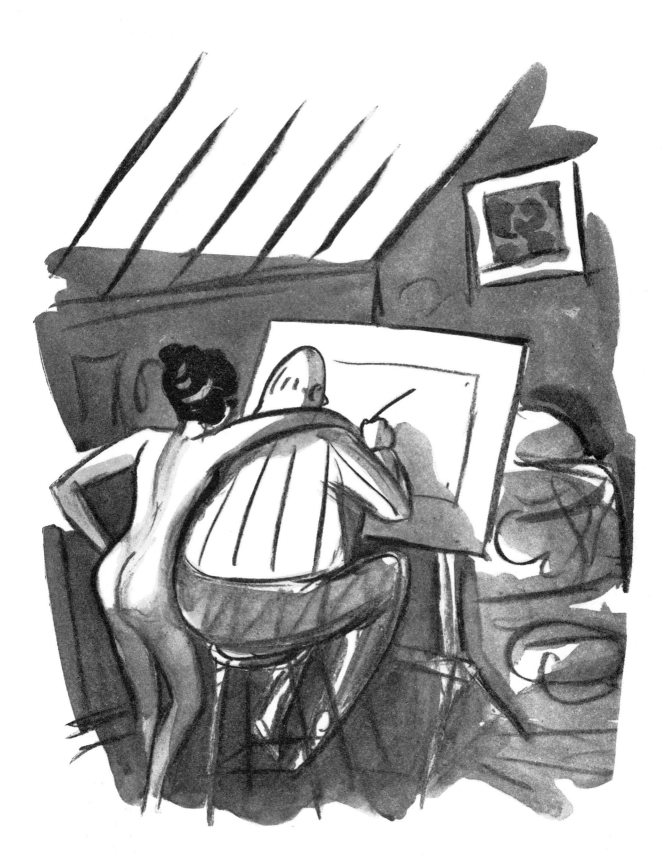

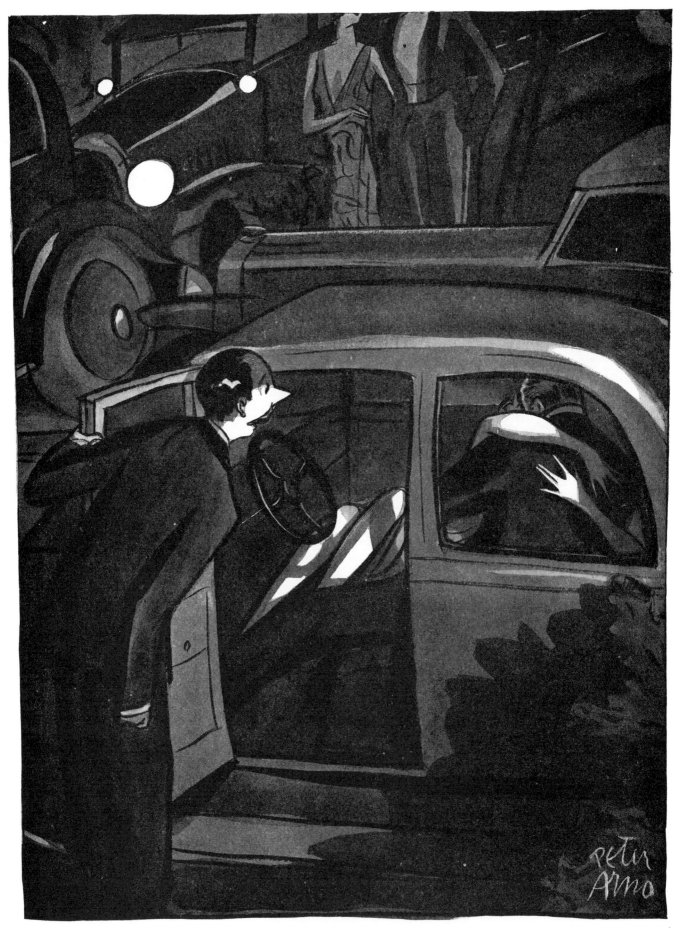

"*Er—is that you, Gwendolyn? I believe this is our dance, Gwendolyn.*"

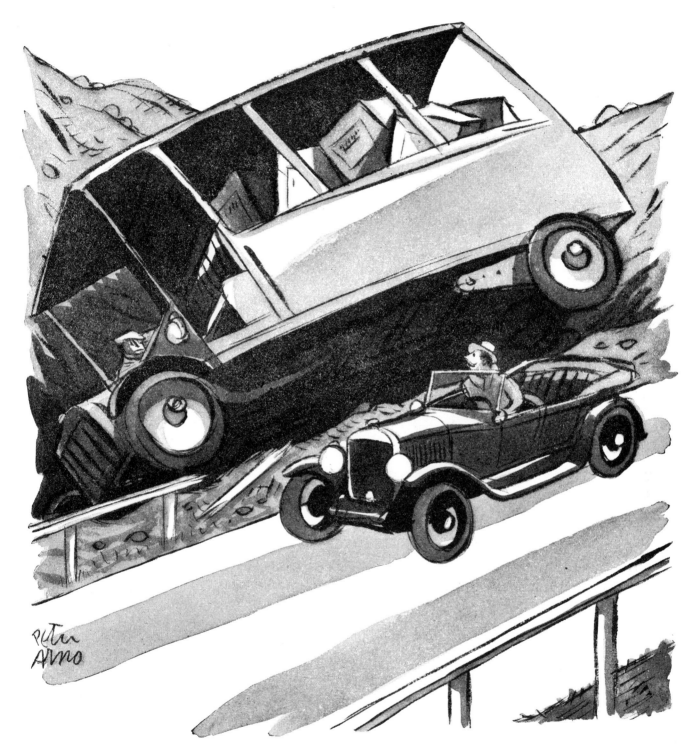

"Tip over?"

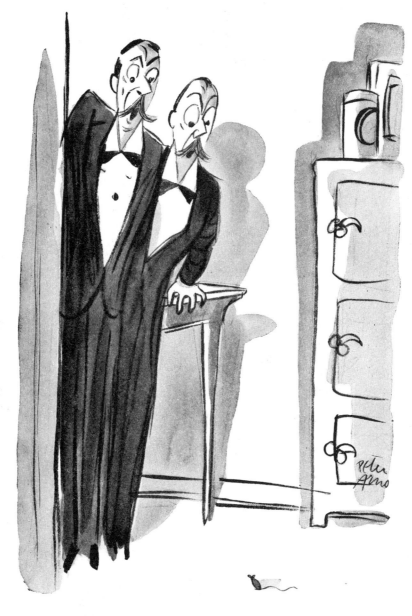

"Cornered, by Gad!"

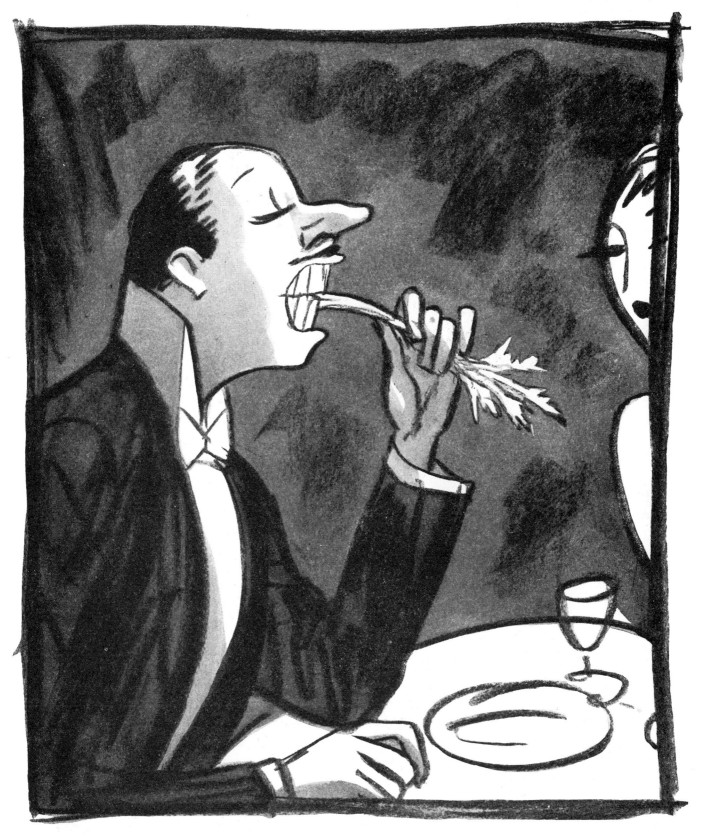

Celery

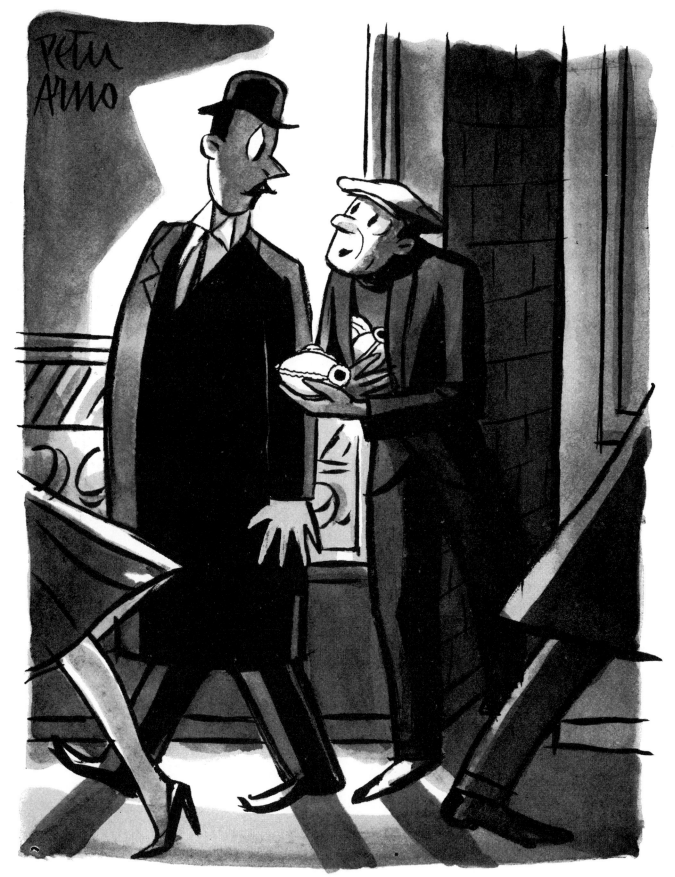

"Feelthy Easter eggs?"

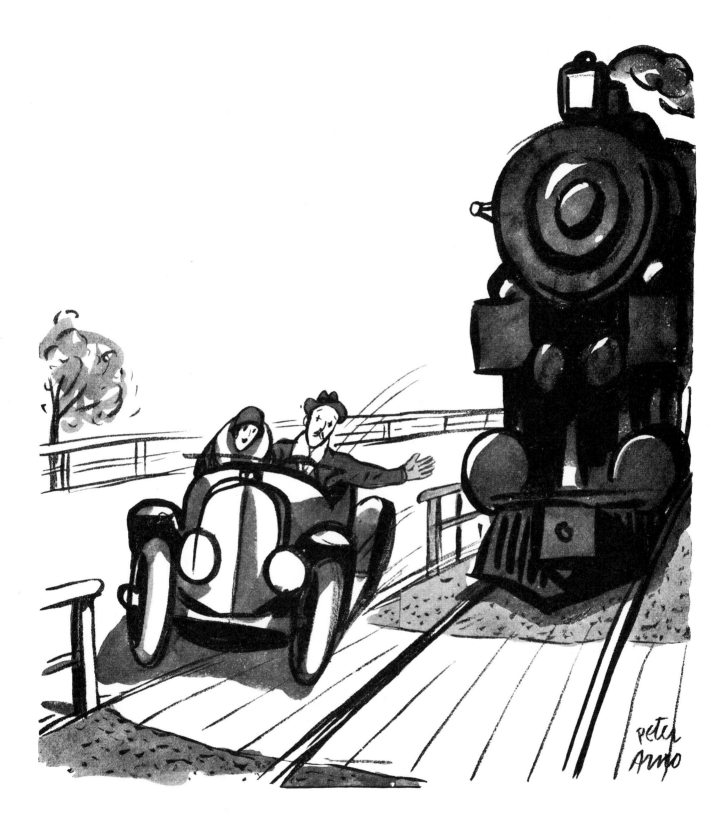

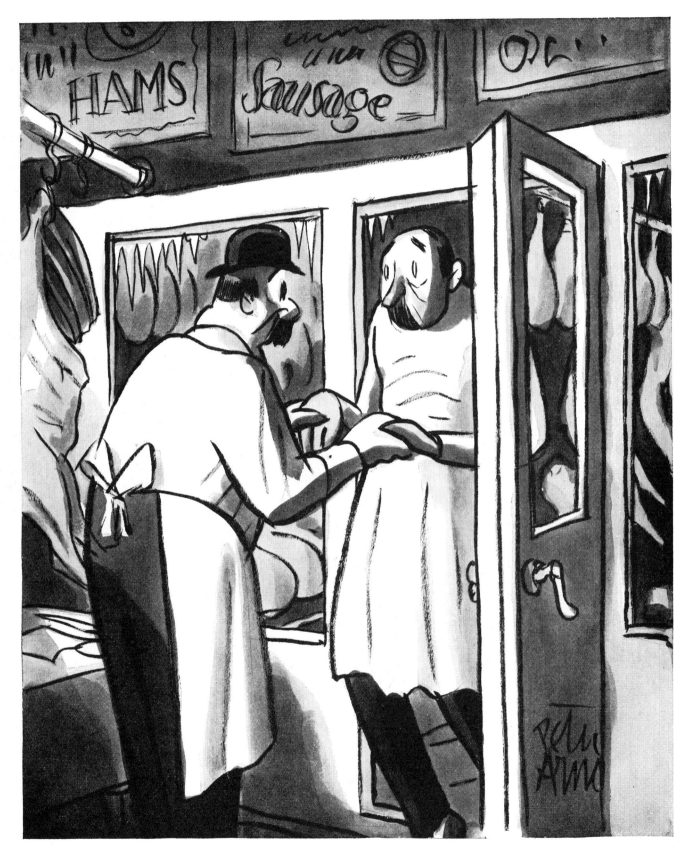

"Why, Alfred! Your hands are like _ice_!"

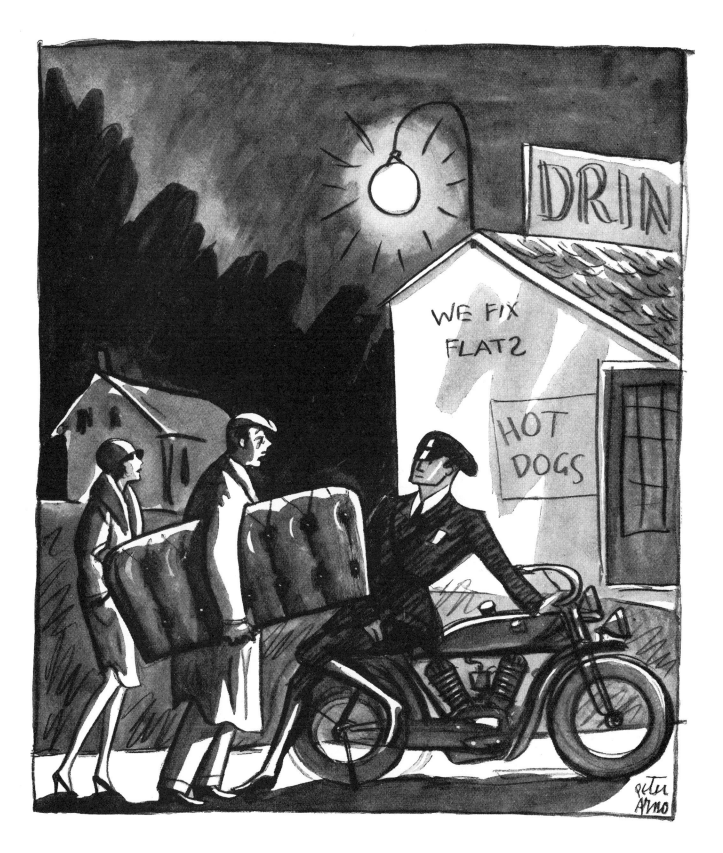

"We want to report a stolen car."

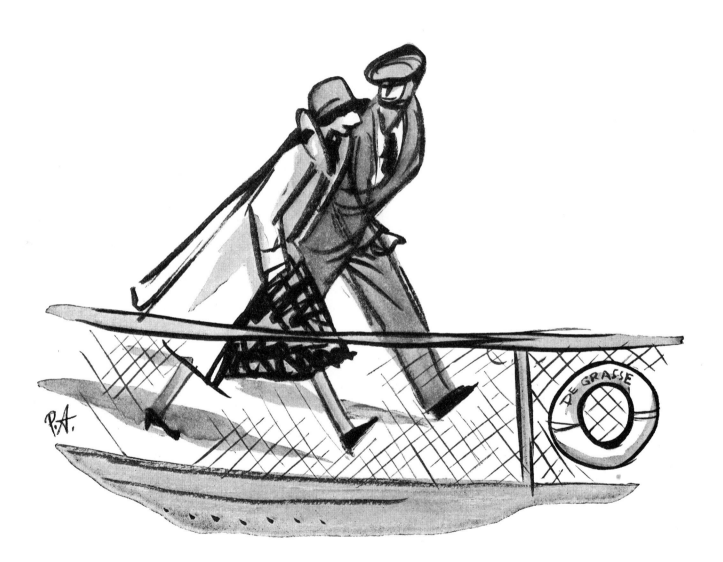

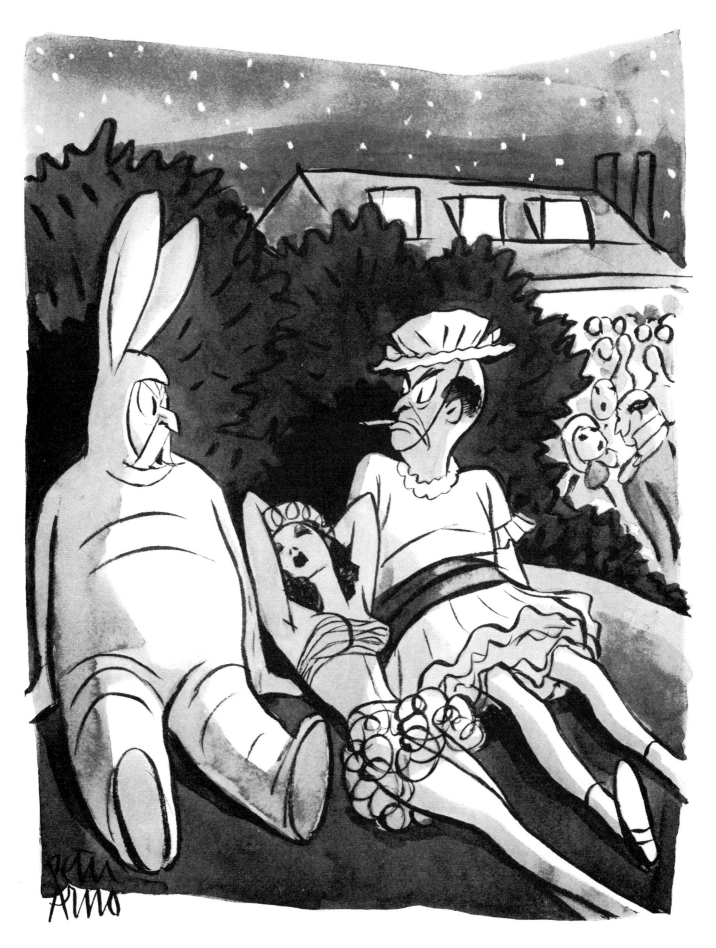

"Look here, Grenville, this isn't geting either of us anywhere."

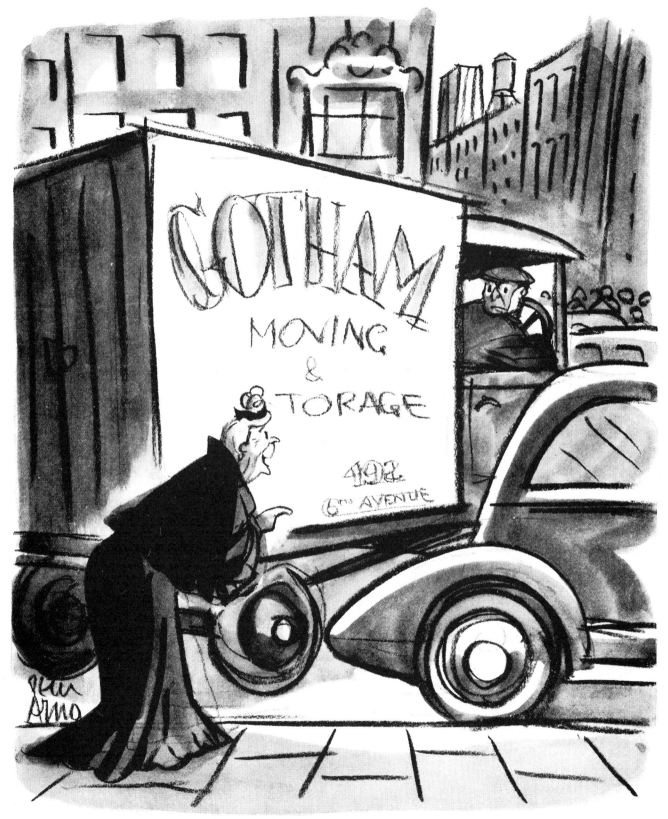

"O.K. Now cut her hard."

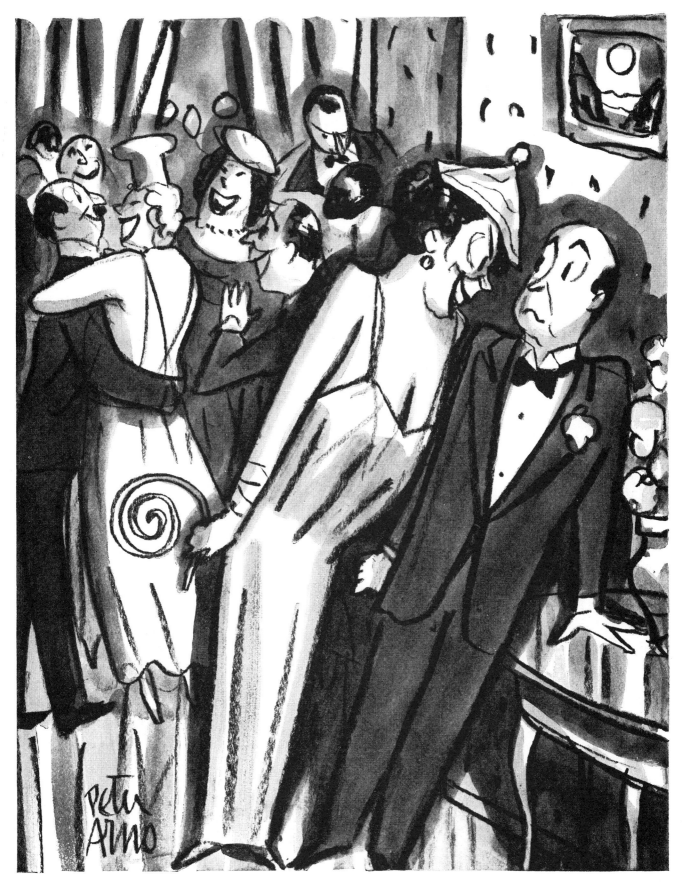

"Whose little husband are you?"

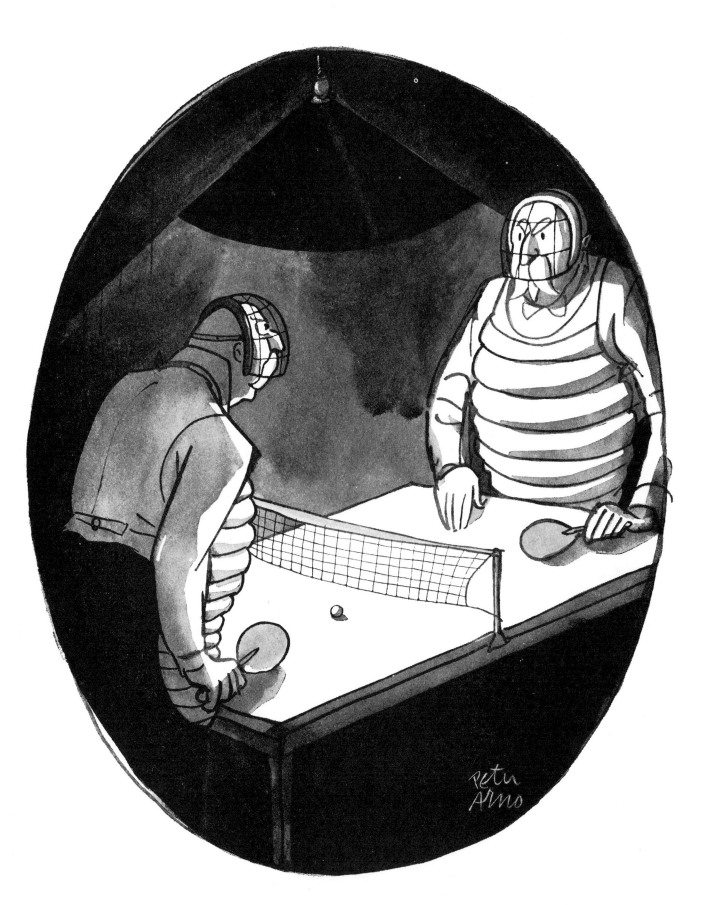

"Let's not lose our tempers, sir!"

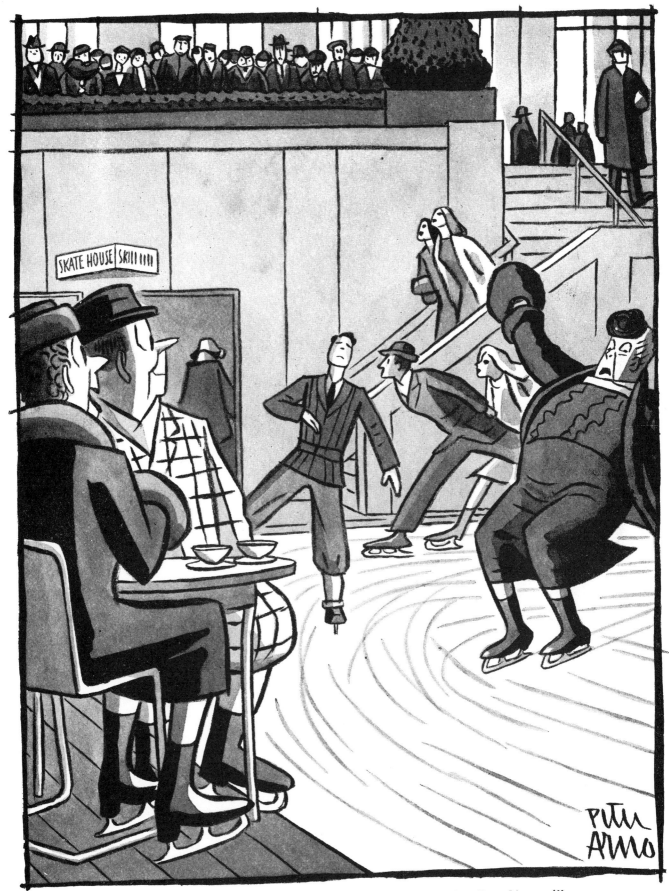

"*Why, it's Mrs. Courtney Richardson, Senior—she's heading this way!*"

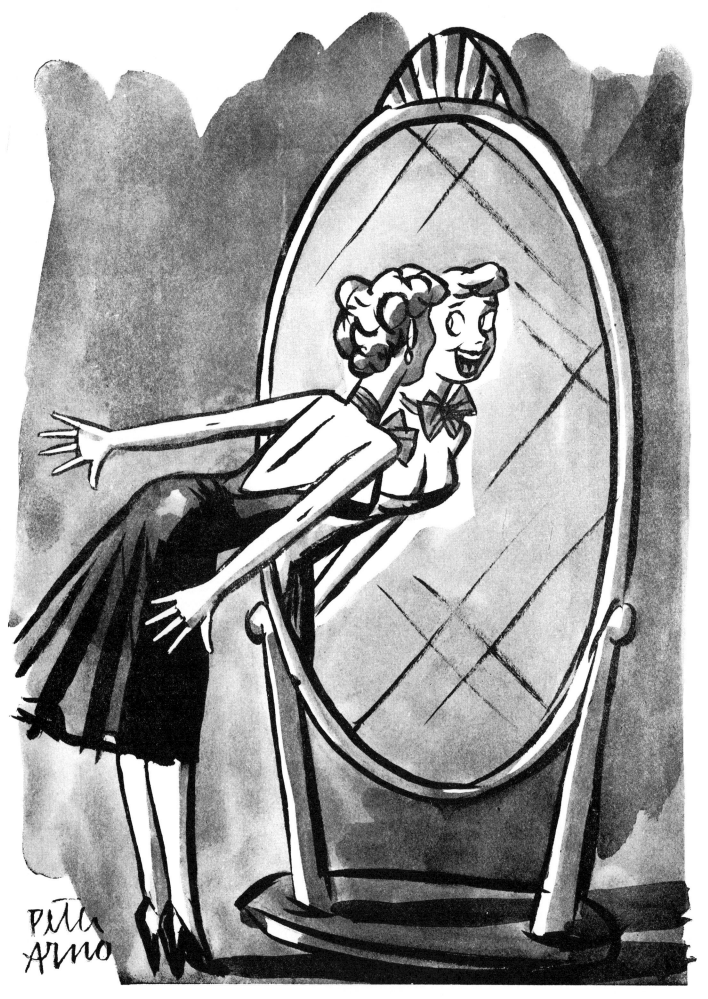

"Boo! You pretty creature!"

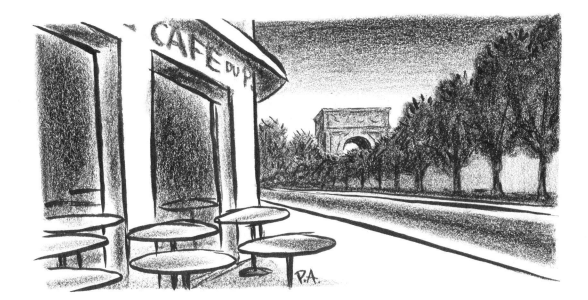

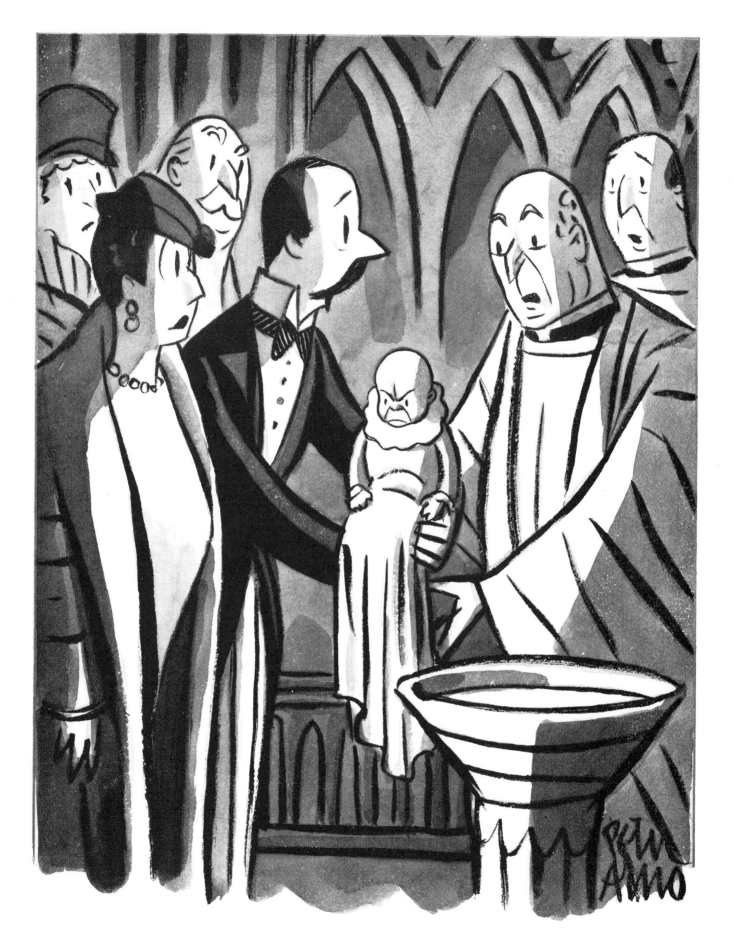

"Watch out, he bites!"

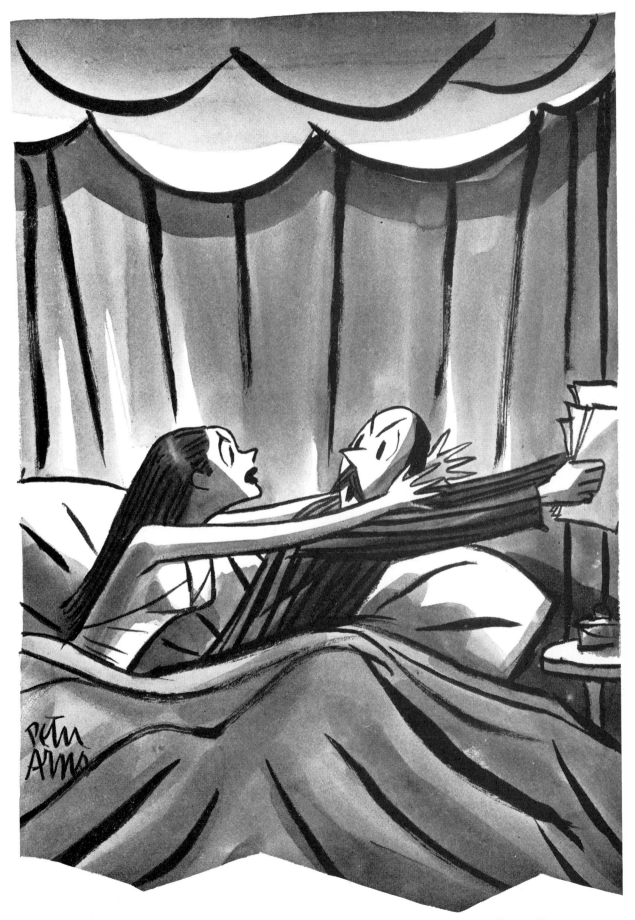

"*I'm not supposed to let <u>anybody</u> see my Consumers' Research Bulletins!*"

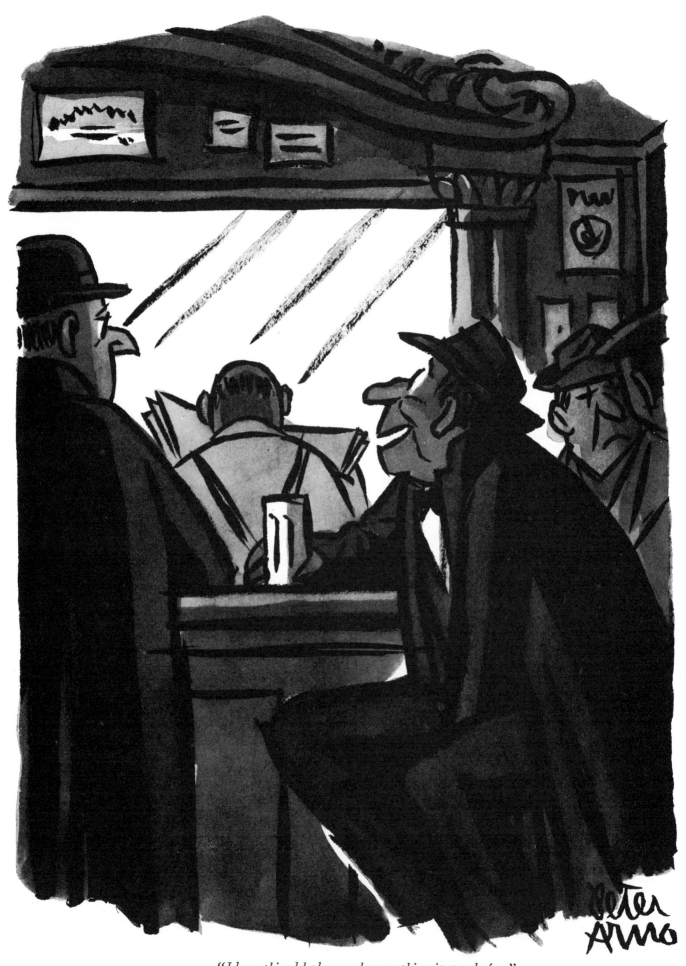

"I love this old place and everything it stands for."

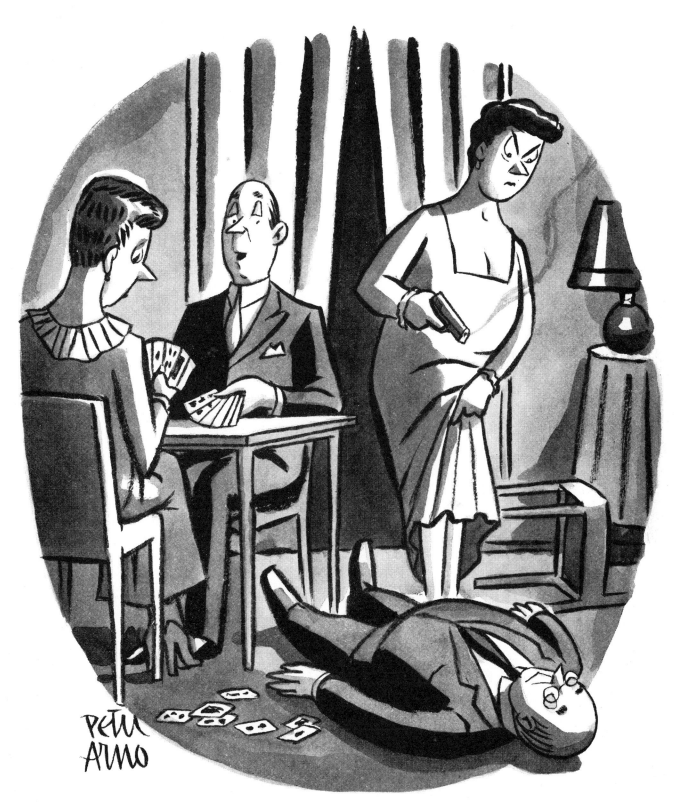

"*Well, I guess that breaks up our little game.*"

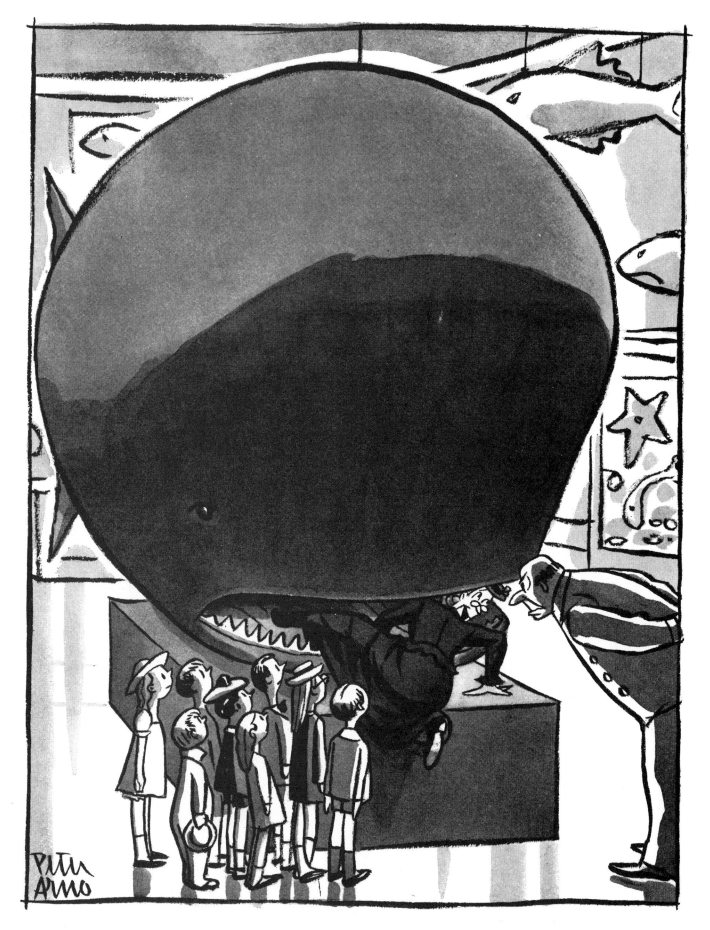

"It's all right. I'm just illustrating a point."

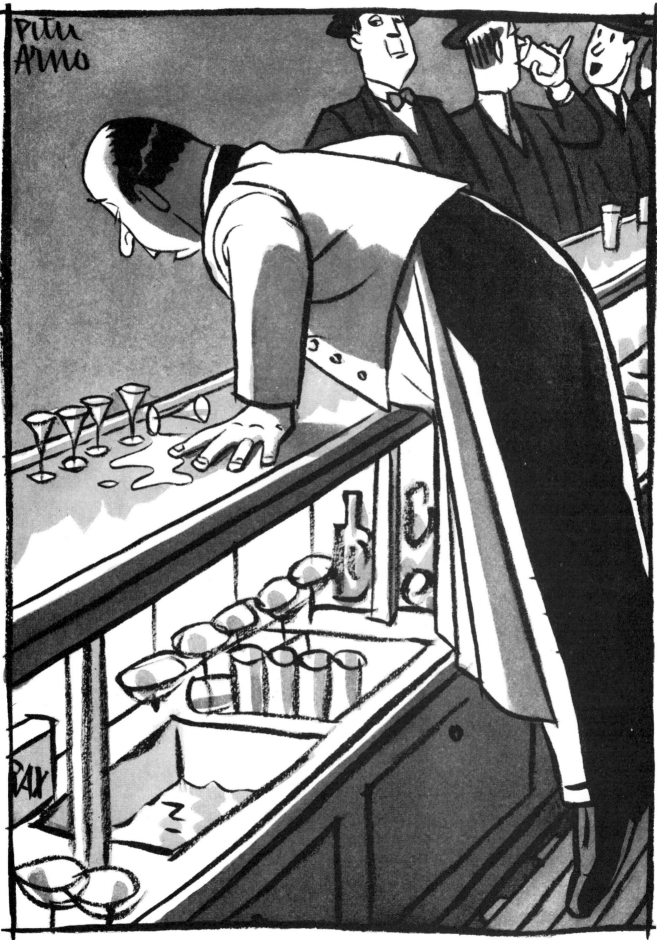

"Will that be all, sir?"

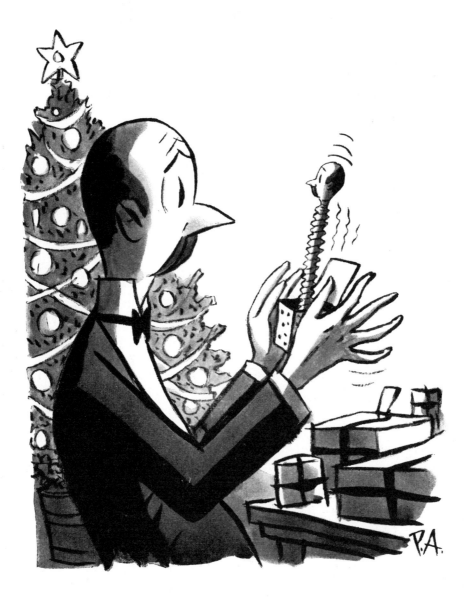

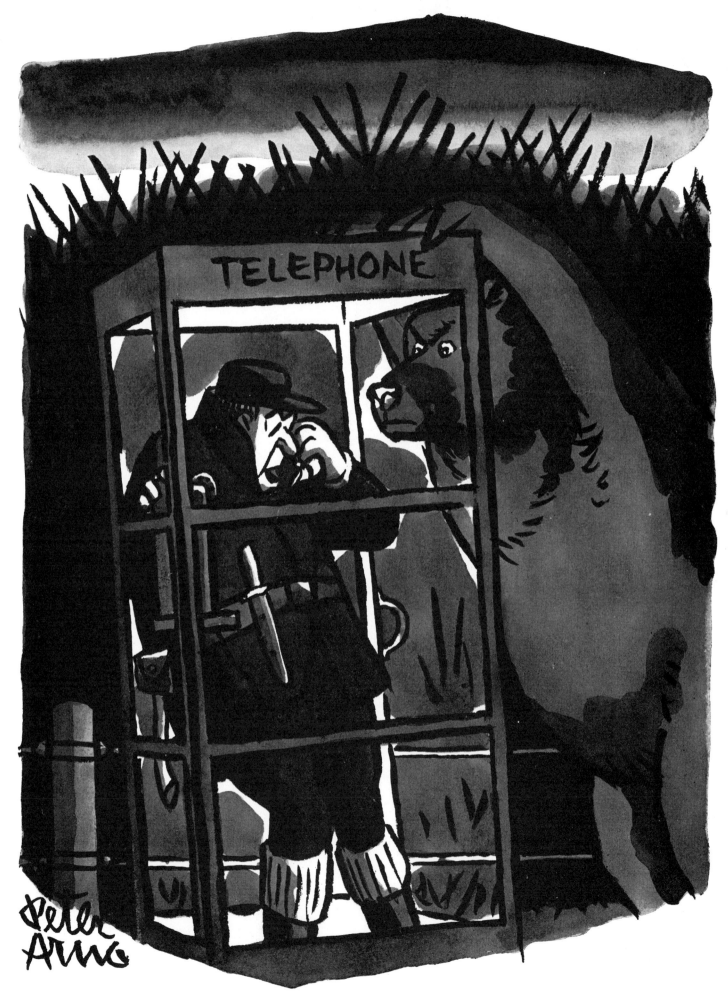

"Hello! Abercrombie & Fitch?"

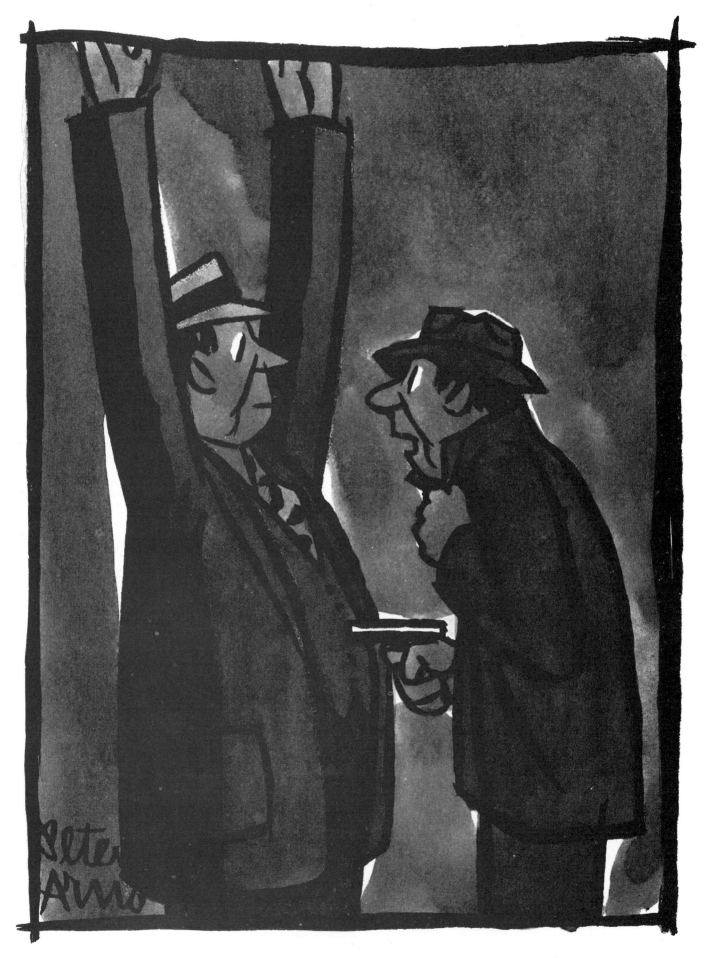

"This is a water pistol—I mean this is a stickup."

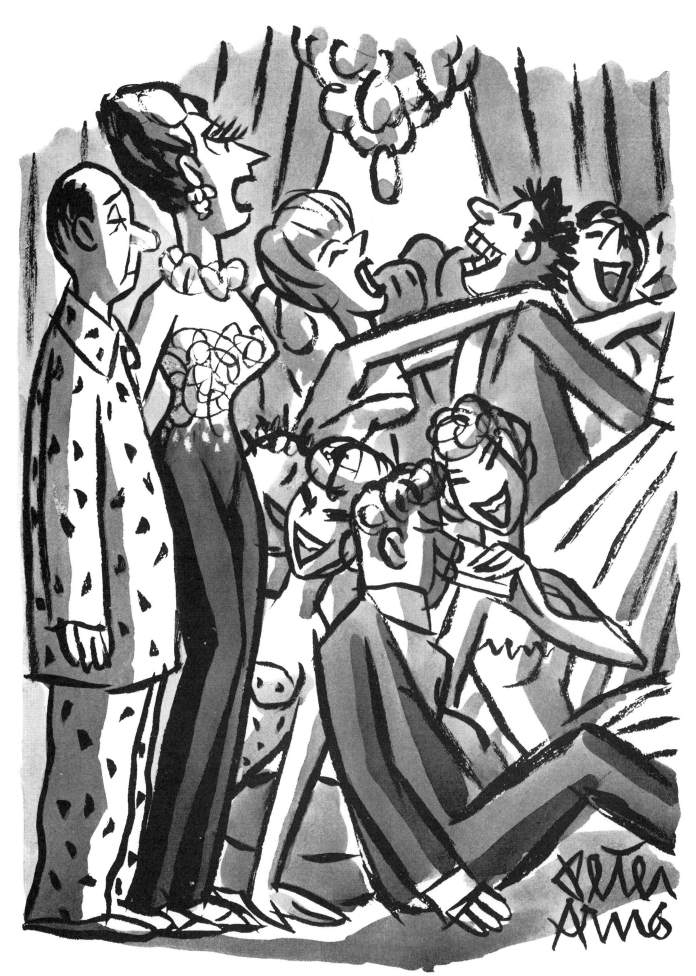

"*Quiet, everybody! Wallace wants to say good night.*"

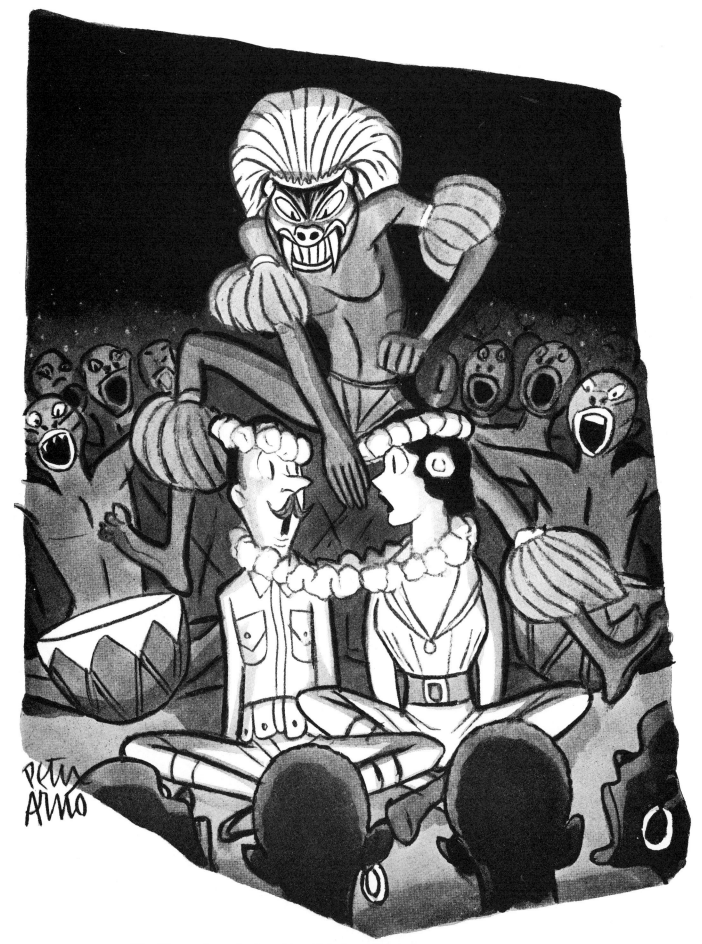

"*I still question whether this will be legally binding in New York State.*"

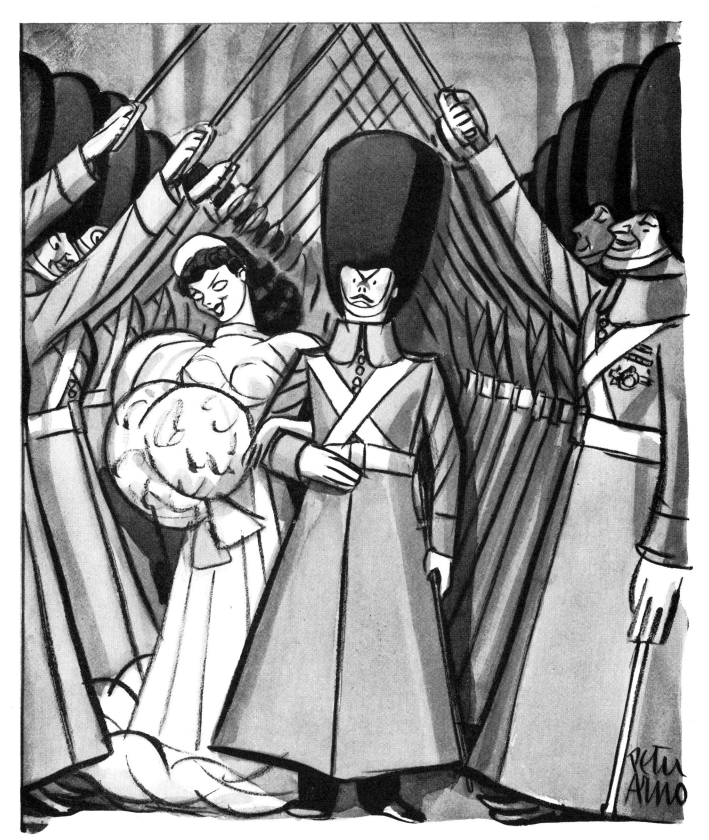

*". . . Hello, Edmund. Hello, Warwick. Hello, Teddy. Hello, Poodgie.
Hello, Freddie . . ."*

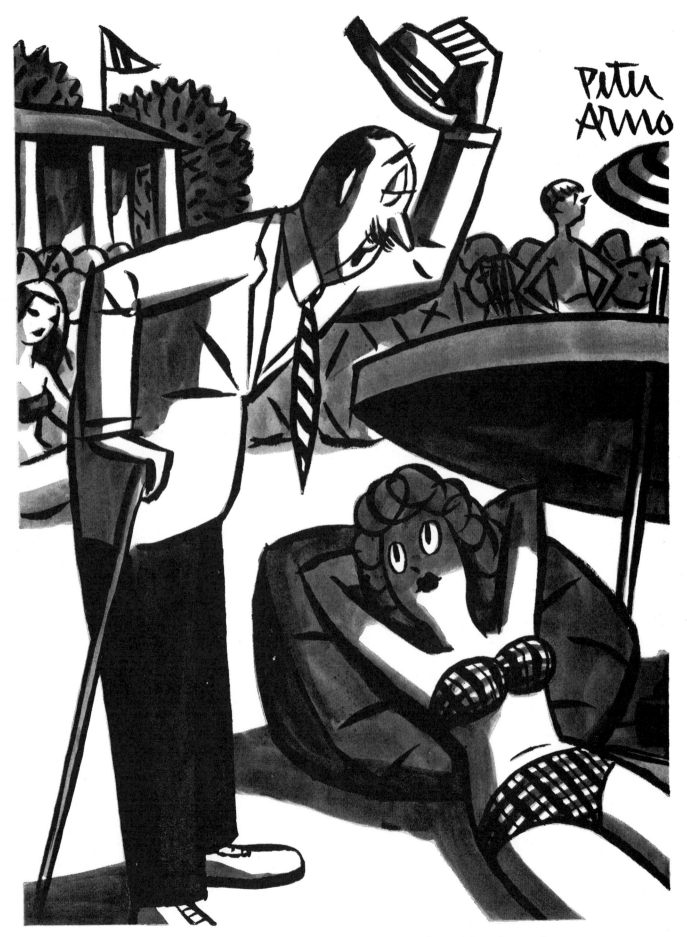

"*I happen to be a MacNab, Miss. I couldn't help noticing that you're
wearing our tartan.*"

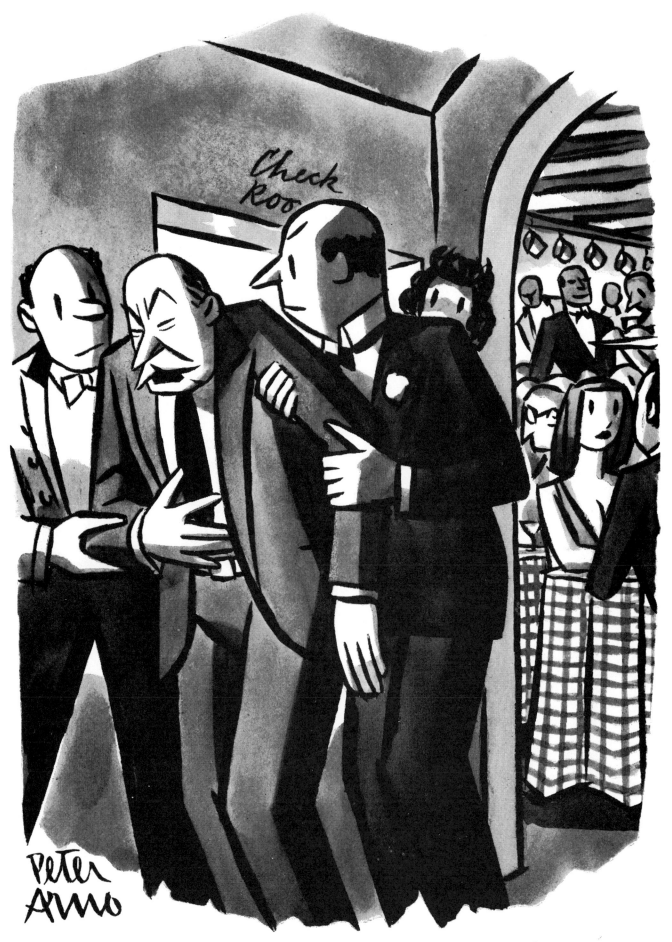

"*I'll be all right in a few minutes. It's just that the people at the next table were drinking Scotch and 7-Up!*"

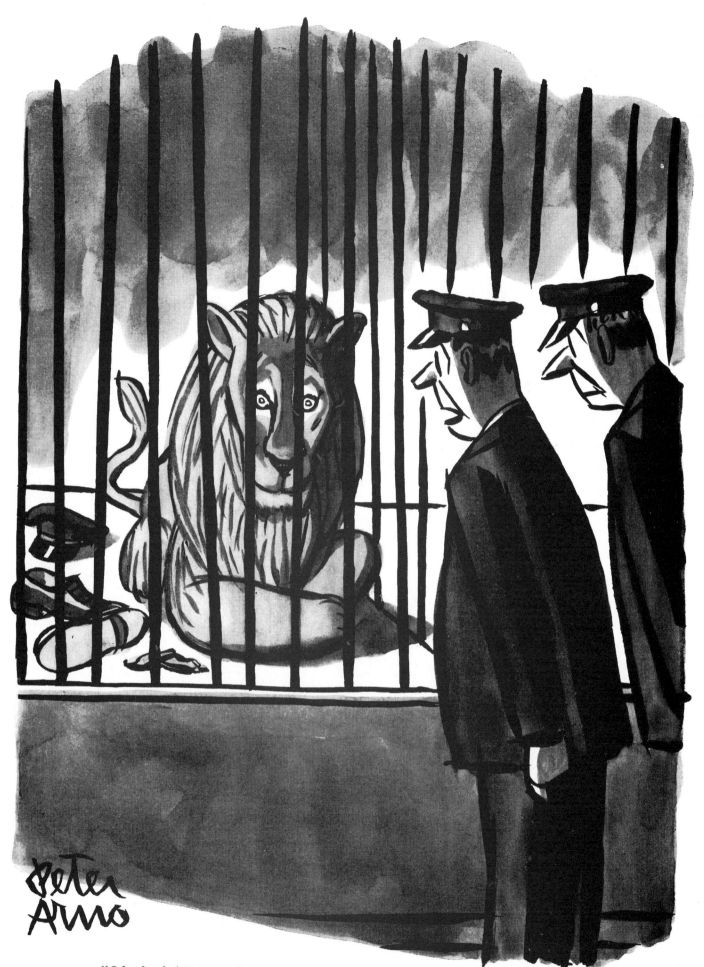

"Oh, shucks! Now we'll have to juggle the whole vacation schedule around again."

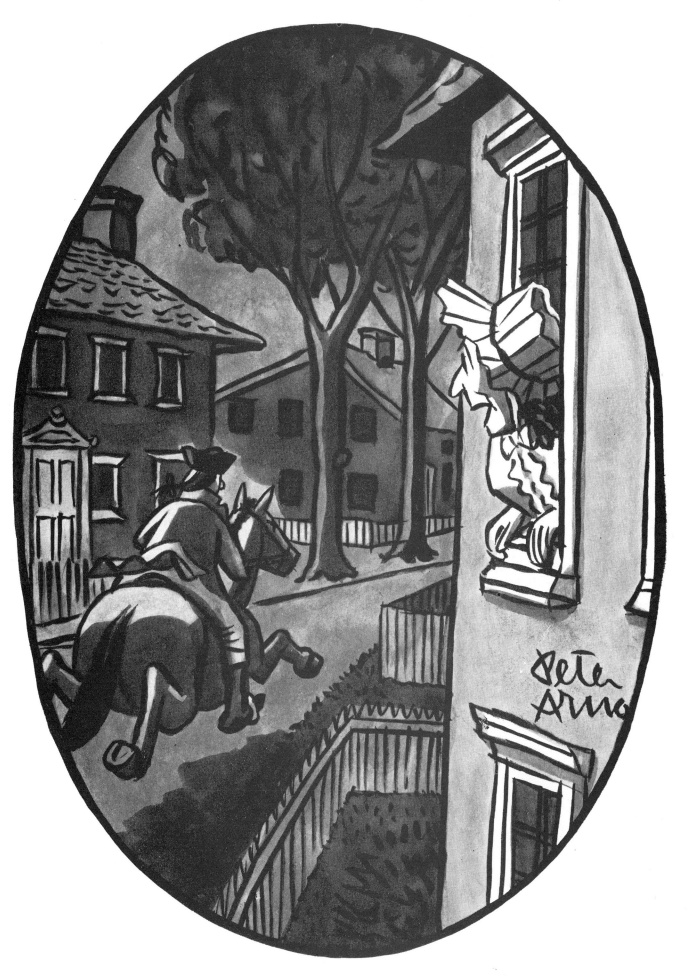

"*Thanks, but what about those silver candlesticks I ordered?*"

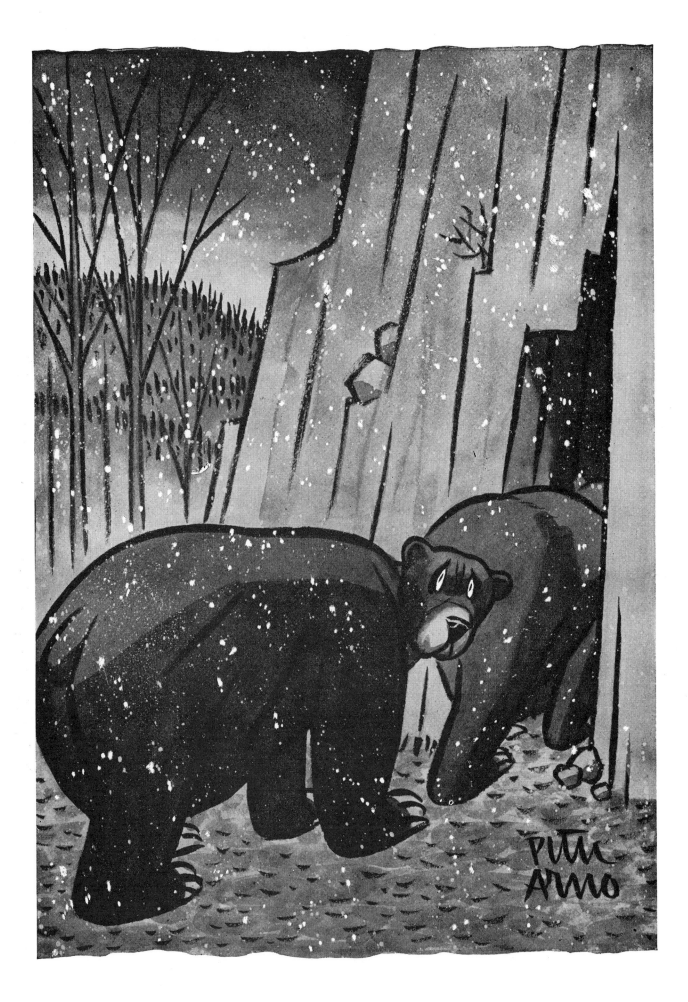

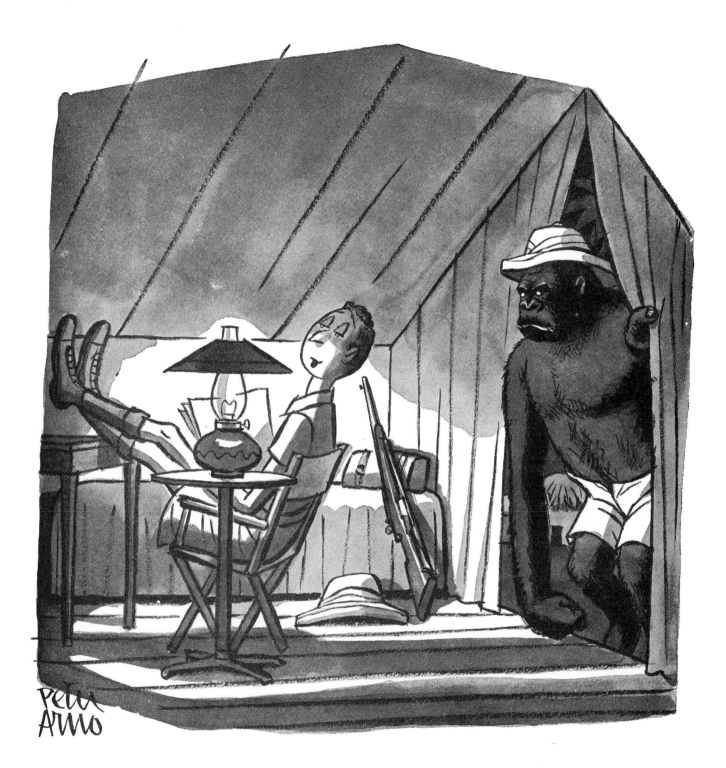

"What ho, Murchison—did you bag him?"

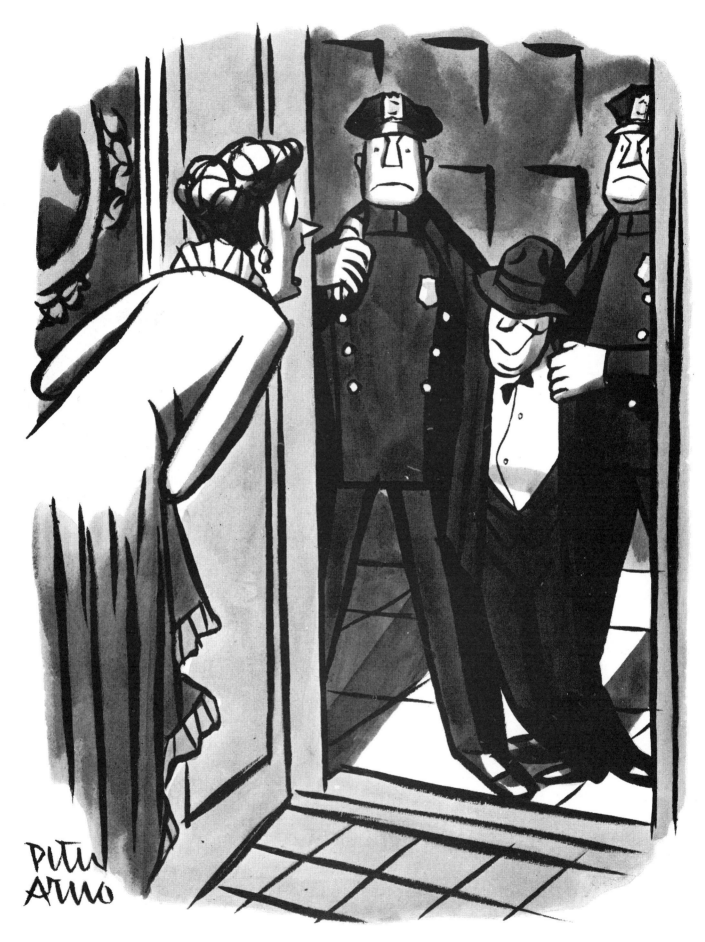

"Edward! Thank heavens! I couldn't imagine <u>what</u> had happened to you!"

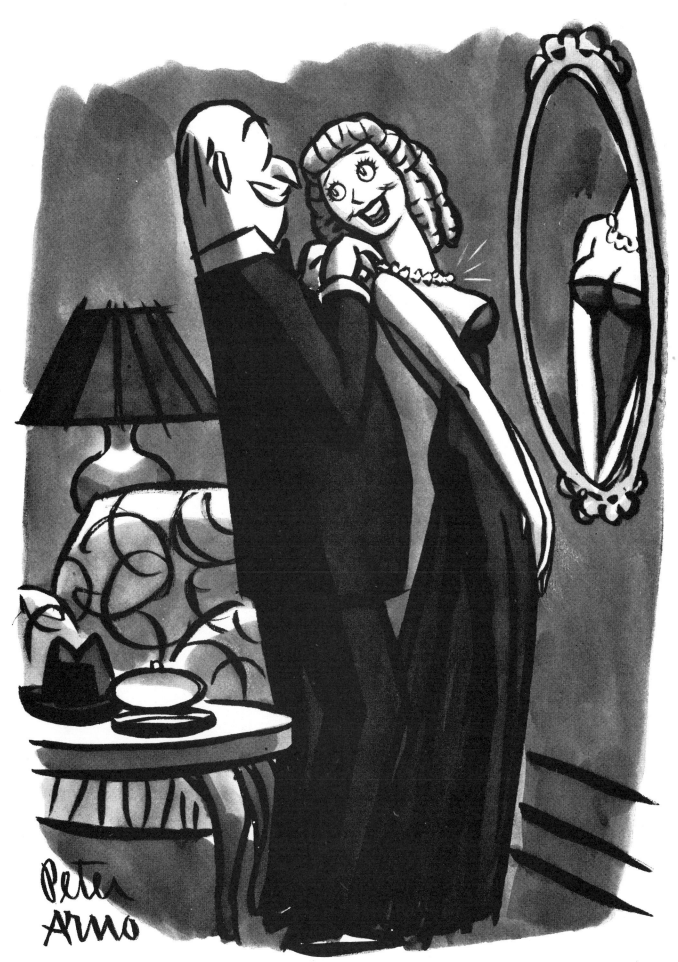

"You certainly know my Achilles' heel, Mr. Benson."

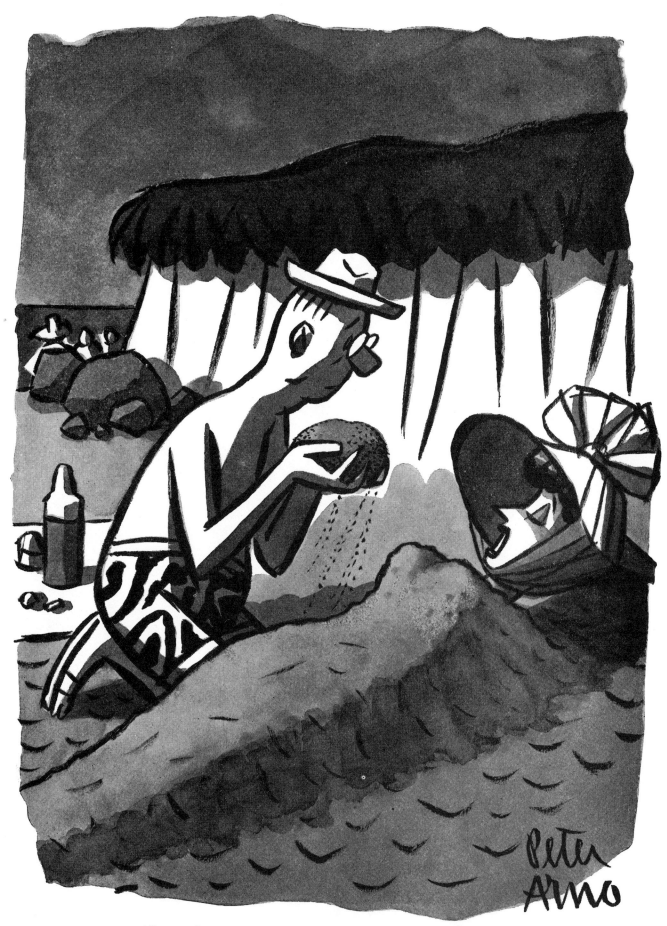

"*Remember, Mr. Kornheiser—no patting it smooth this time.*"

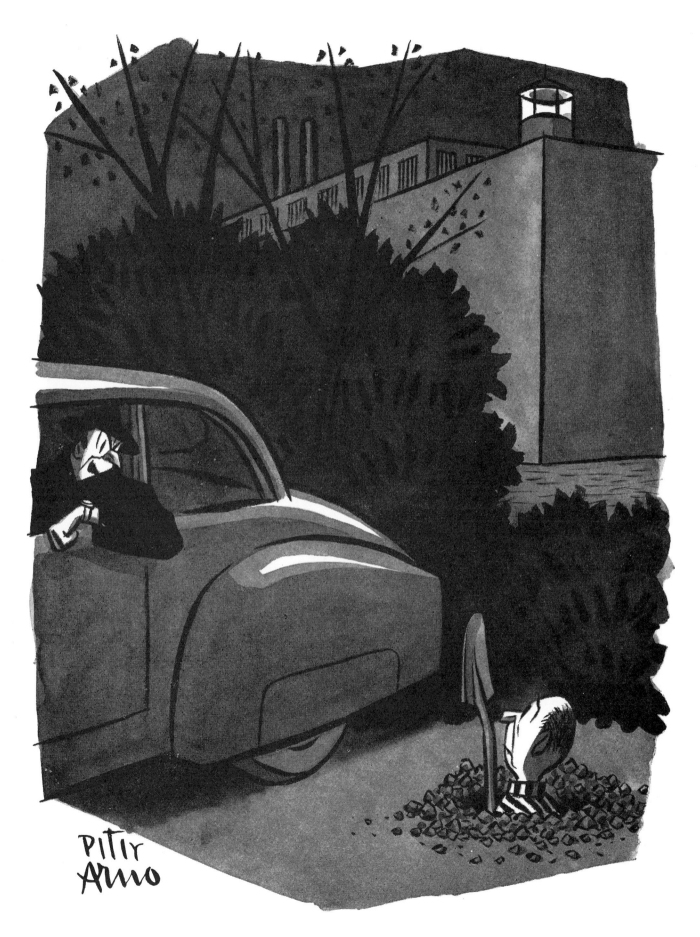

"Well! Finally!"

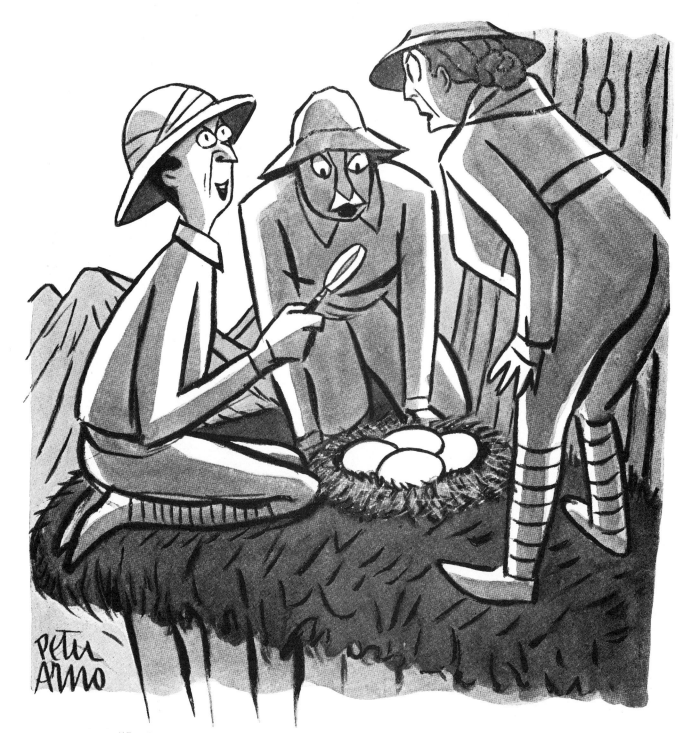

"*In the interests of science, Miss Mellish, I'm going to make a rather strange request of you.*"

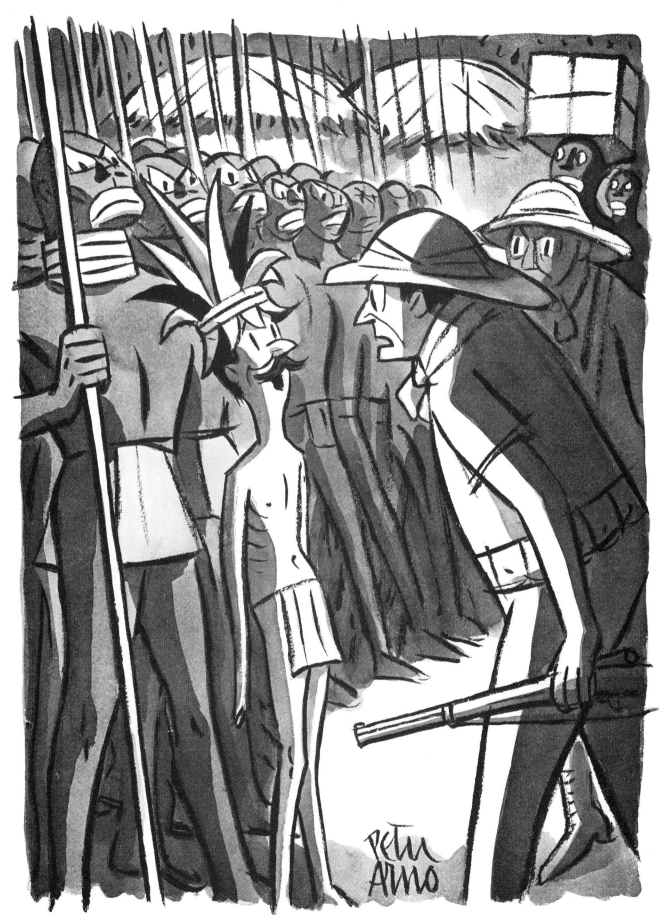

"They think I'm God."

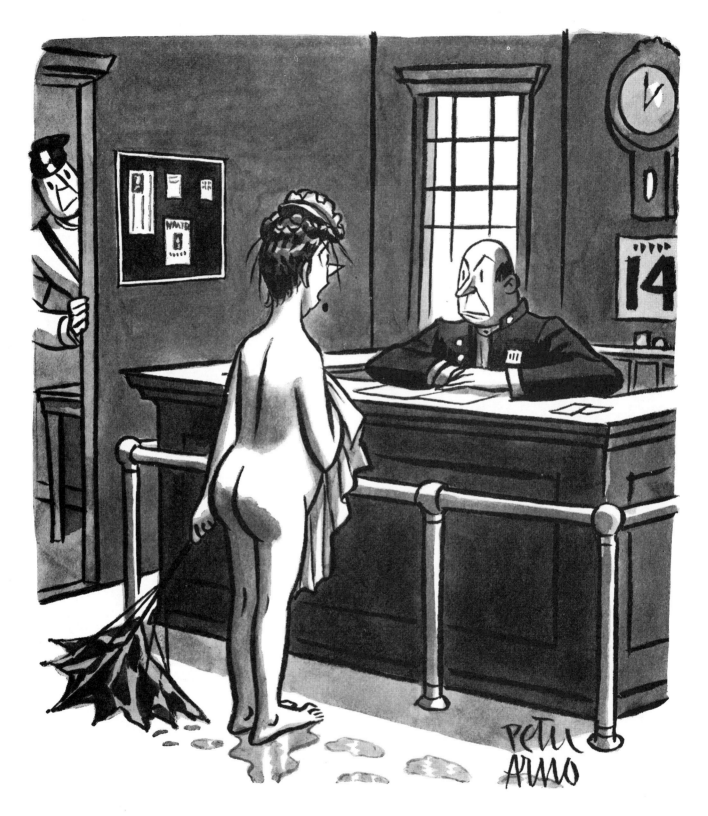

"I want to report a tornado."

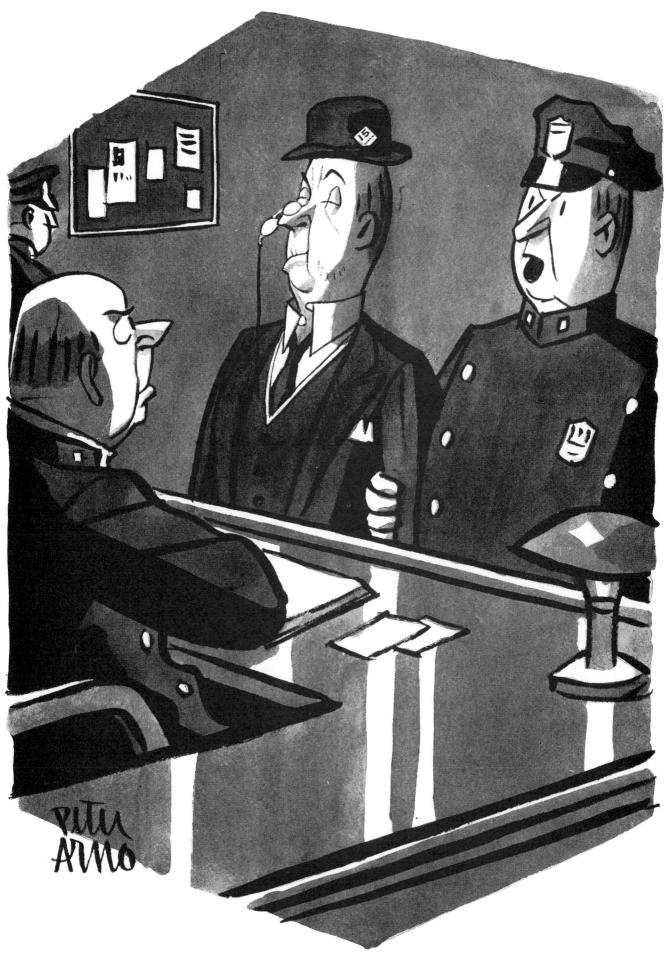

"*He can't remember his name, Sergeant. All he remembers is he's somebody pretty damned important.*"

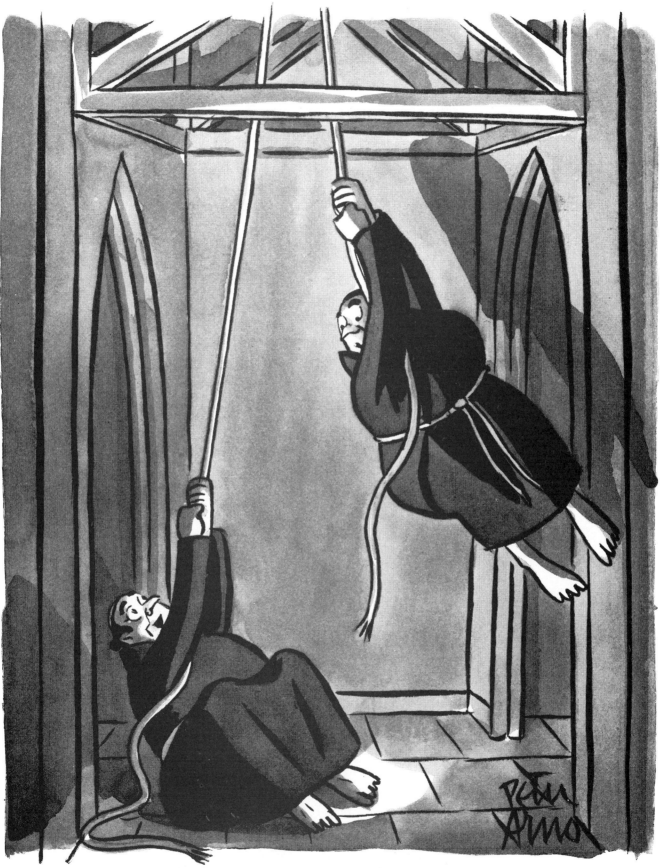

"Take it, Andrew!"

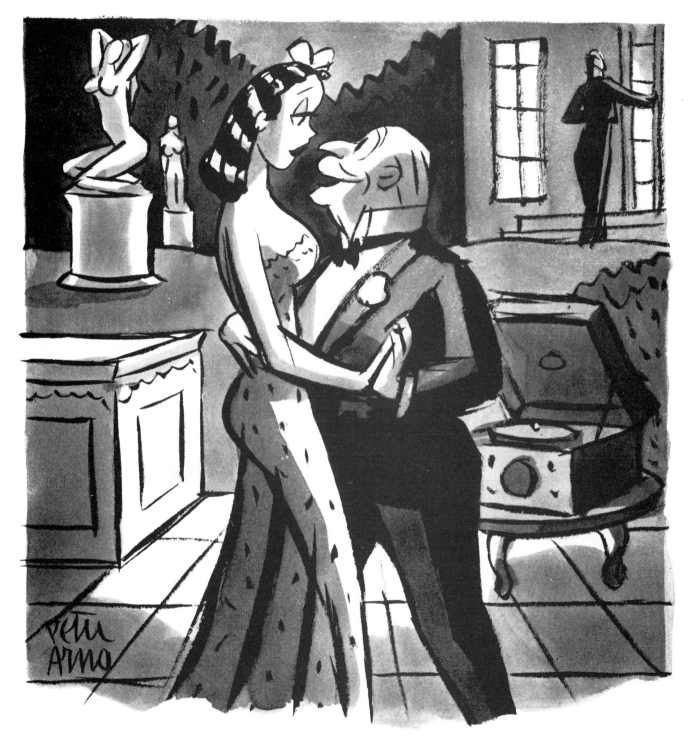

"I keep wanting to put you on a pedestal."

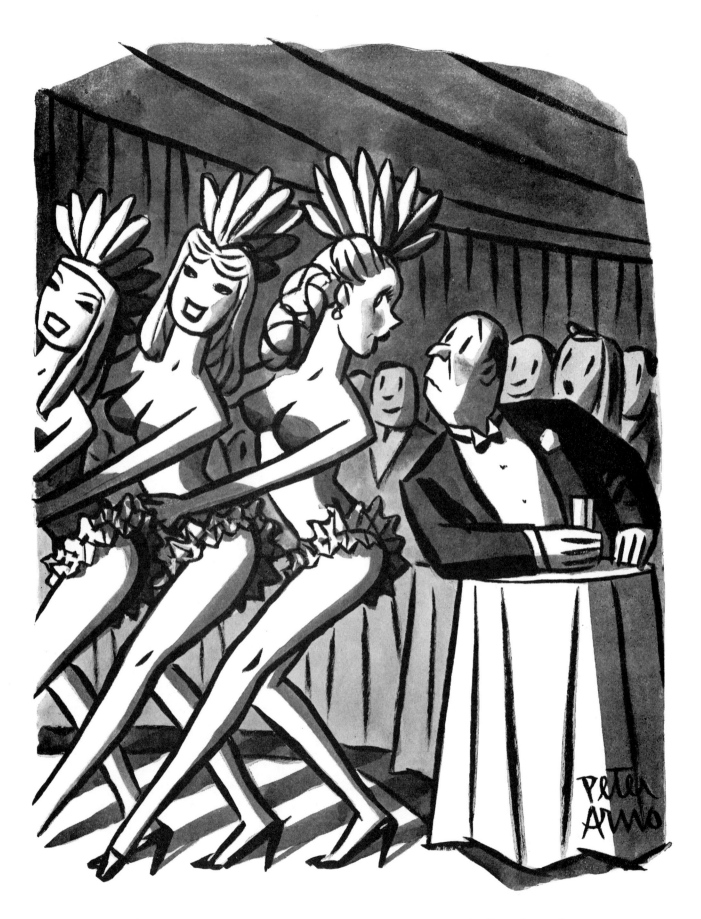

"Valerie won't be around for several days. She backed into a sizzling platter."

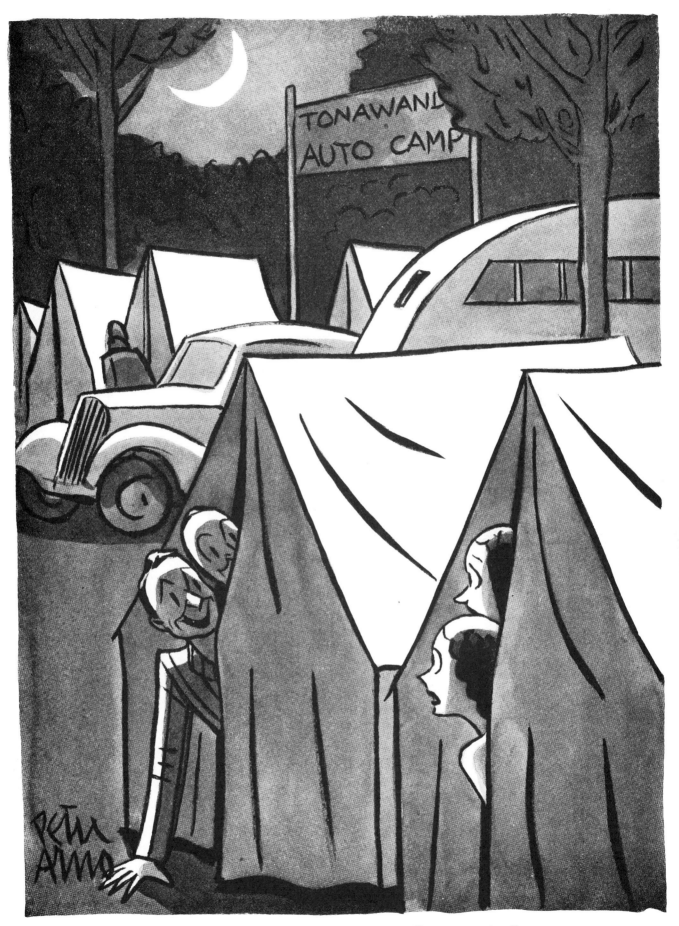

"*Armbruster here has what I think is a marvellous suggestion.*"

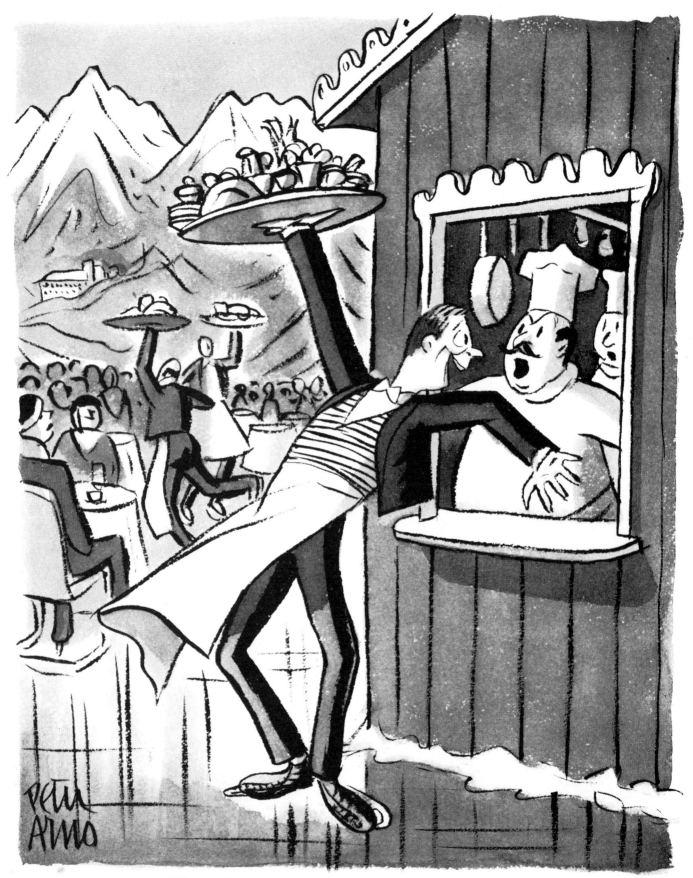

"Now don't expect __too__ much. This is my first time on skates."

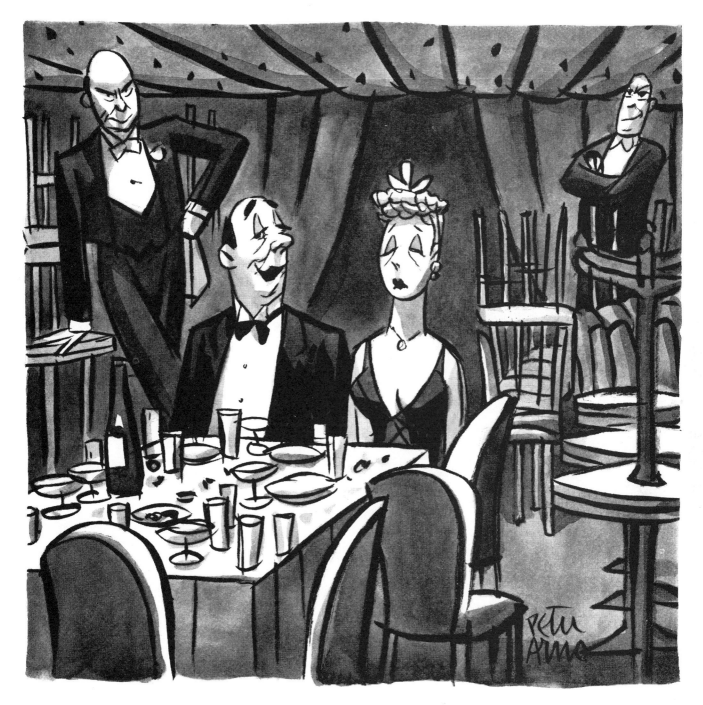

"Sleepy?"

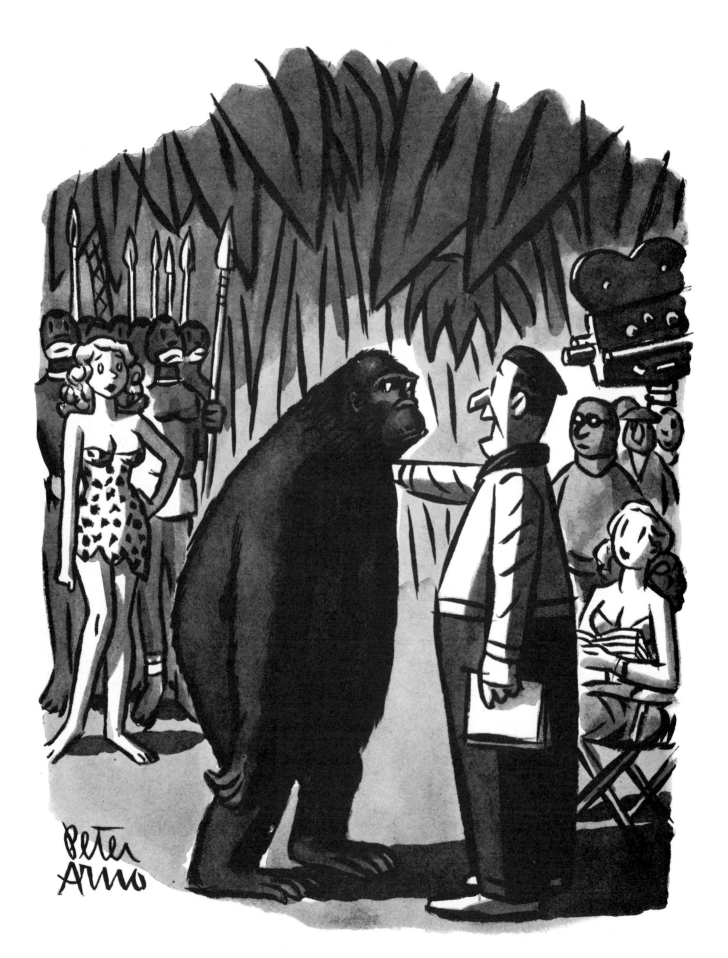

"*What you really want is to marry
the girl and settle down. But you can't, because you're a gorilla.*"

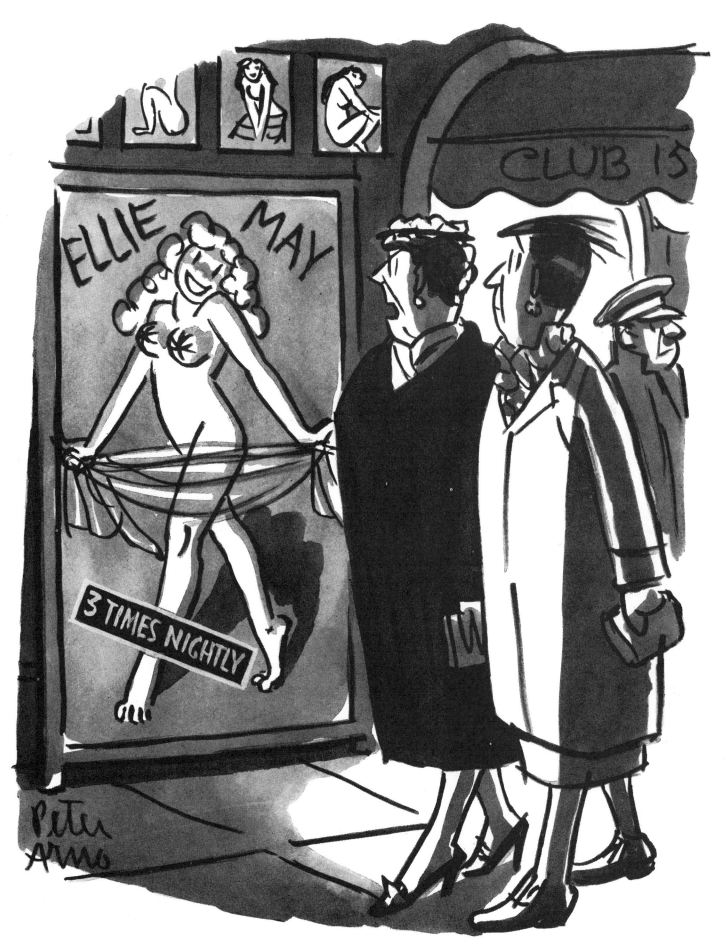

"I'd starve first!"

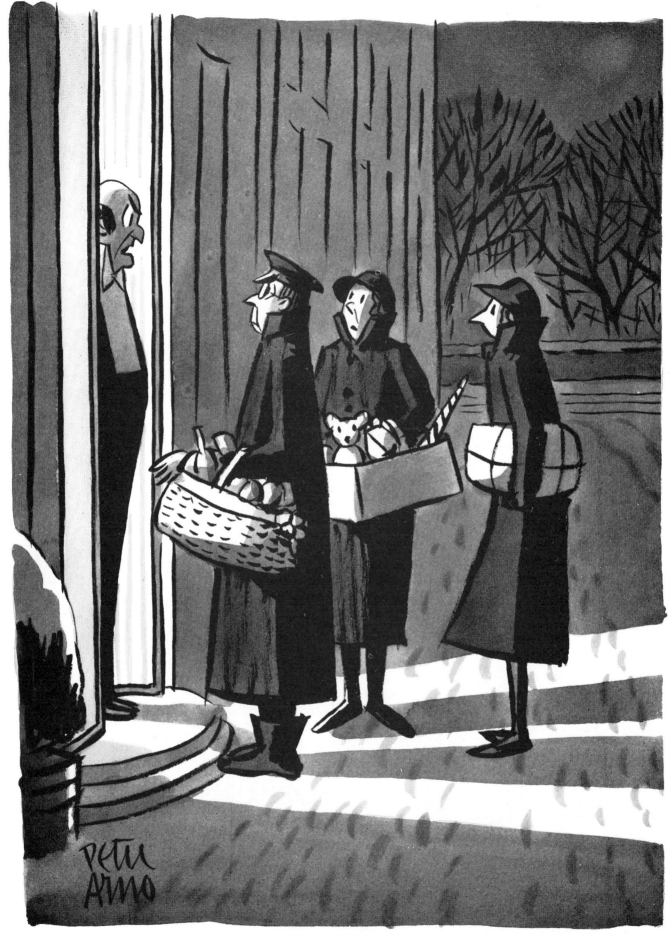

"I can't help what address you have. We are not a needy family."

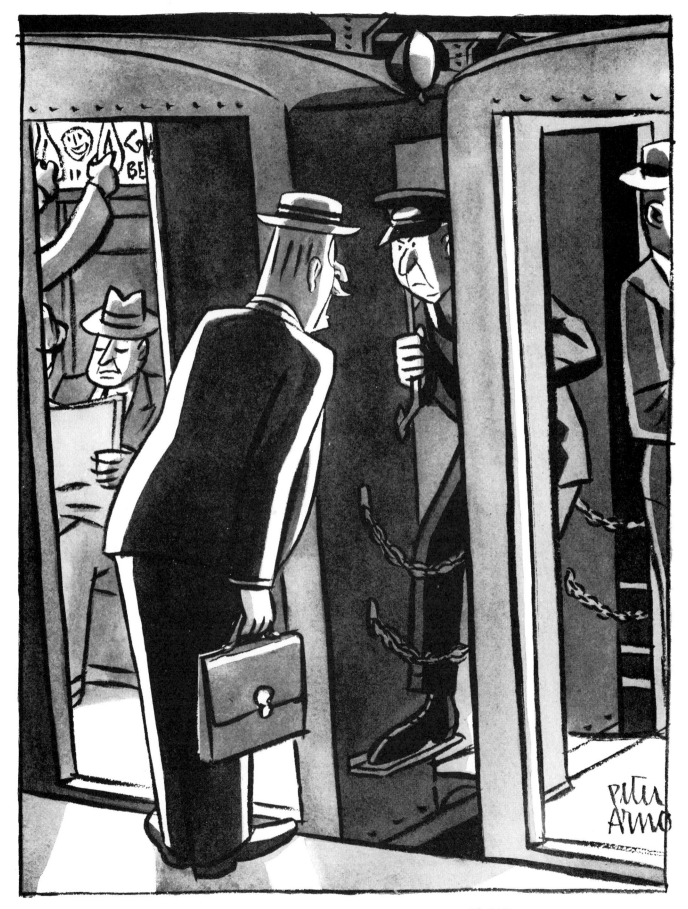

"Will this train take me anywhere near the Racquet Club?"

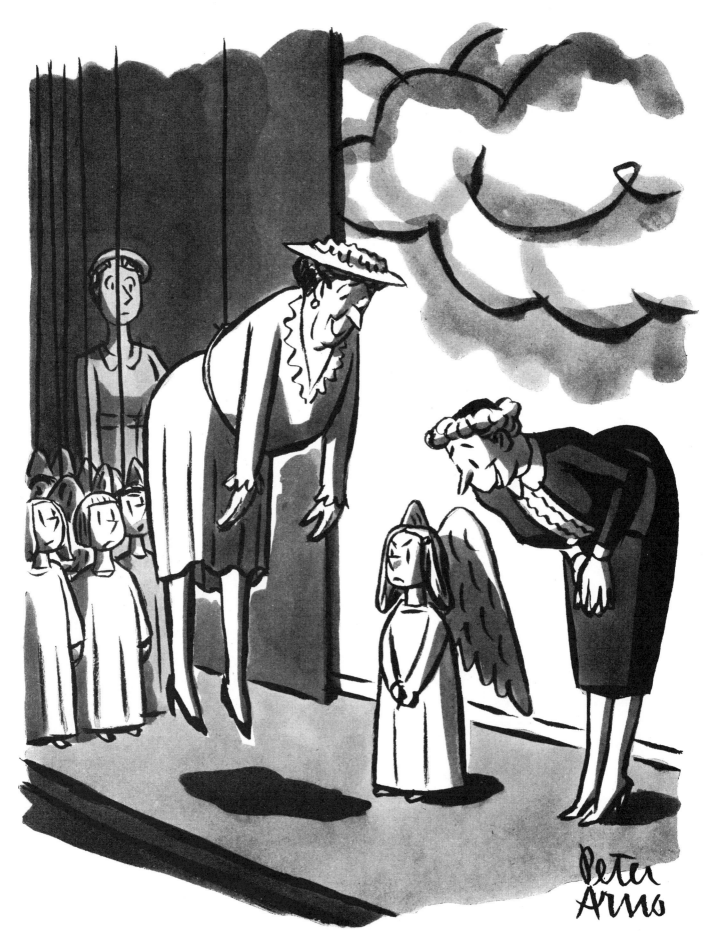

"See? Mrs. Bentley isn't falling."

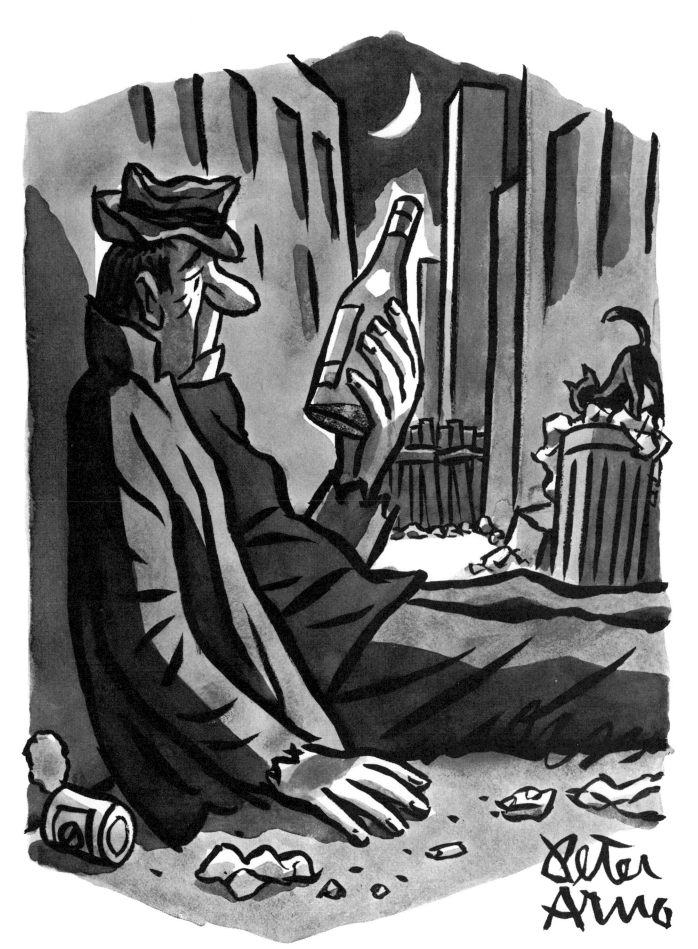

"*. . . It is a pleasant accompaniment to fish, shellfish, and the lighter meats,
but its delicate flavor is perhaps even more appreciated at the end of the meal
with melon or dessert.*"

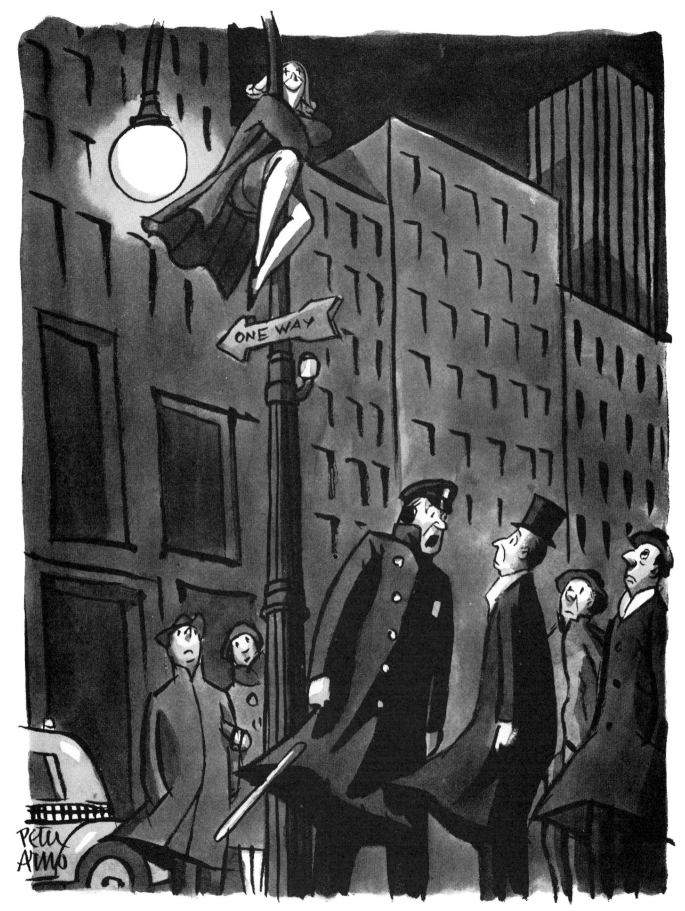

"You the husband?"

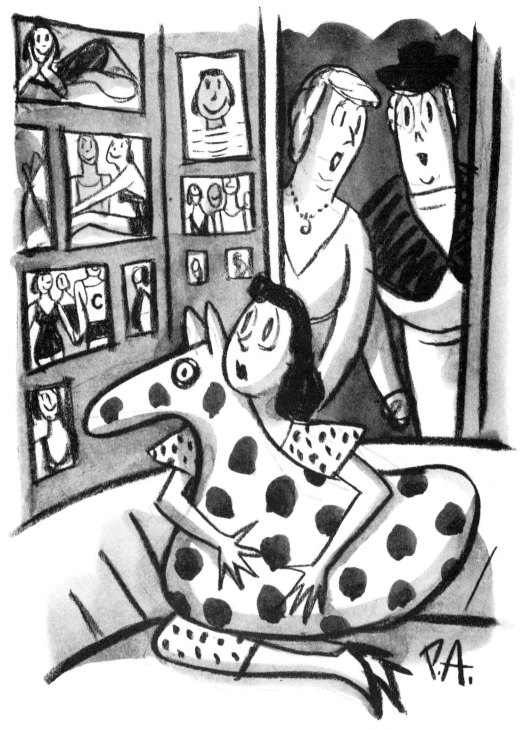

"*It sort of tides her over the winter months.*"

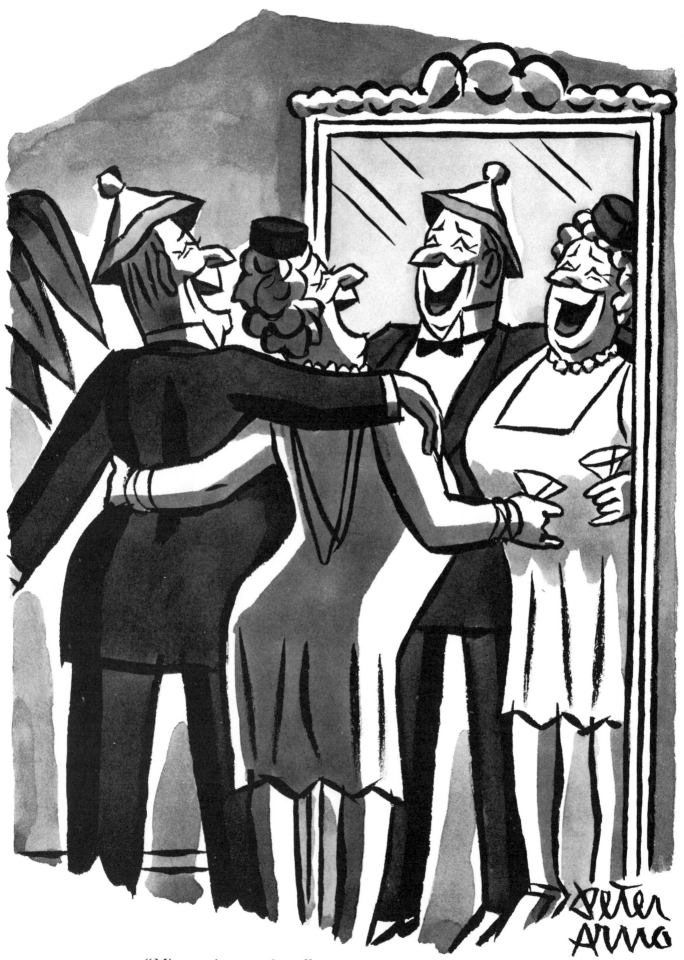

"Mirror, mirror, on the wall, what fun couple is the most fun of all?"

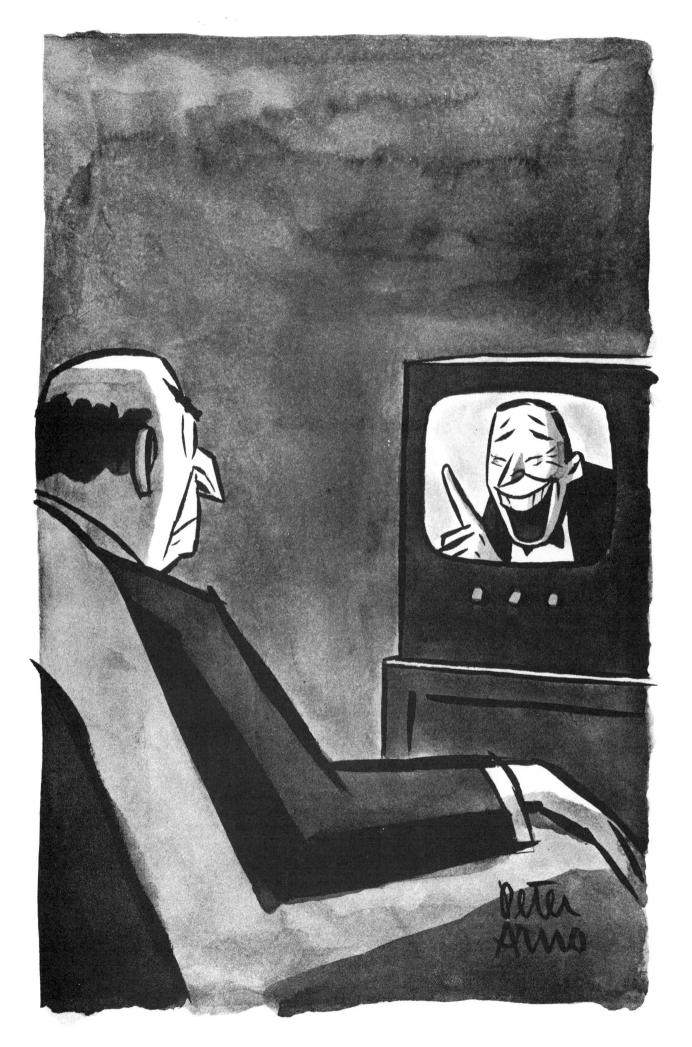

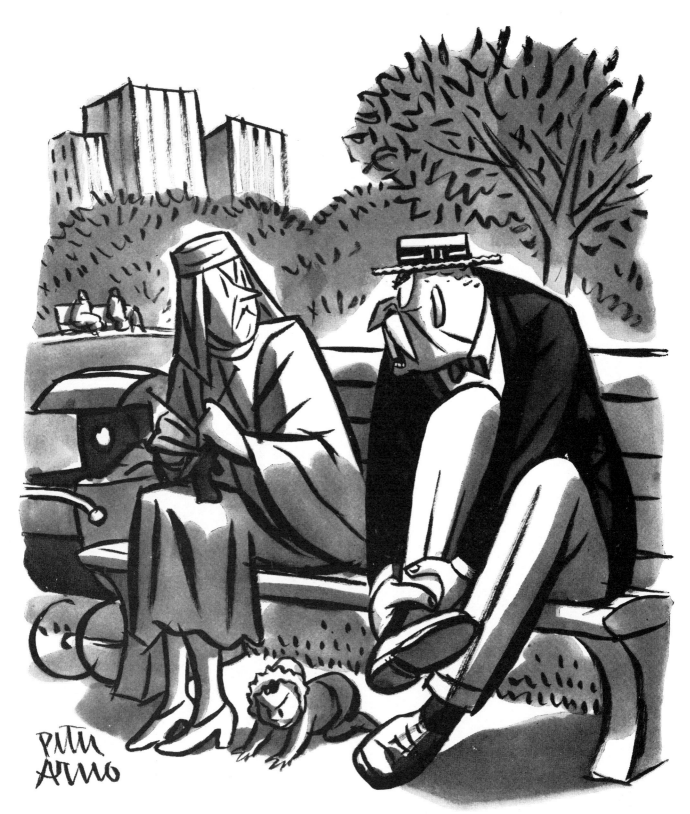

"Well, by gad, Madam, something nipped me!"

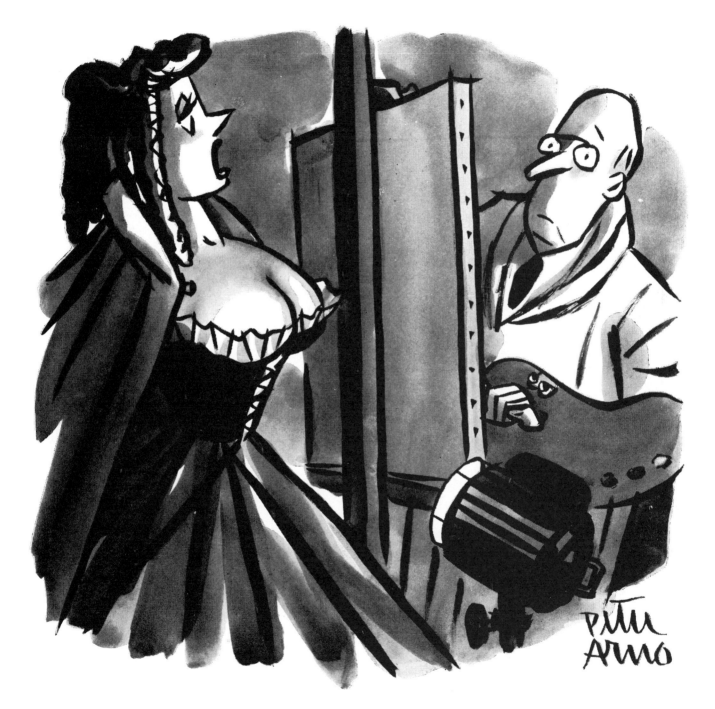

"Don't you ever do anything but covers for historical novels, Mr. Carmichael?"

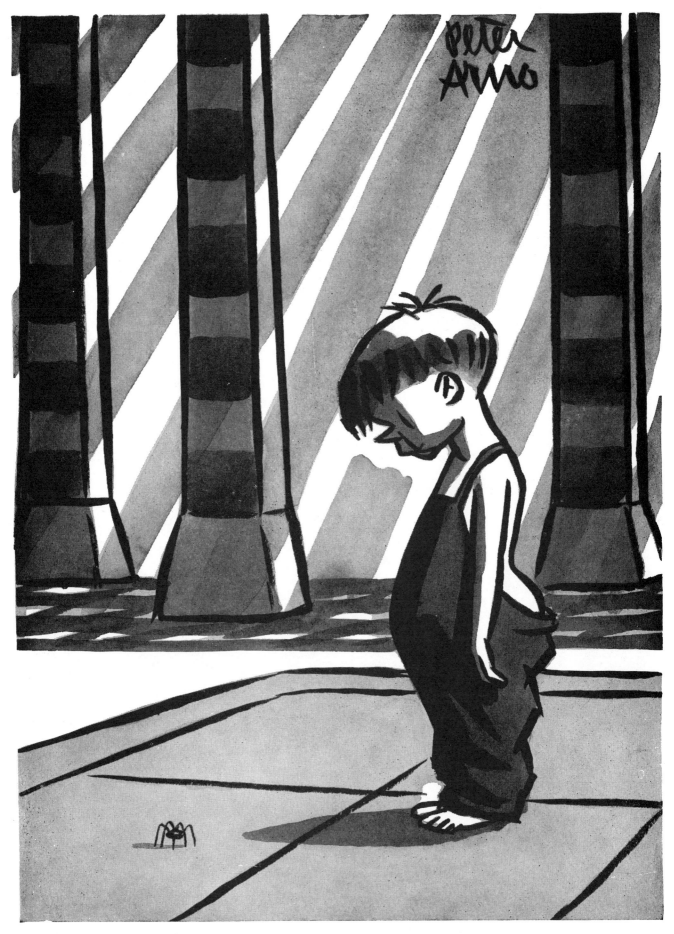

Spring in the City

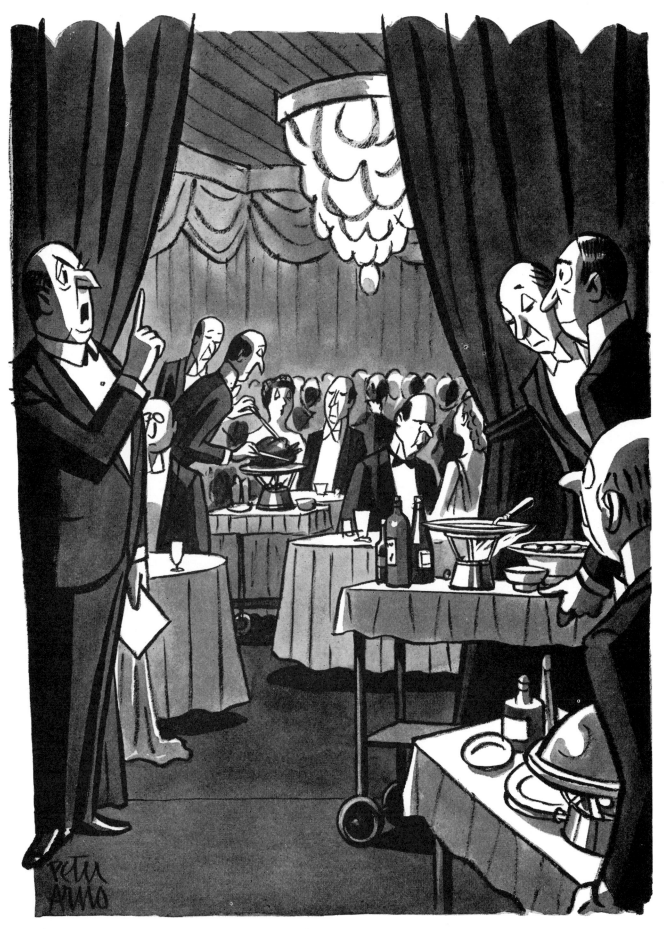

"Ready, Marcel! You're on next."

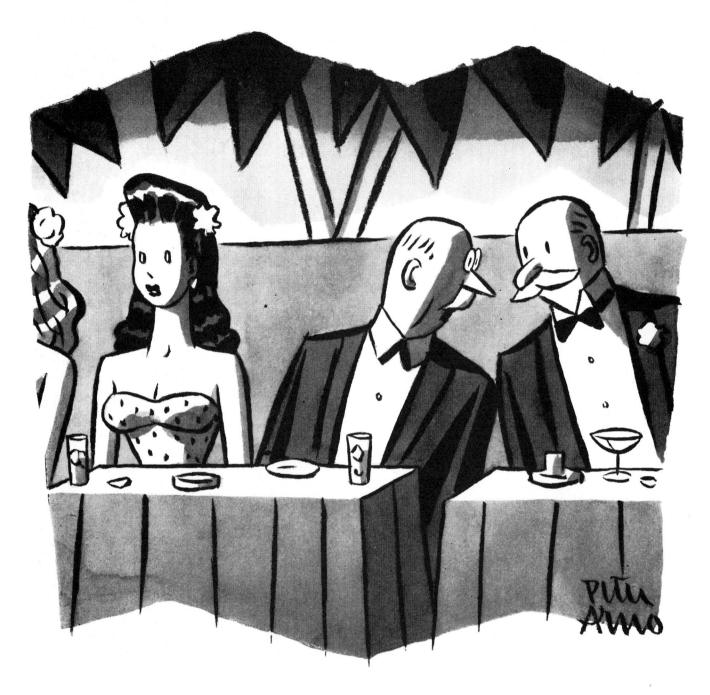

"She's sort of a secretary. With the new tax setup, I figure she's only costing
me eight cents on the dollar."

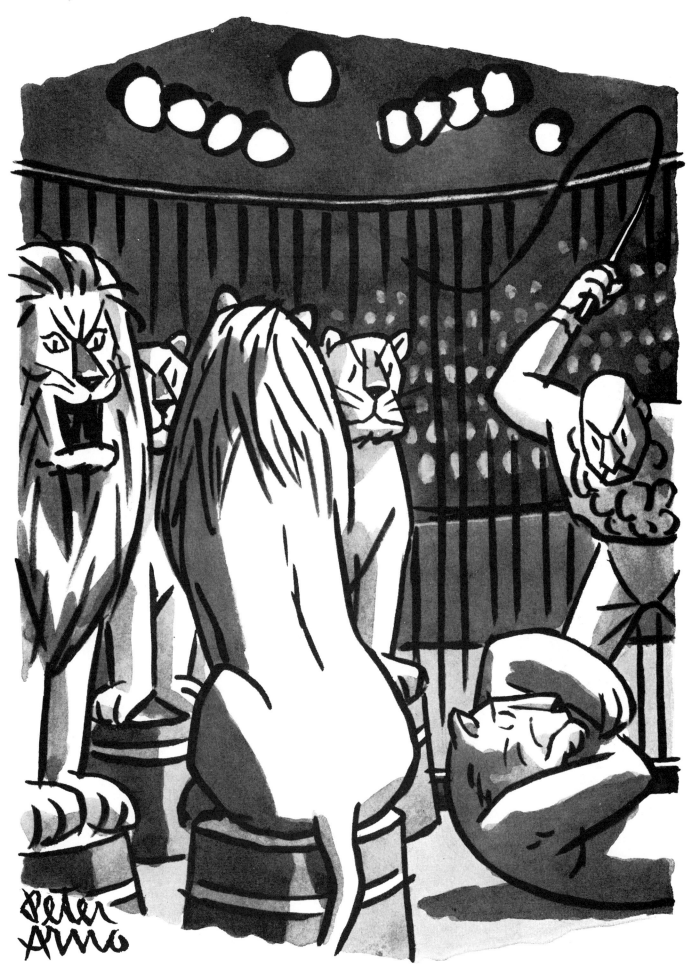

"If I were only twenty years younger and had my teeth!"

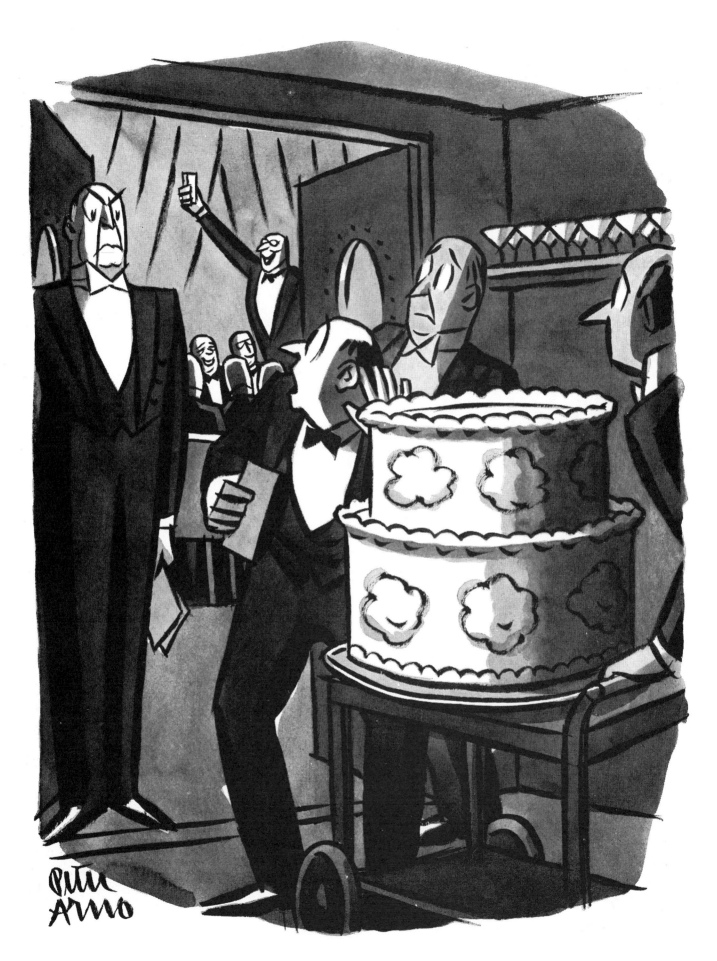

"She wants a drink of water."

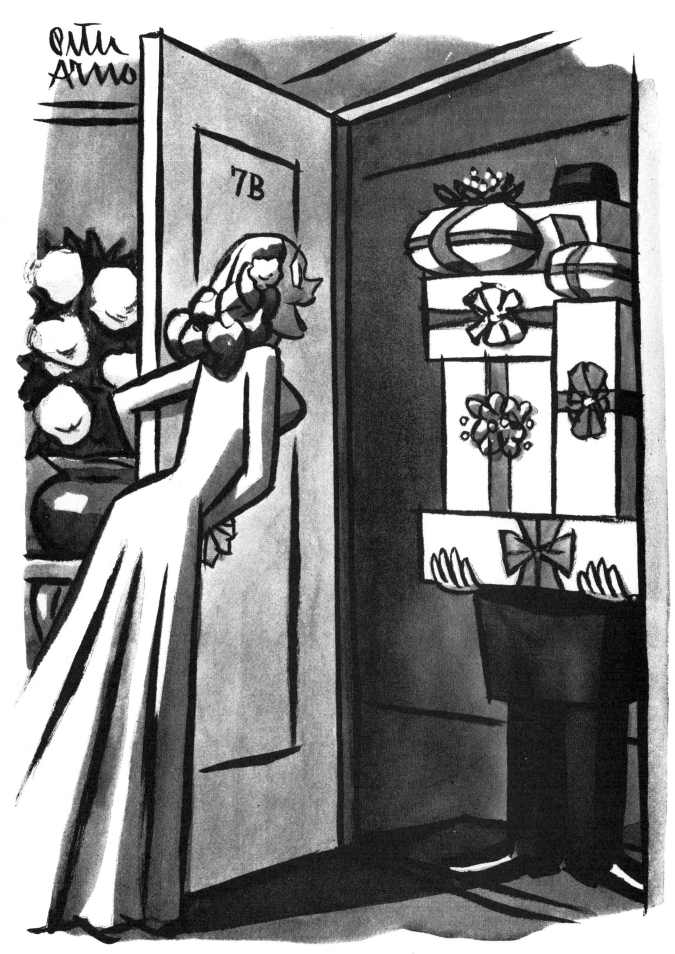

"Come in, come in, whoever you are."

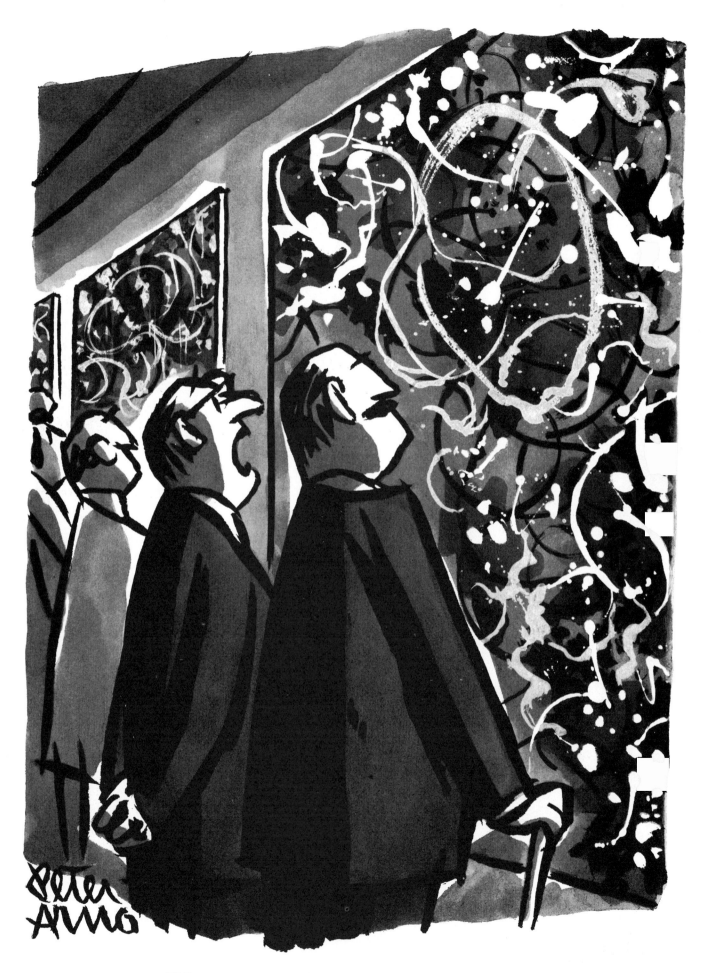

"*His spatter is masterful, but his dribbles lack conviction.*"

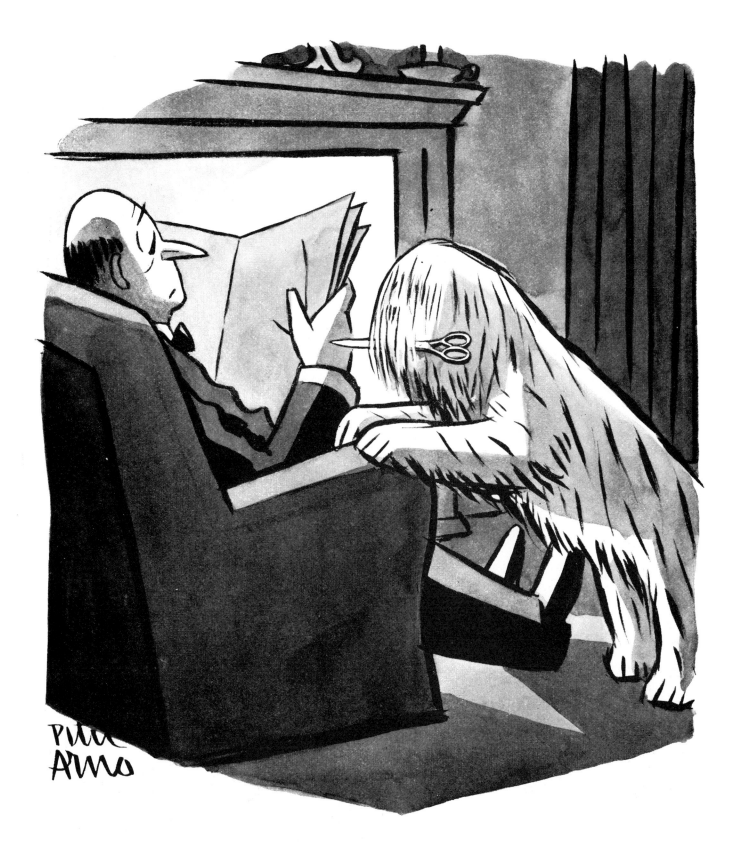

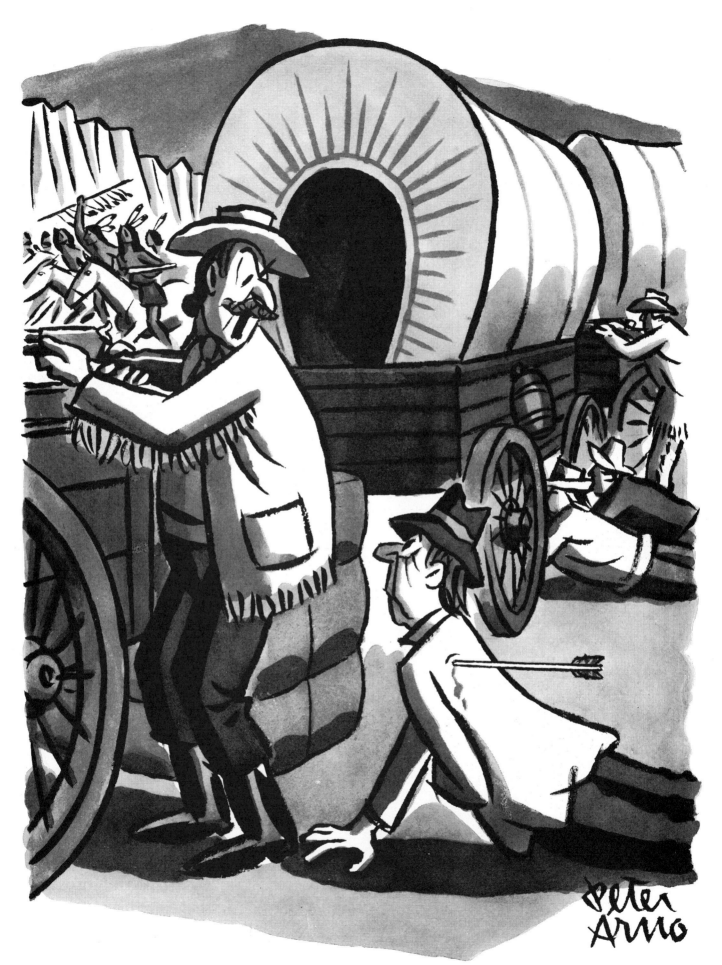

"Judson, you've done nothing but complain the whole trip!"

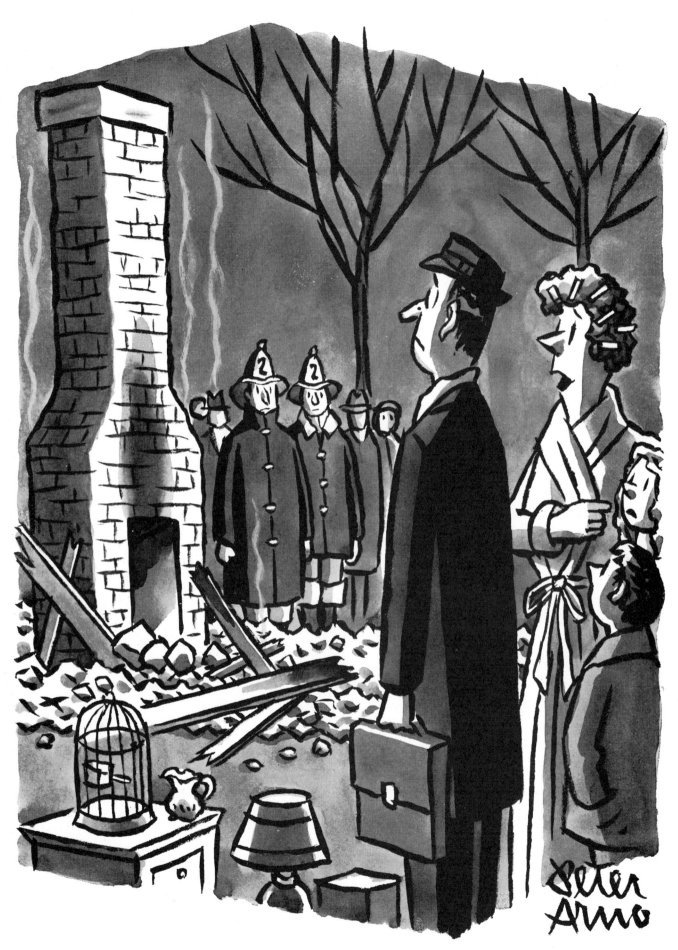

"Well, enough about me. What sort of a day did *you* have?"

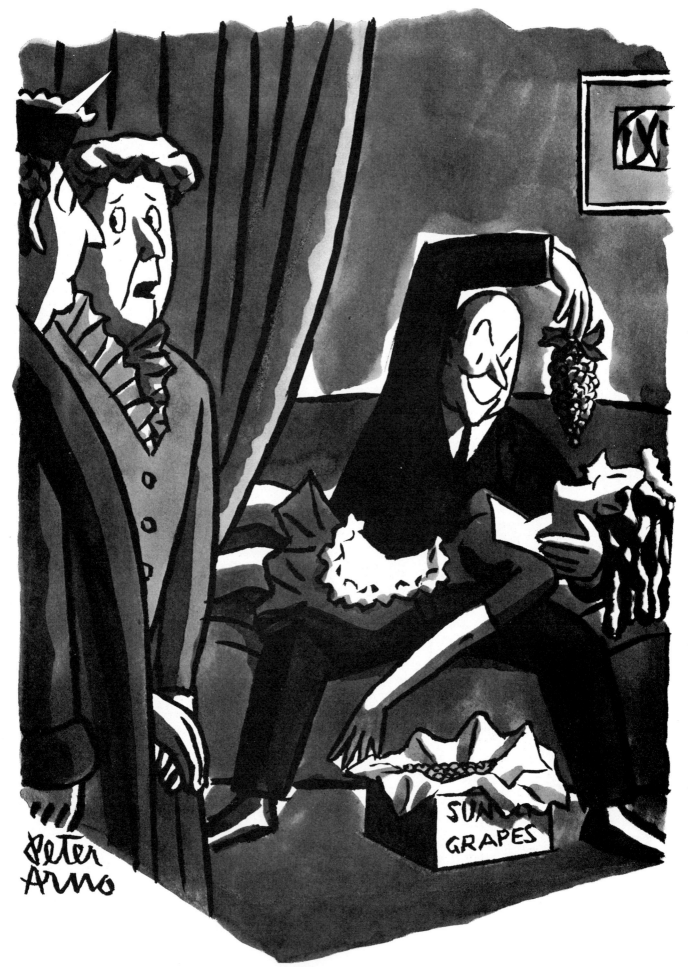

"Oh dear, I'll be so glad when our membership in the Fruit-of-the-Month Club expires!"

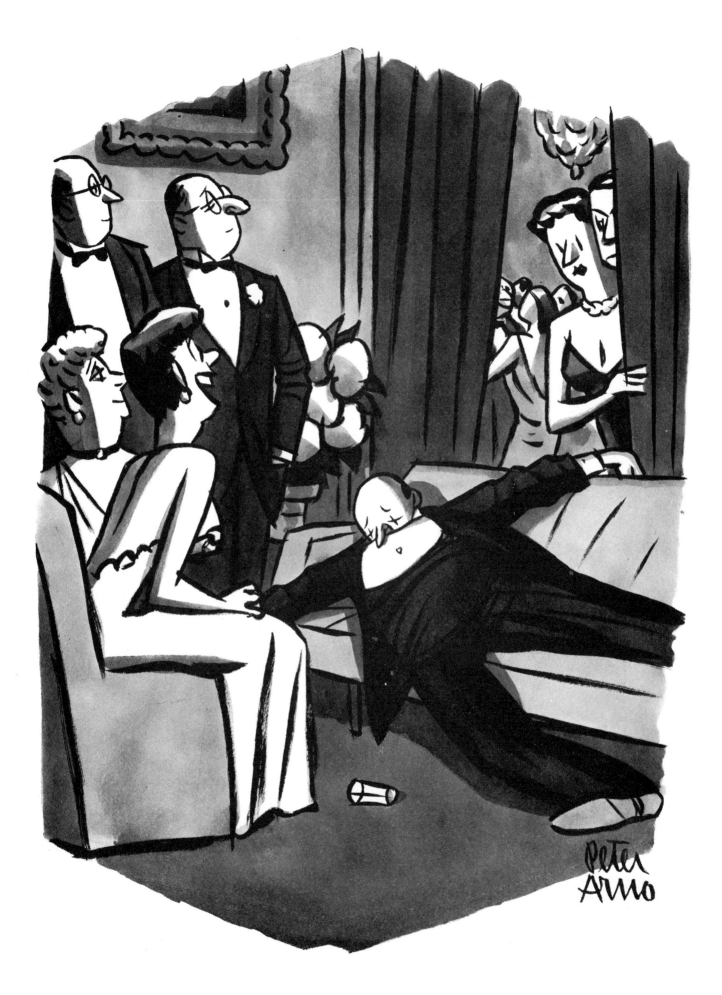

"Oh, you just missed it! Mr. Casey's been absolutely scintillating!"

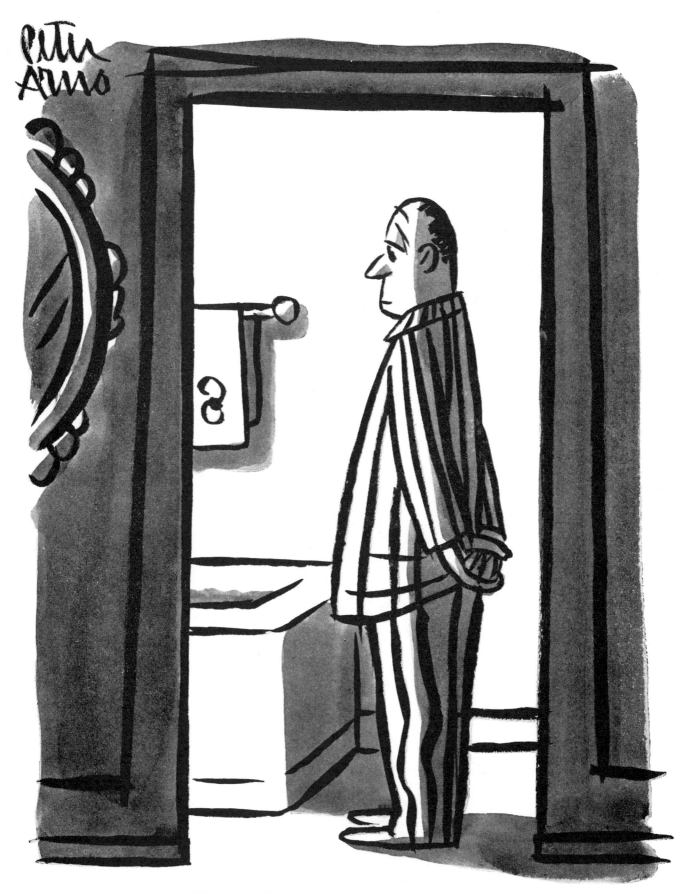

"Of *course* they float. What did you think?"

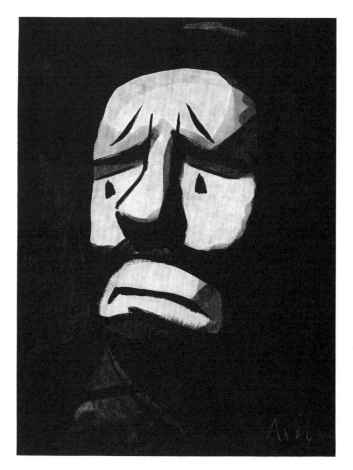

Sad Clown

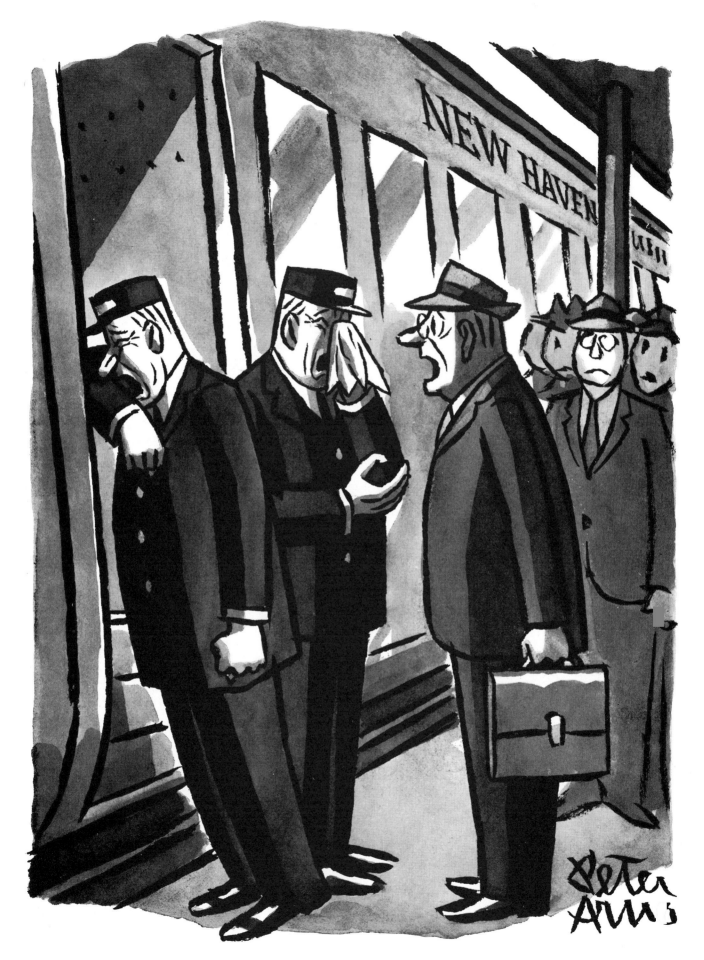

"Great Scott! Now what's happened?"

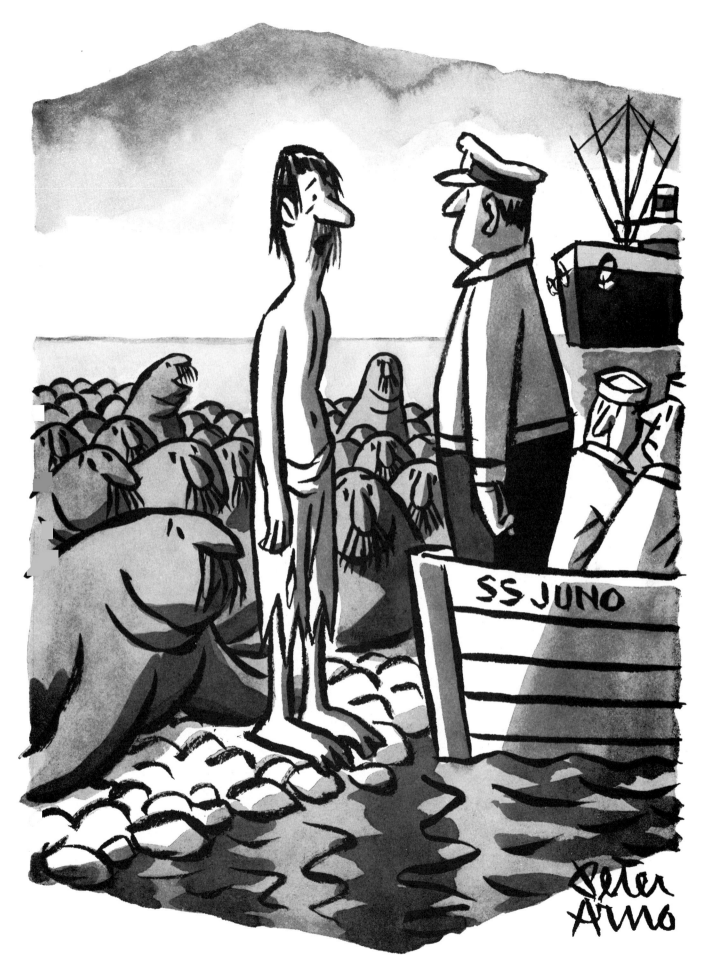

"They think I'm their leader."

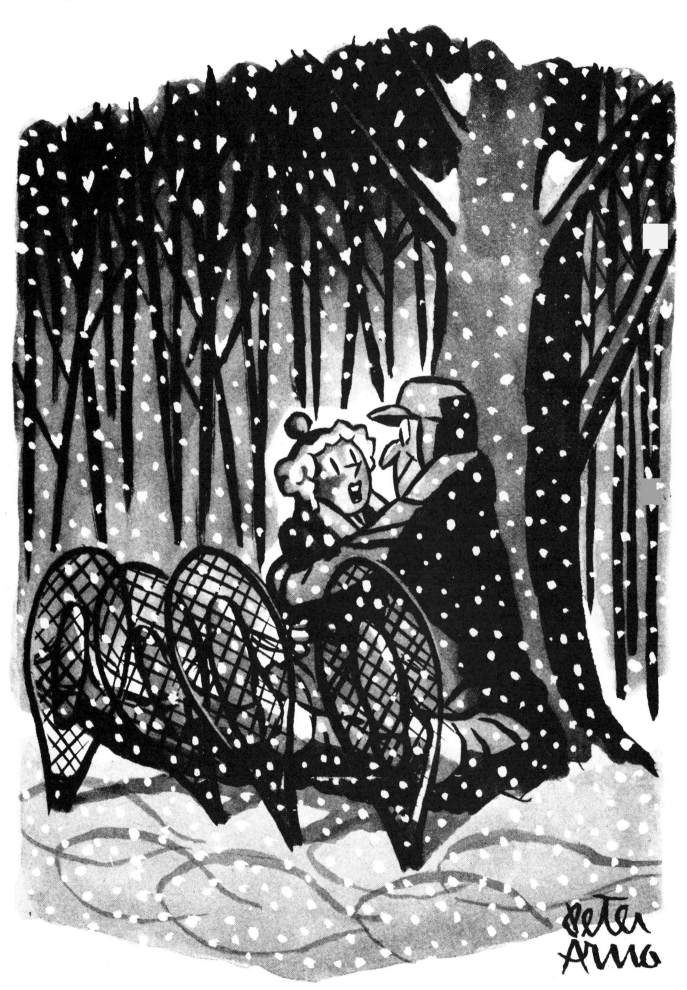

"But Mr. Deming, shouldn't we look for help before we huddle together for warmth?"

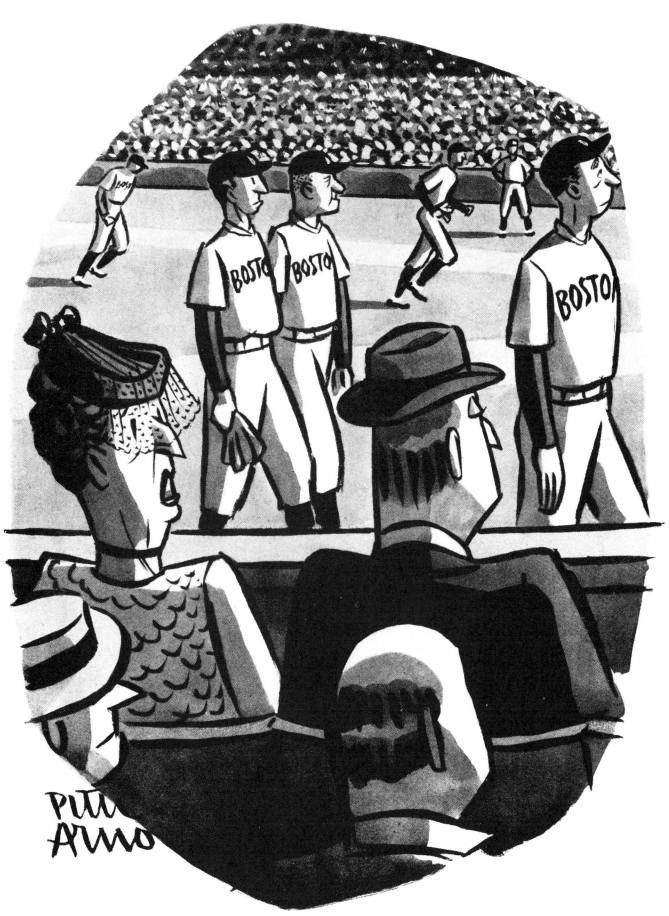

"They don't look Bostonian."

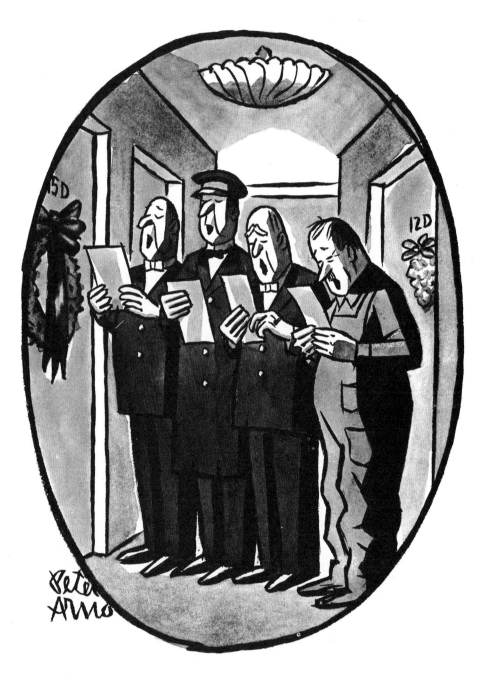

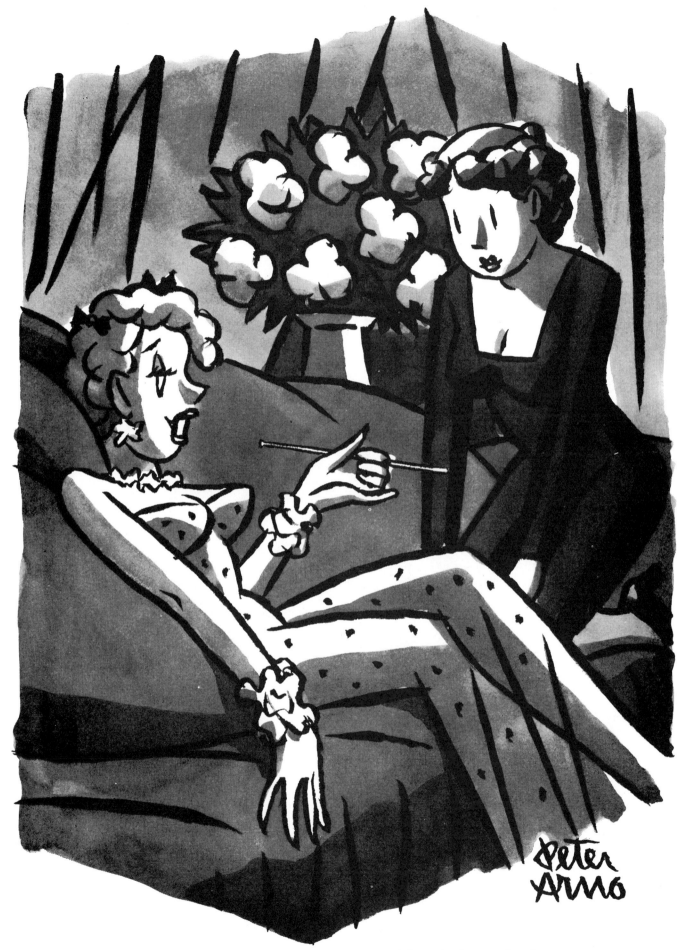

"Of course I still have my room at the 'Y'—a girl can do that much to keep her mother happy."

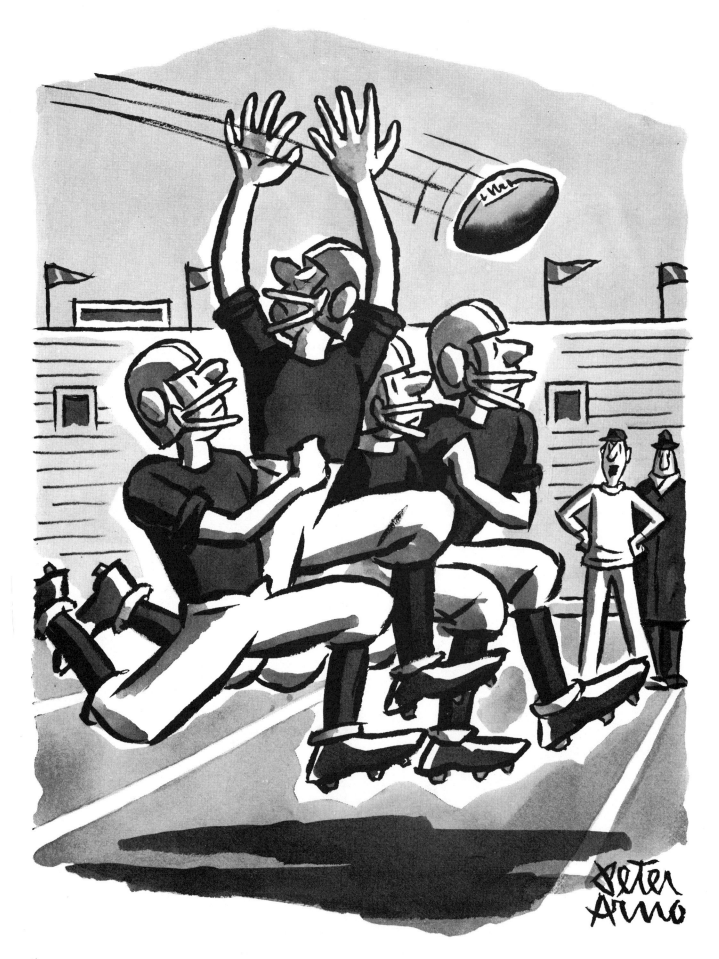

"*There they go, the Four Horsemen—Famine, Pestilence, Death, and Butterfingers.*"

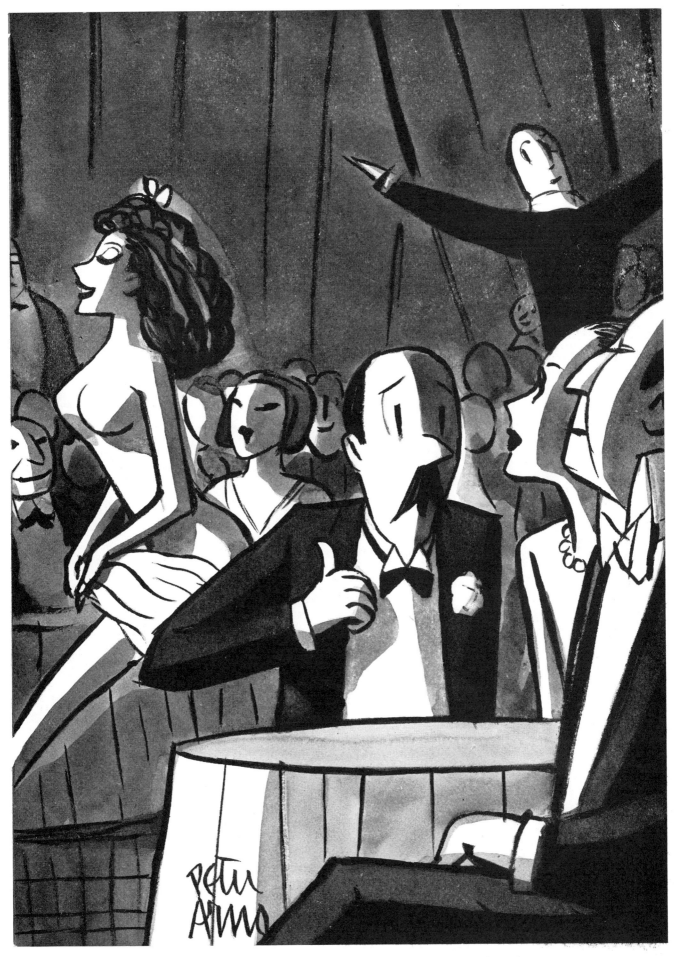

"One would think she'd be subject to a series of nasty colds."

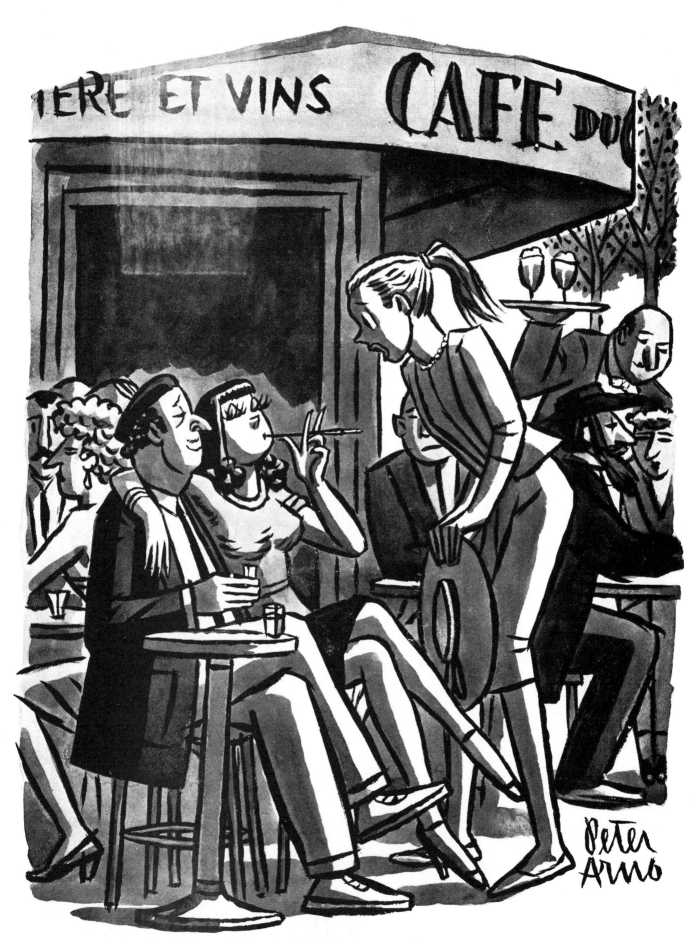

"But Mary Lou! You mean you're not going back to Bryn Mawr _ever_?"

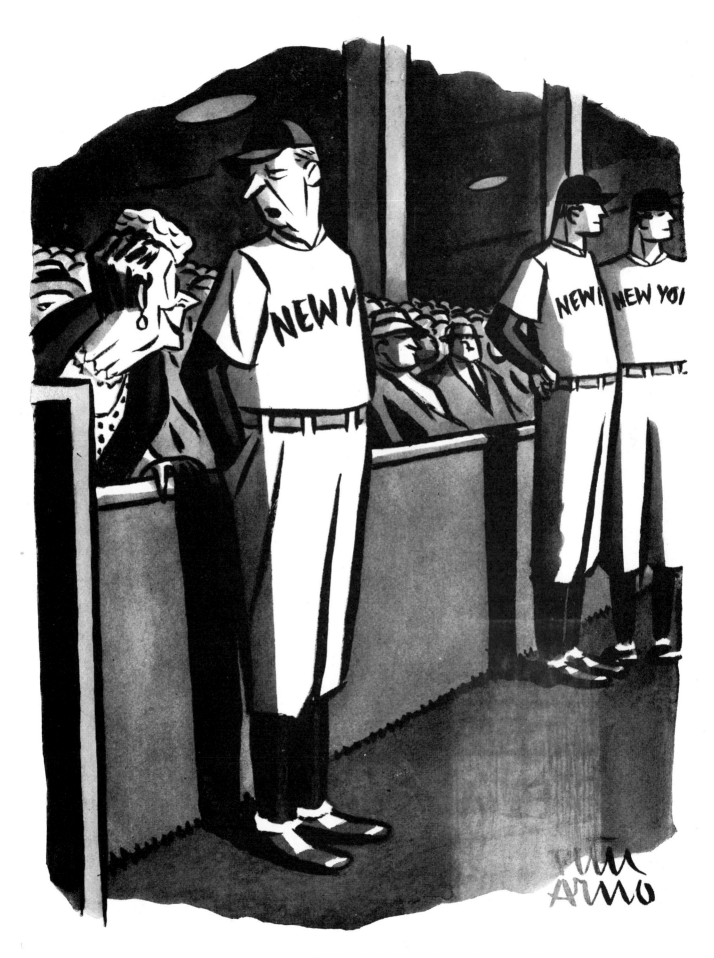

"Sometimes we sell them, lady, but only to other teams."

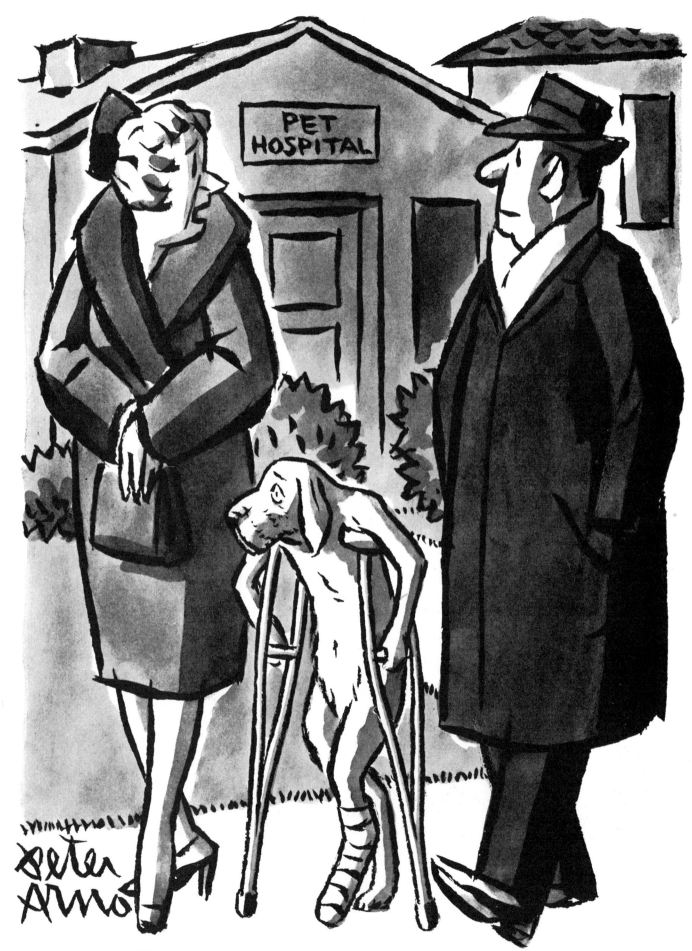

"He may be a fine veterinarian, but we're going to get some funny looks."

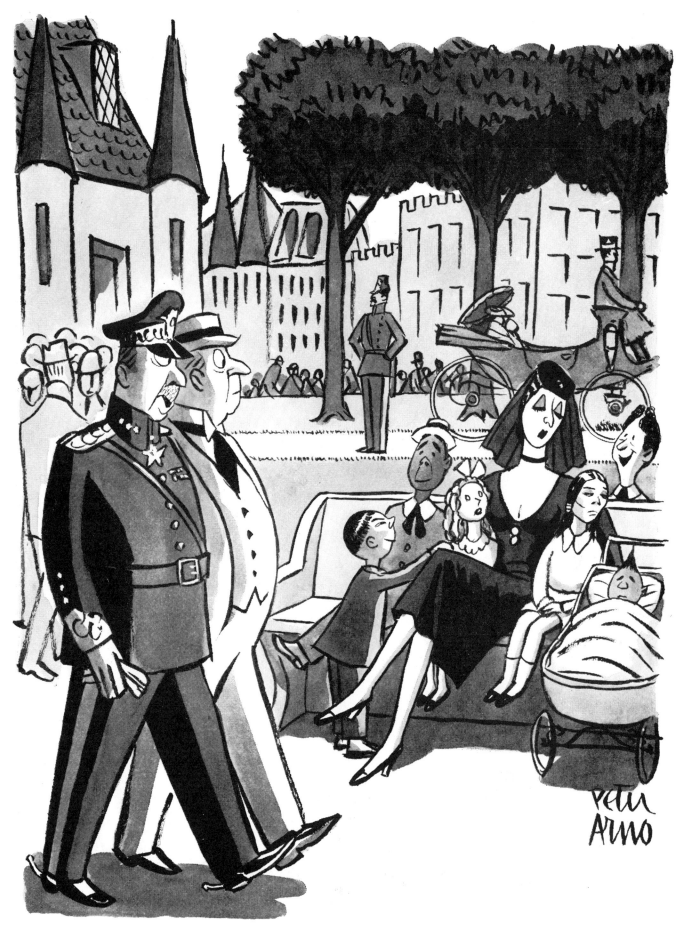

"That's Q37, in her day one of the most effective secret agents this country ever had."

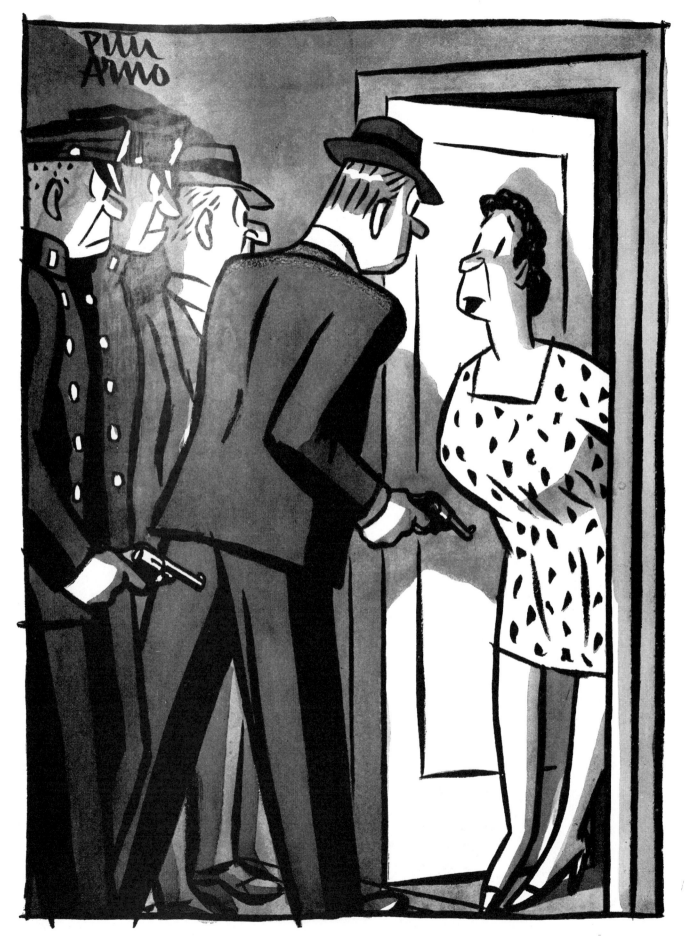

"*I hate to think of waking him. He didn't get in till all hours.*"

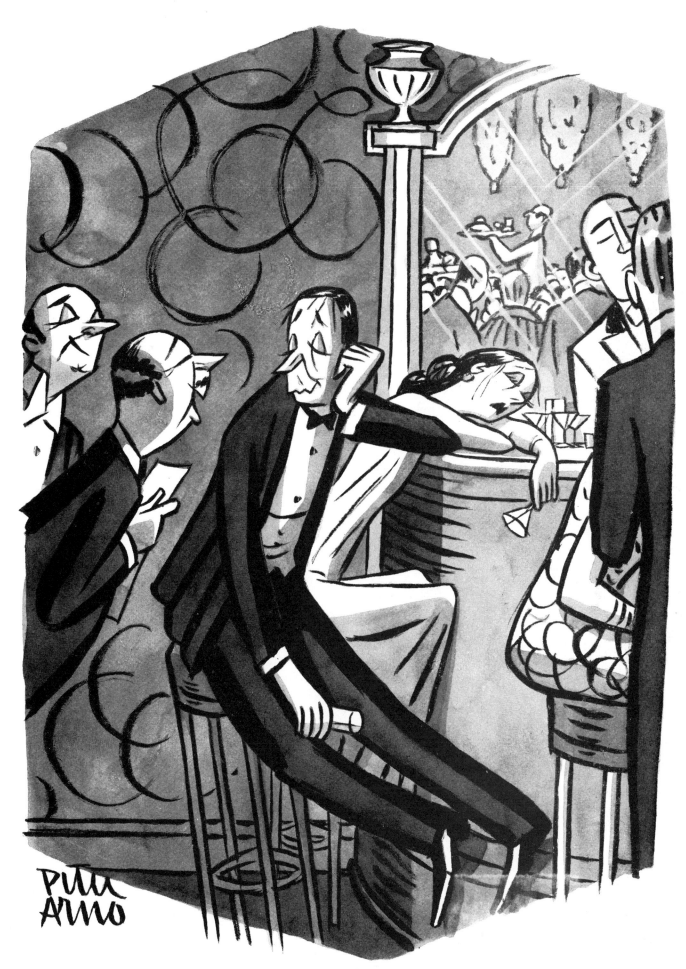

"Ah, M'sieu, I have a table for you now."

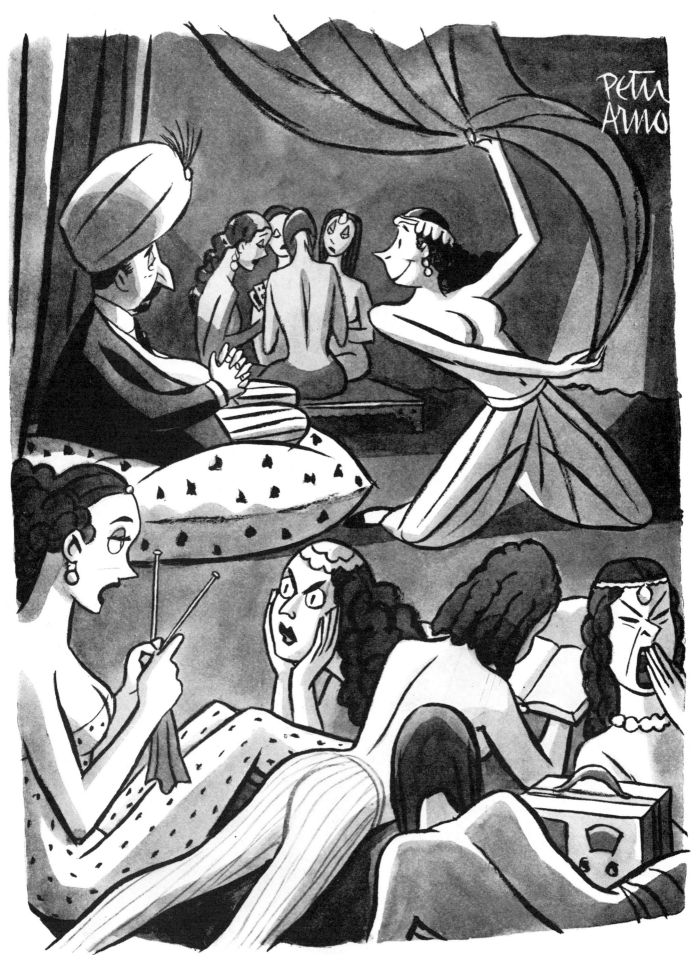

"You can certainly tell it's her first day here."

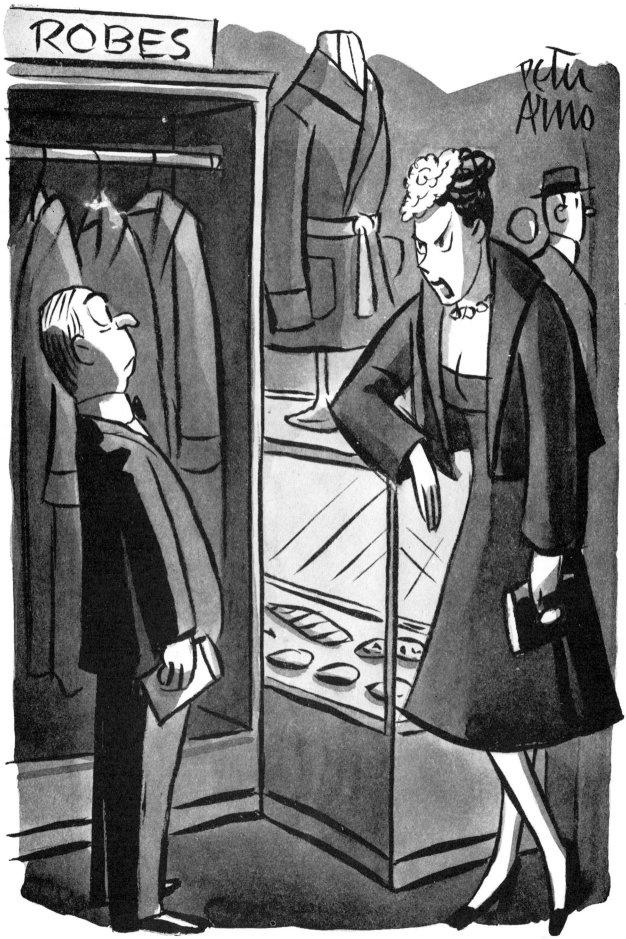

"He's just about your size—damn it!"

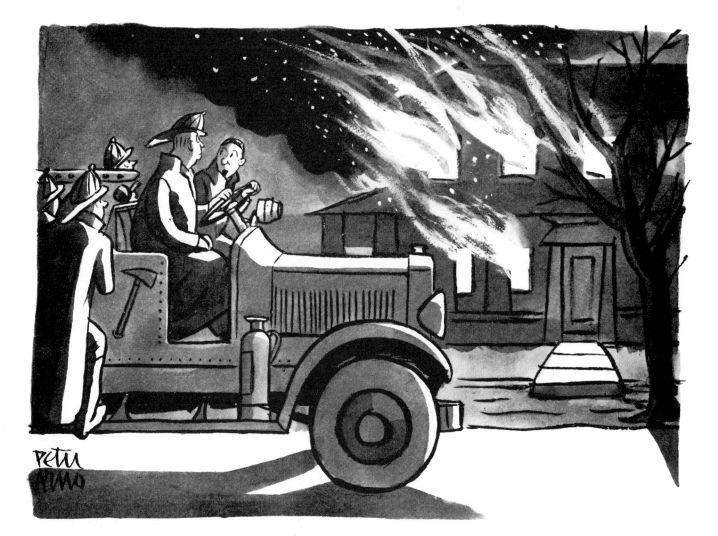

"This place certainly fits the description."

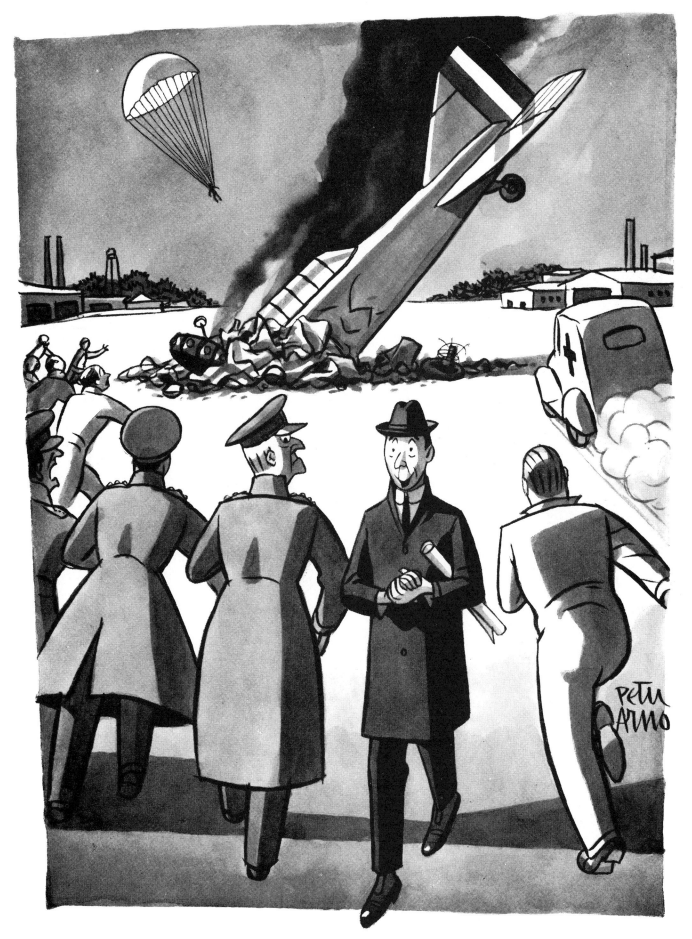

"Well, back to the old drawing board."

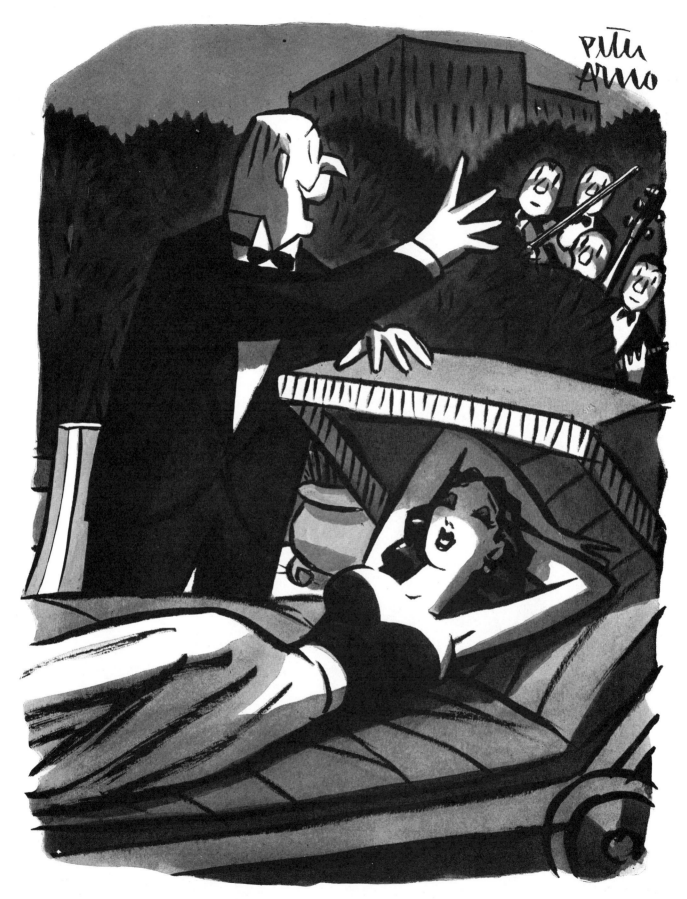

"Thank you, boys. I'll take it from here."

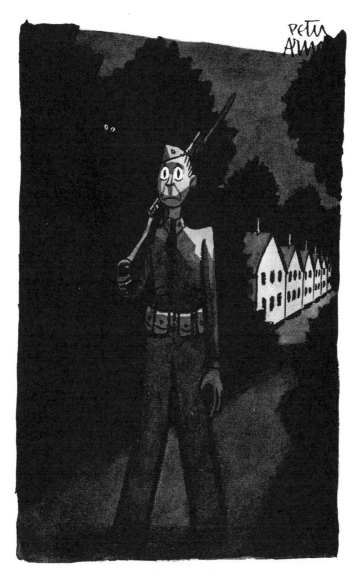

"To—wit, to—whoo! To—wit, to—whoo!"

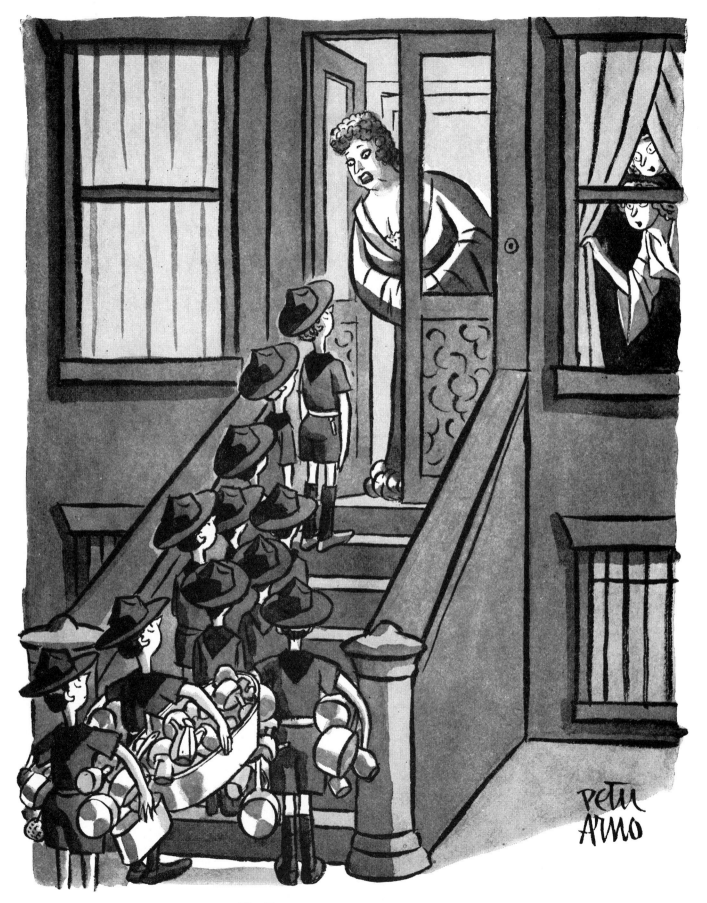

"*I tell you we haven't got any aluminum!*"

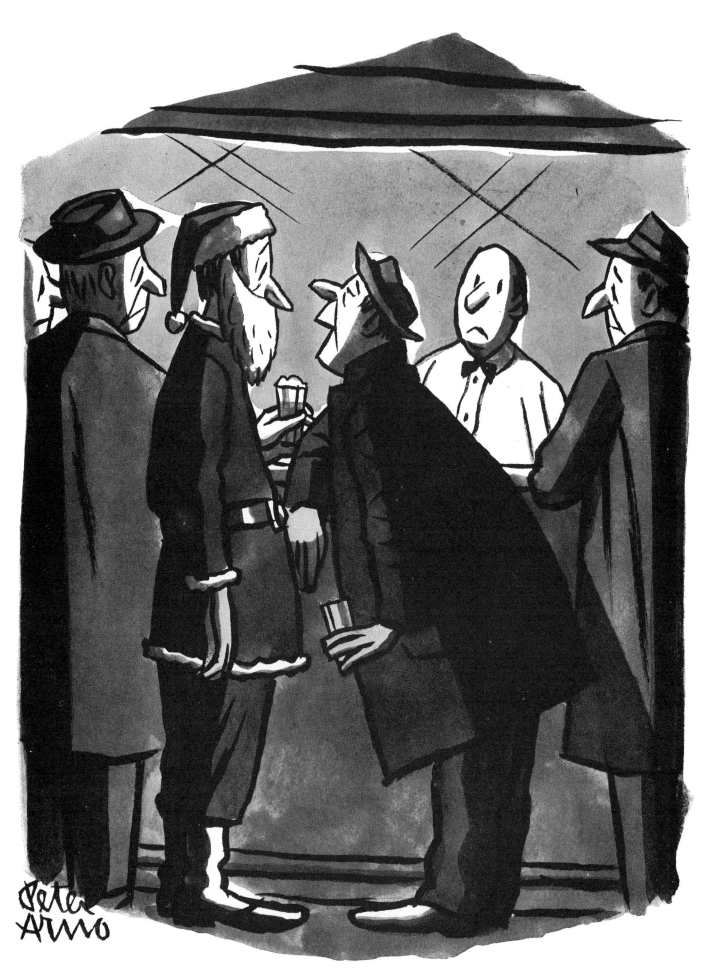

"*Five dollars says you can't tell me the names of all your reindeer.*"

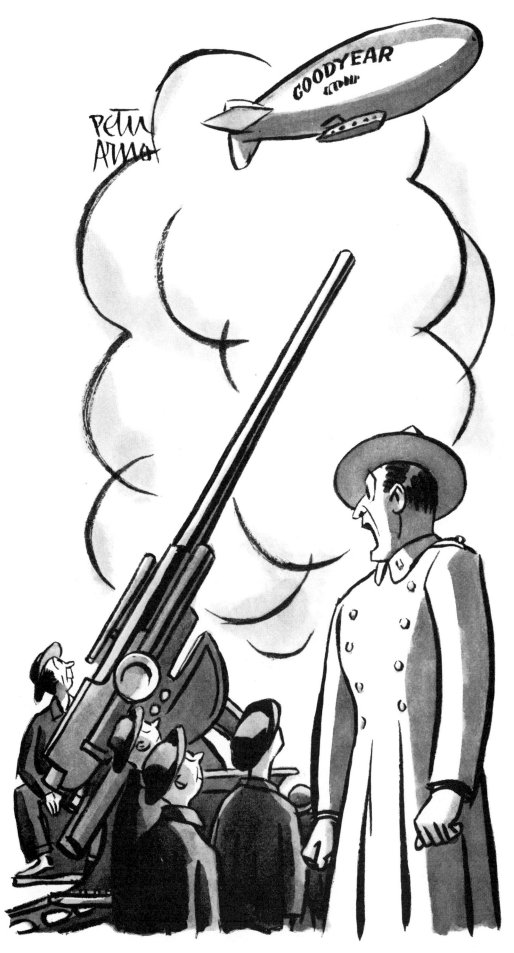

"*Easy now, men! Watch those itching fingers!*"

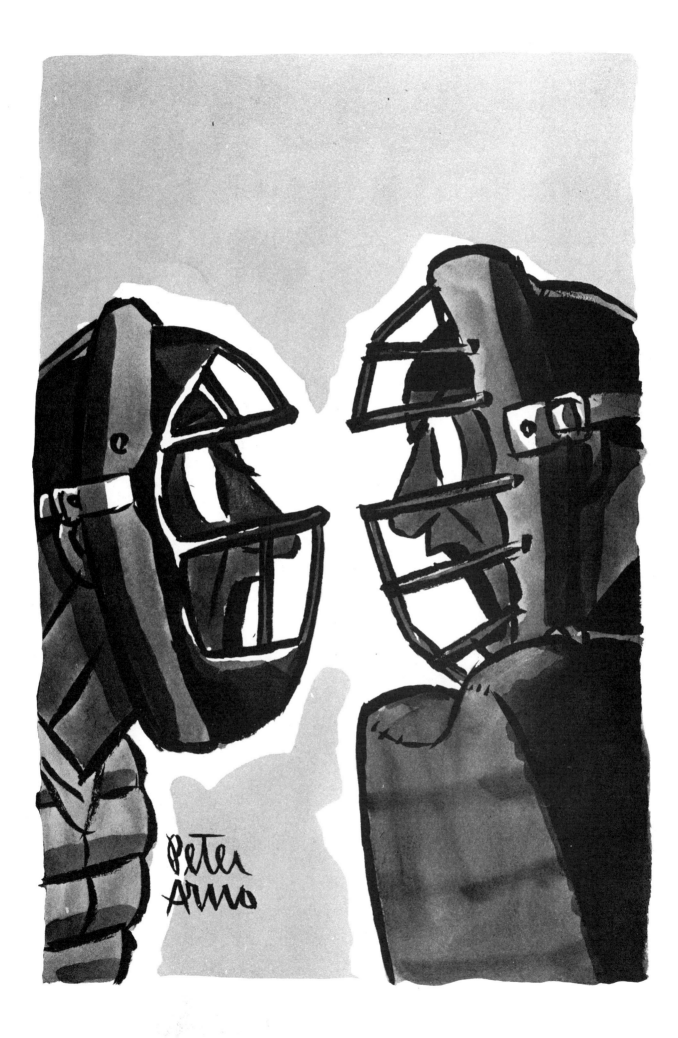

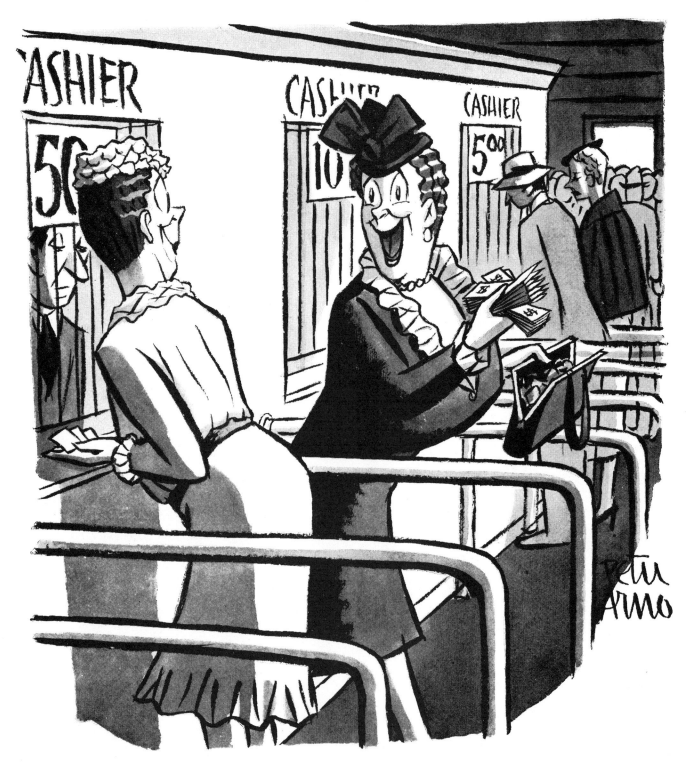

"Don't you just <u>adore</u> it?"

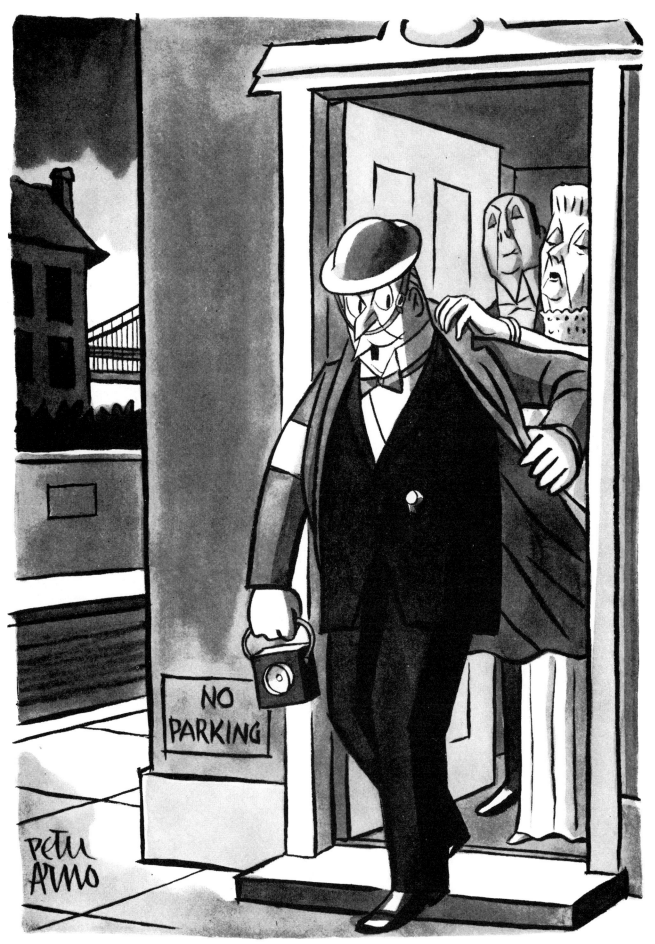

"*Of course, if they <u>don't</u> bomb Sutton Place, I'm going to look like a damn fool.*"

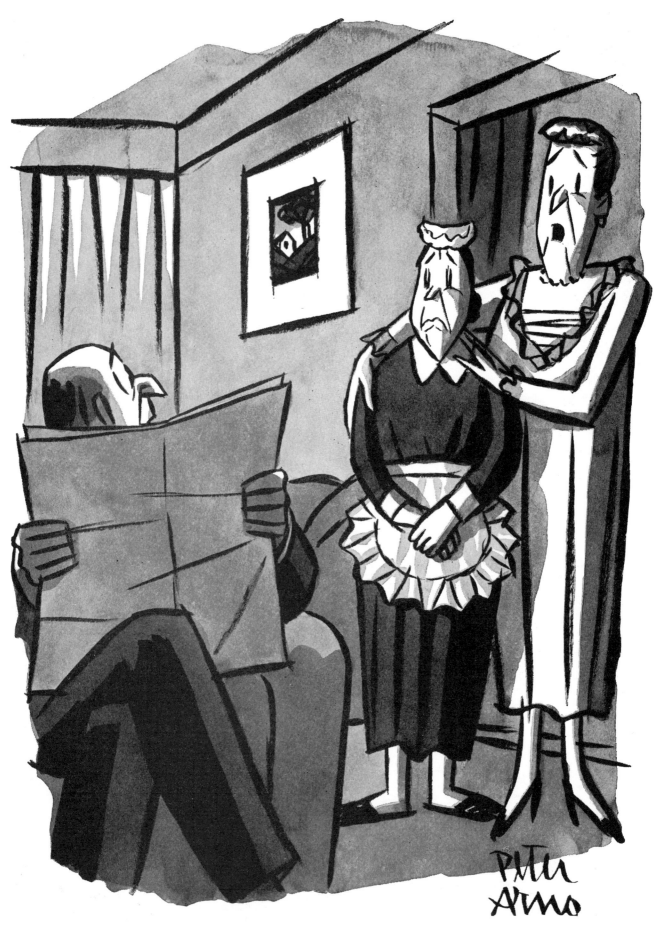

"Charles! Douglas Aircraft has alerted Theodora!"

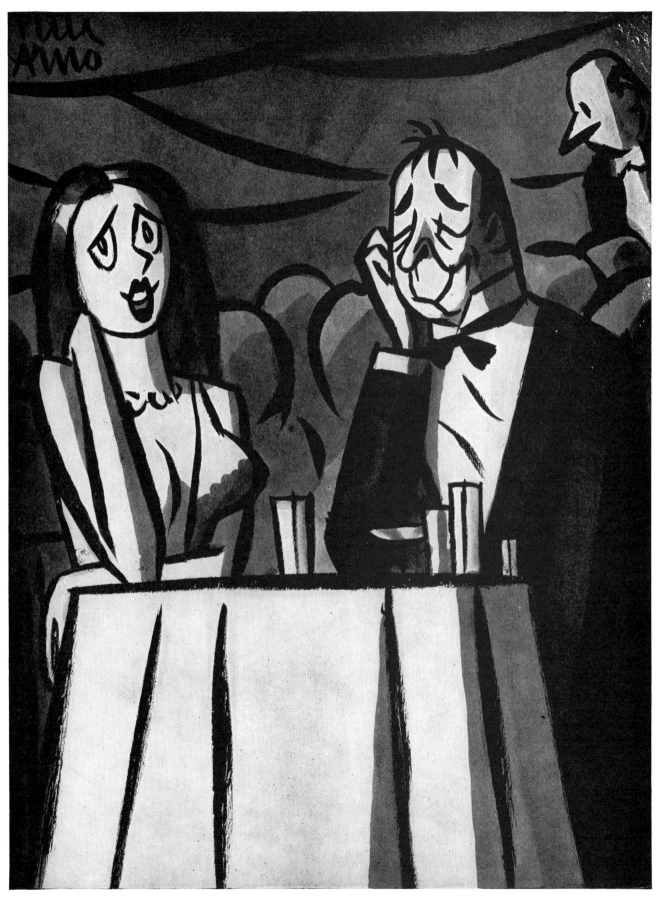

"You're a mystic, Mr. Ryan. _All_ Irishmen are mystics."

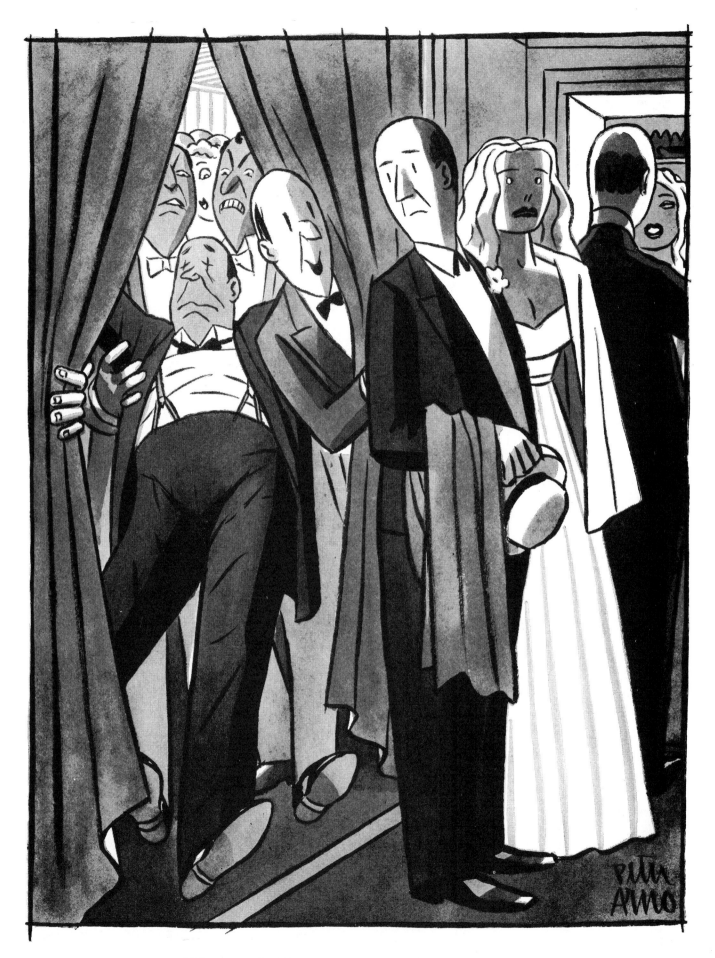

"*Please stand aside, sir. There's a gentleman coming out.*"

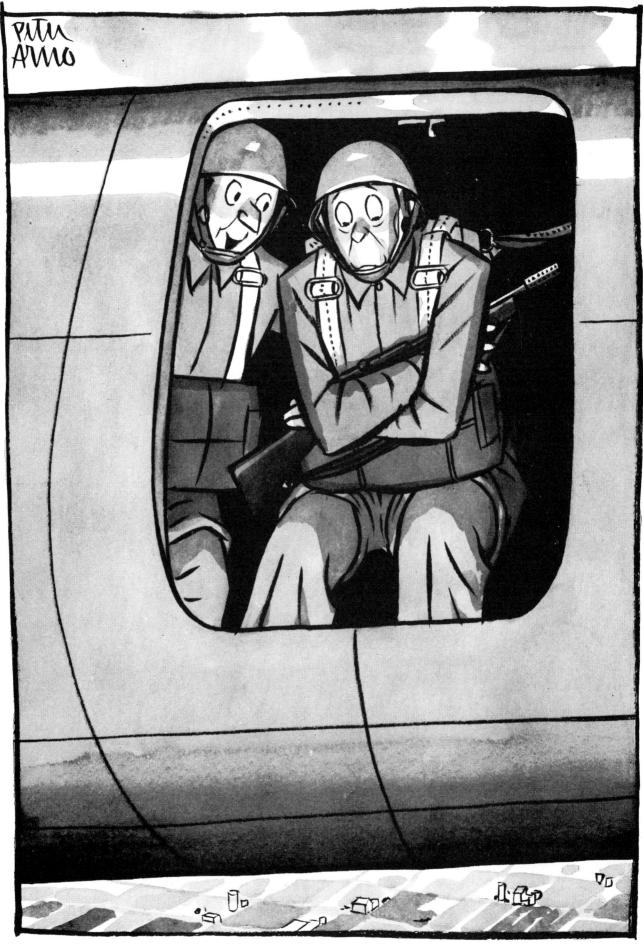

"Look at it this way—you're the baby sparrow and I'm the mamma sparrow."

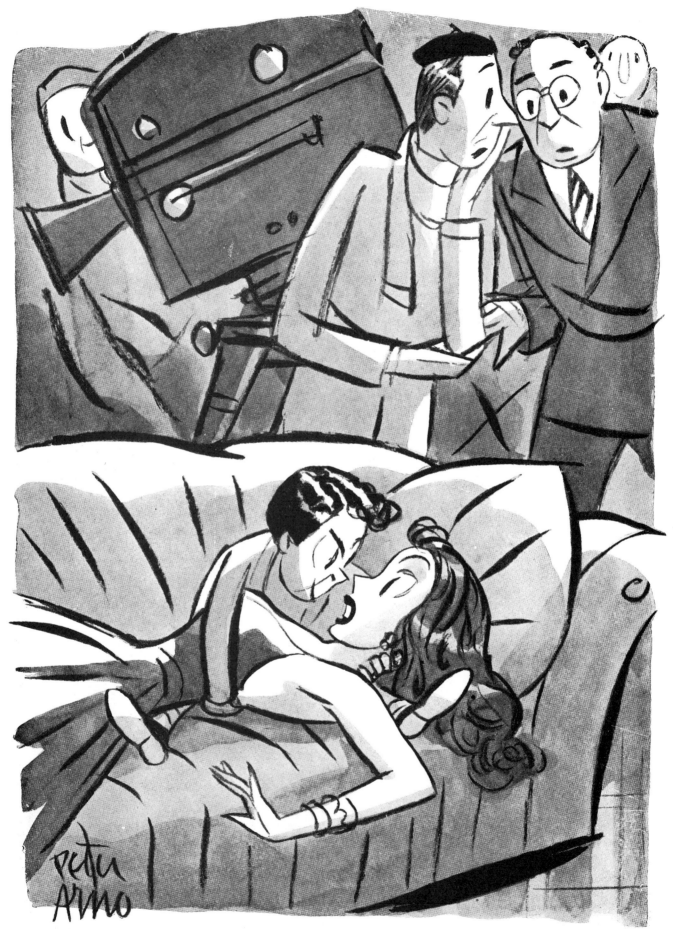

"*I'm afraid as a kid star he's through.*"

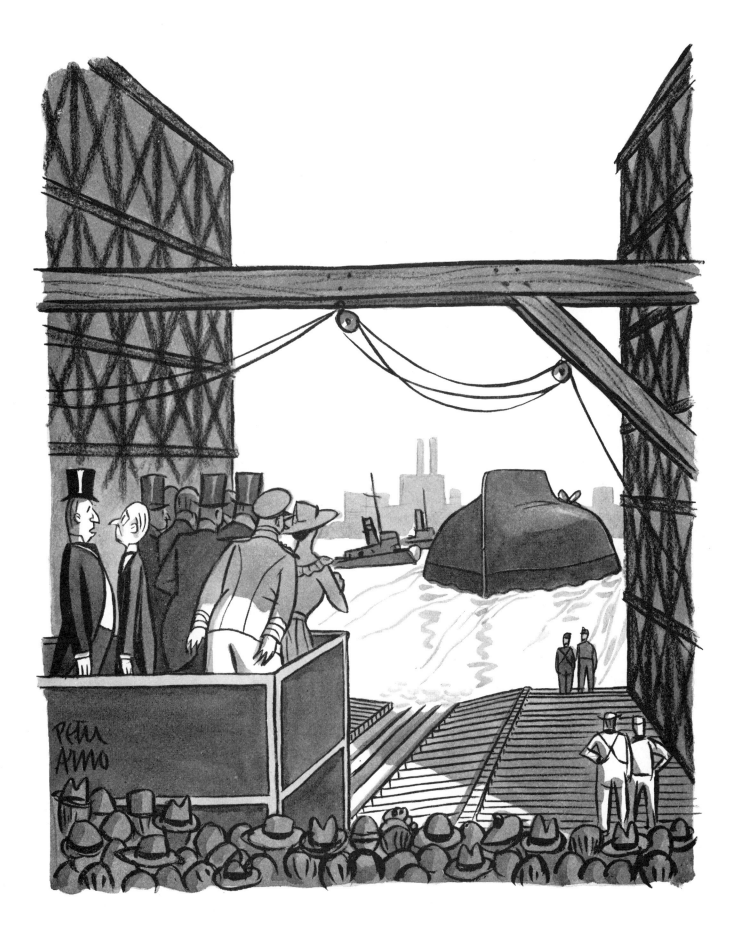

"Well, what's the excuse this time?"

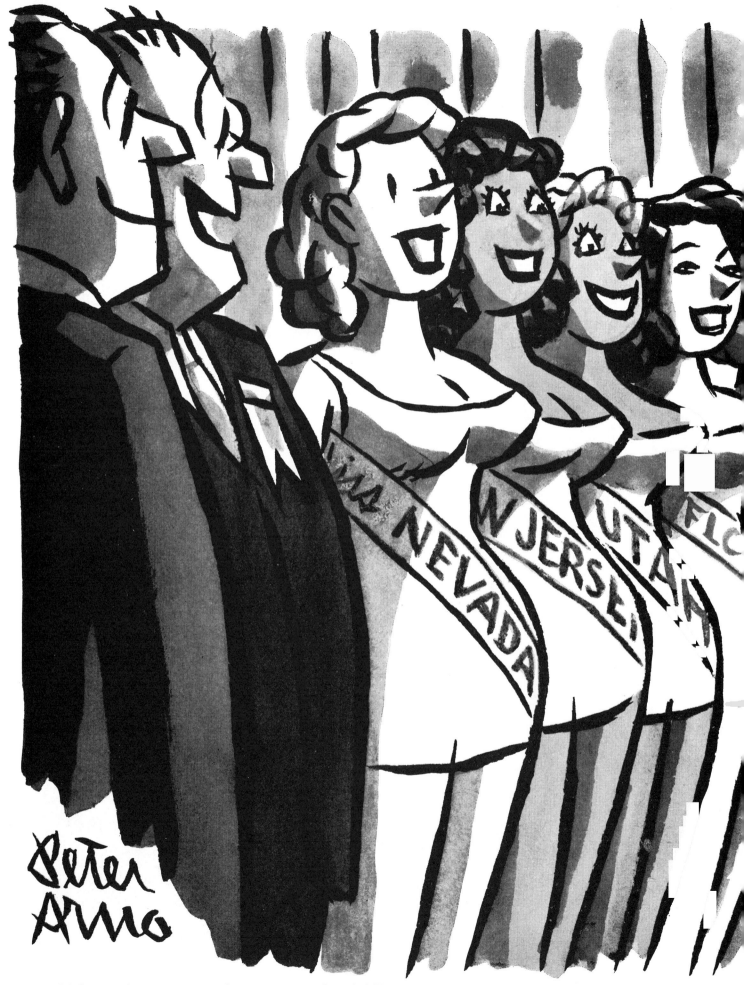

"Makes you kind of proud to be an American, doesn't it?"

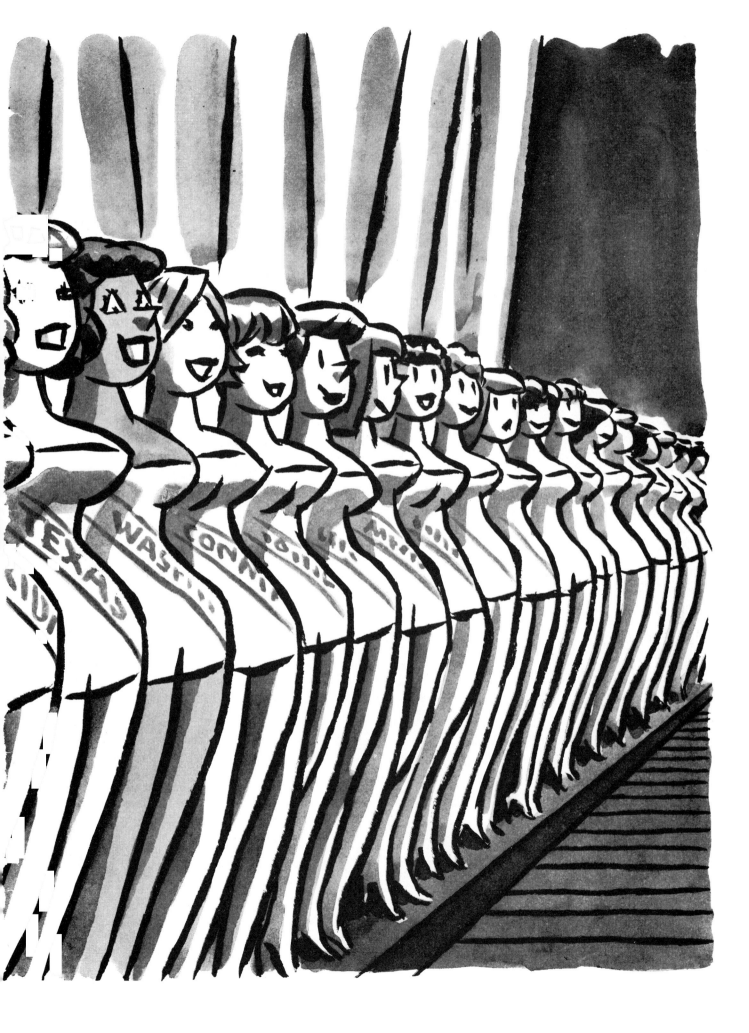

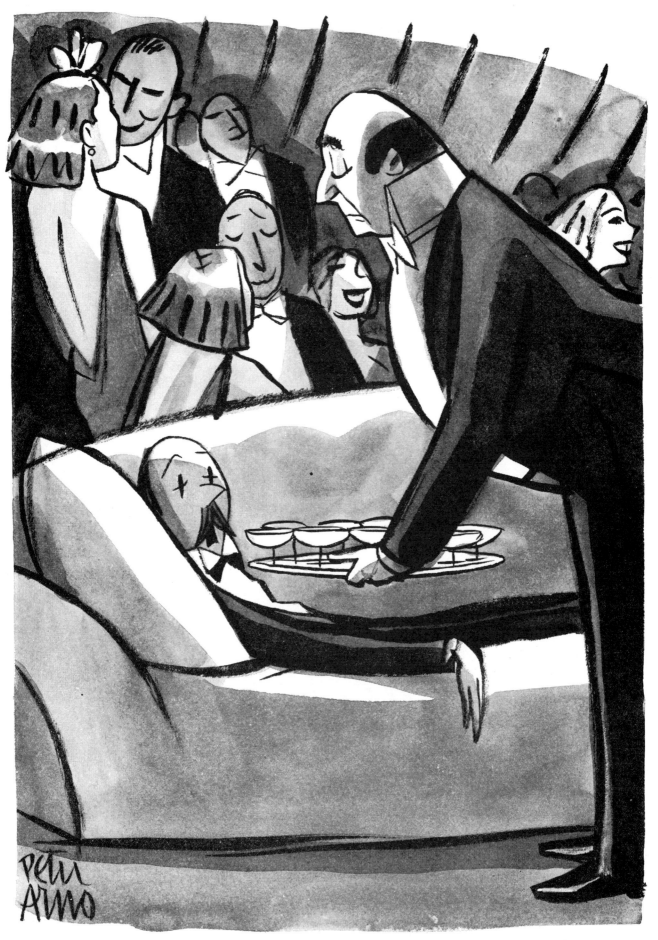

"No, thanks, I've been drinking brandy."

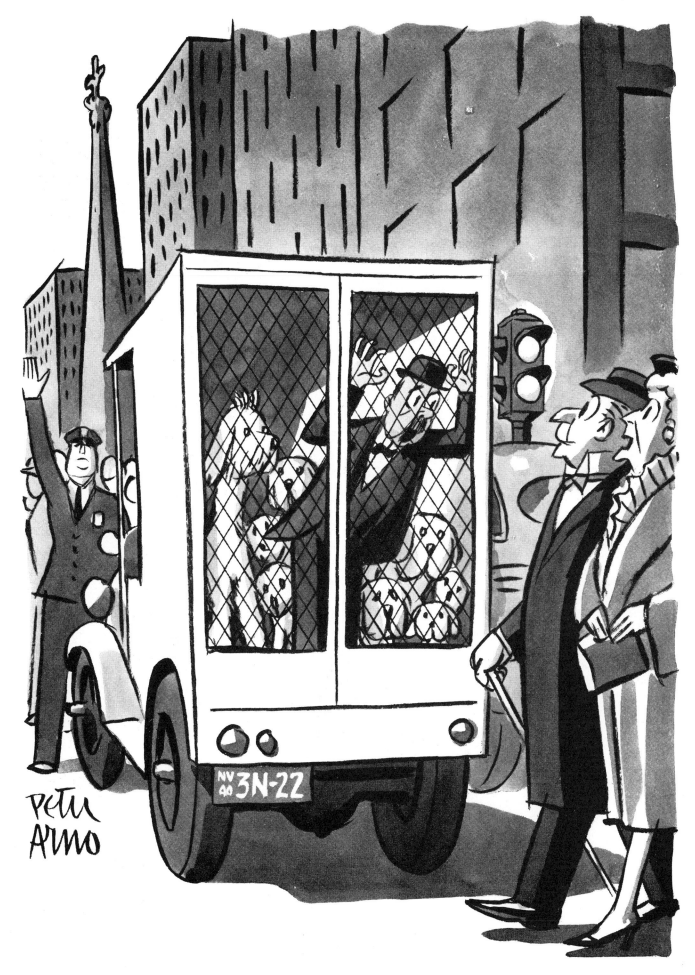

"*I'm Edmund J. Murchison of 222 Morton Street! A horrible mistake has been made!*"

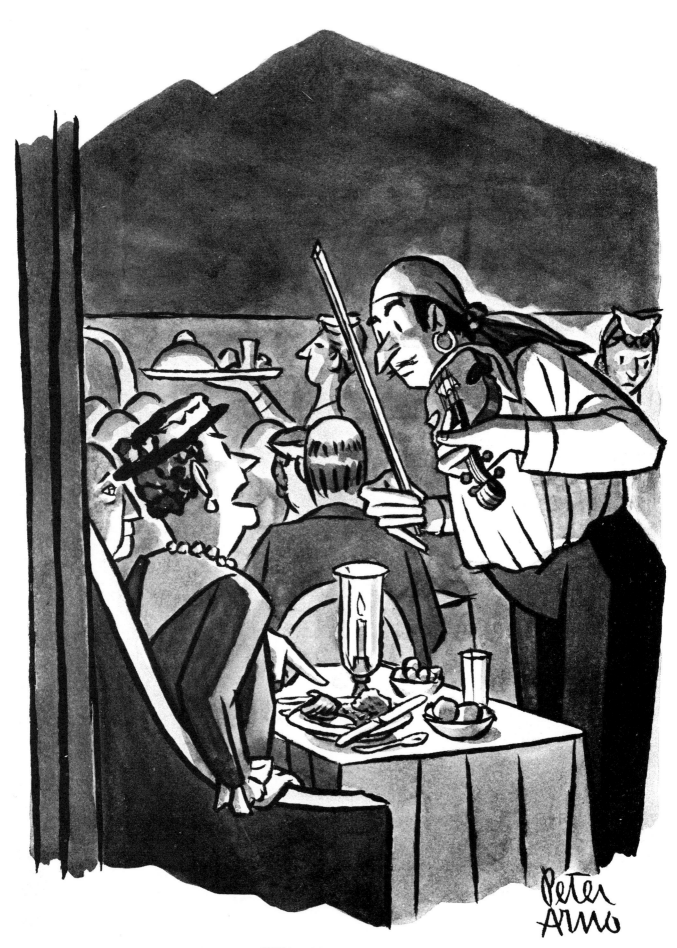

"This giblet gravy is lumpy!"

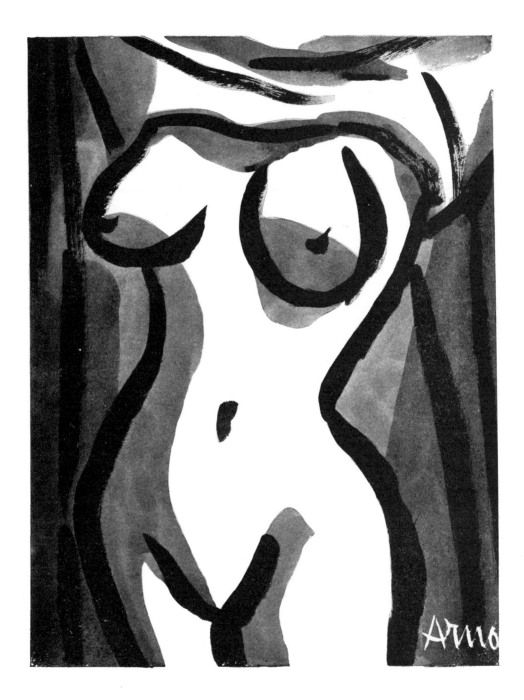

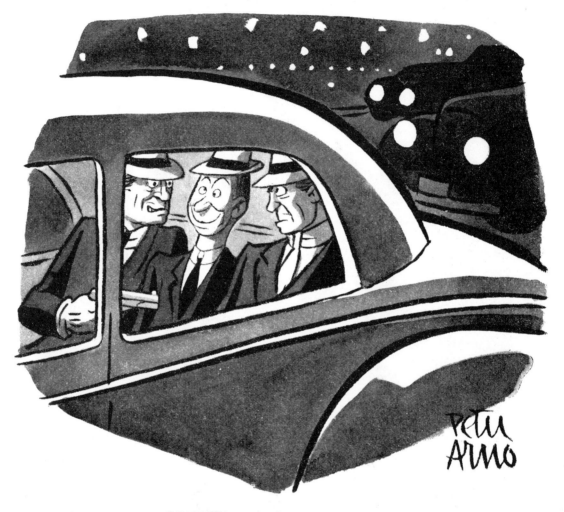

"*O'Hallihan, you know too much.*"

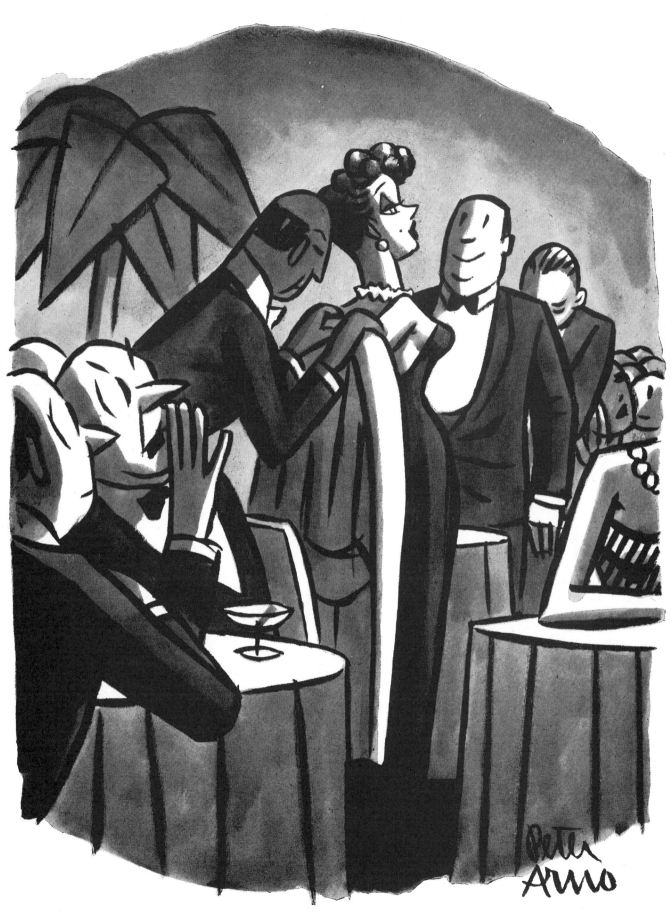

"*I very nearly married her once. Fortunately, I had a cracking good lawyer.*"

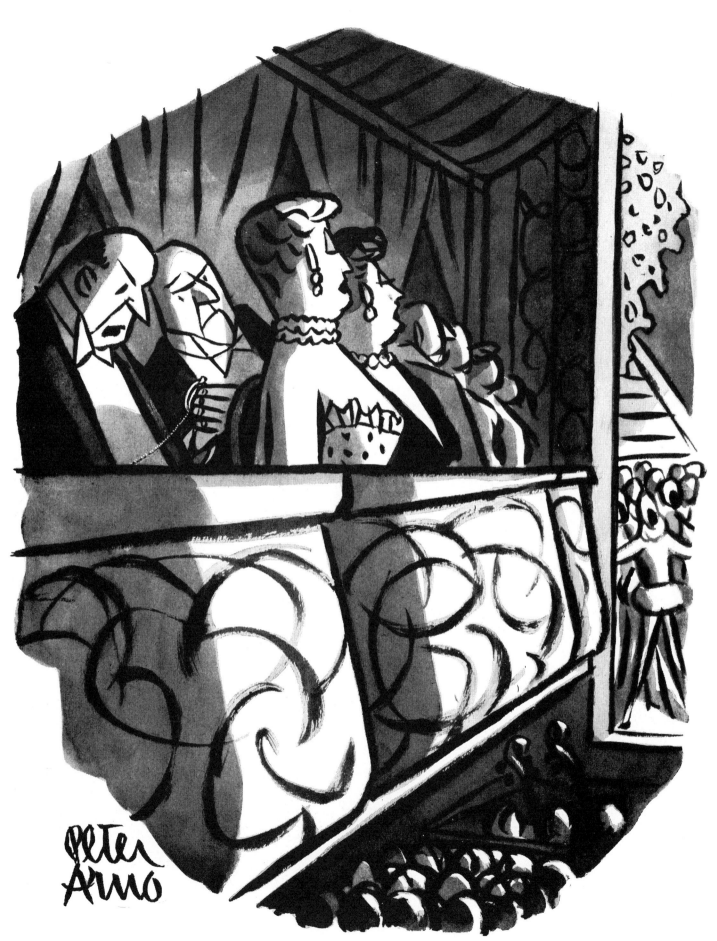

"Well, we're over the hump."

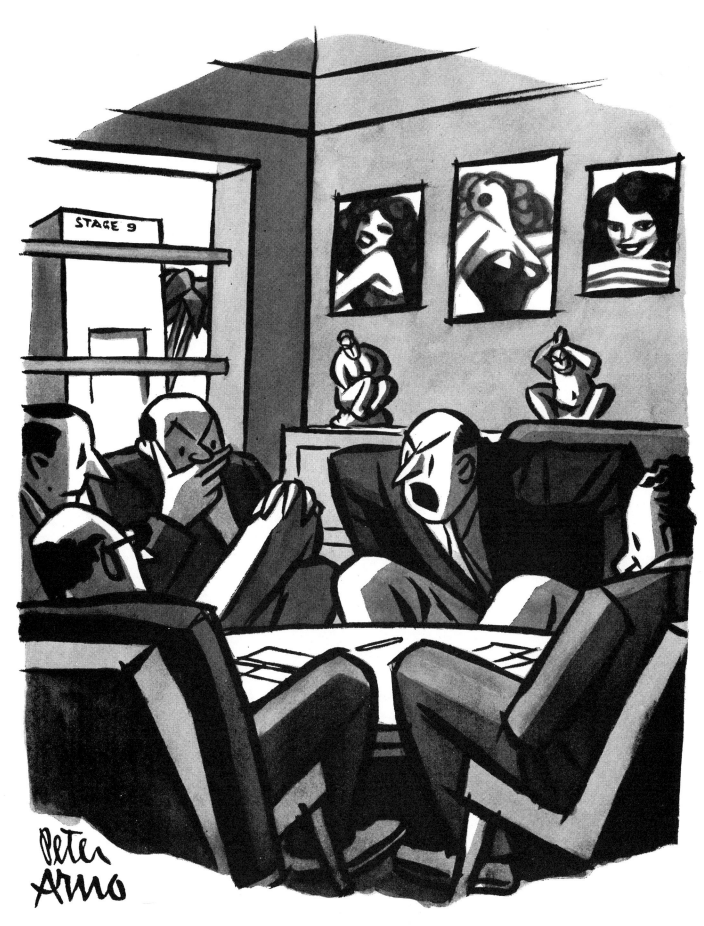

"*Damn it , there must be <u>some</u> taboo subject we can approach honestly and fearlessly!*"

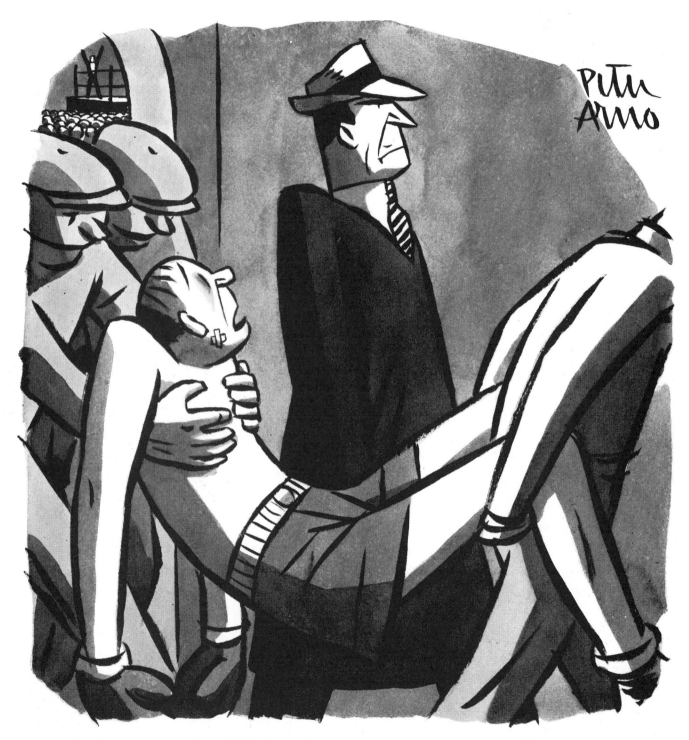

"All of a sudden you stop saying 'we.'"

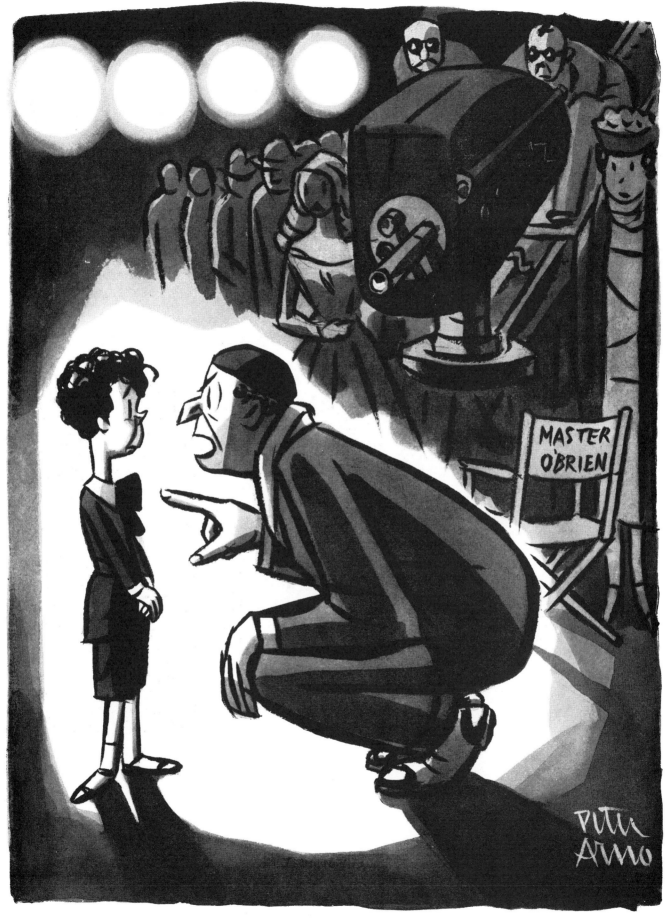

"You're unhappy, see? You're an unwanted child. You were born out of wedlock."

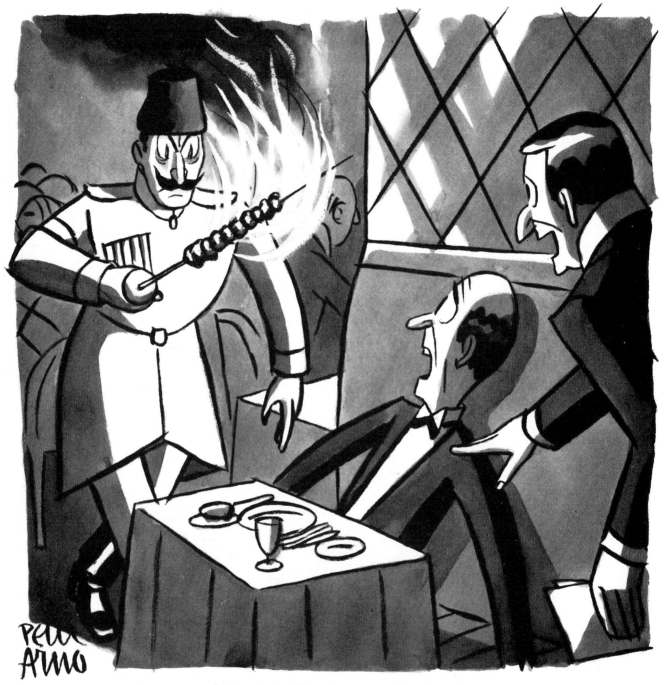

"Steady sir! There's no cause for alarm."

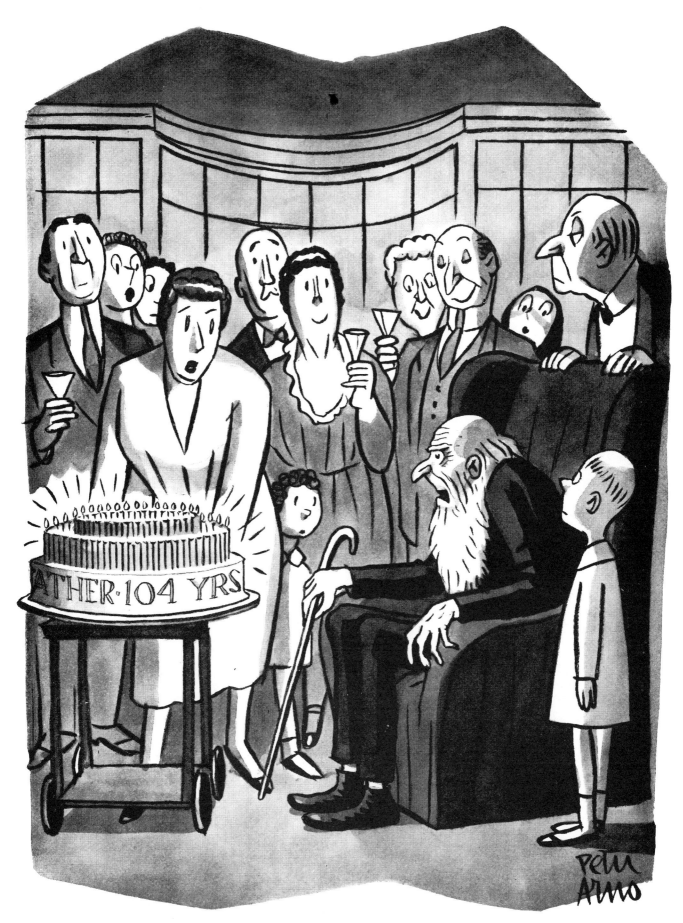

"*Never mind the damned cake! Where are the reporters?*"

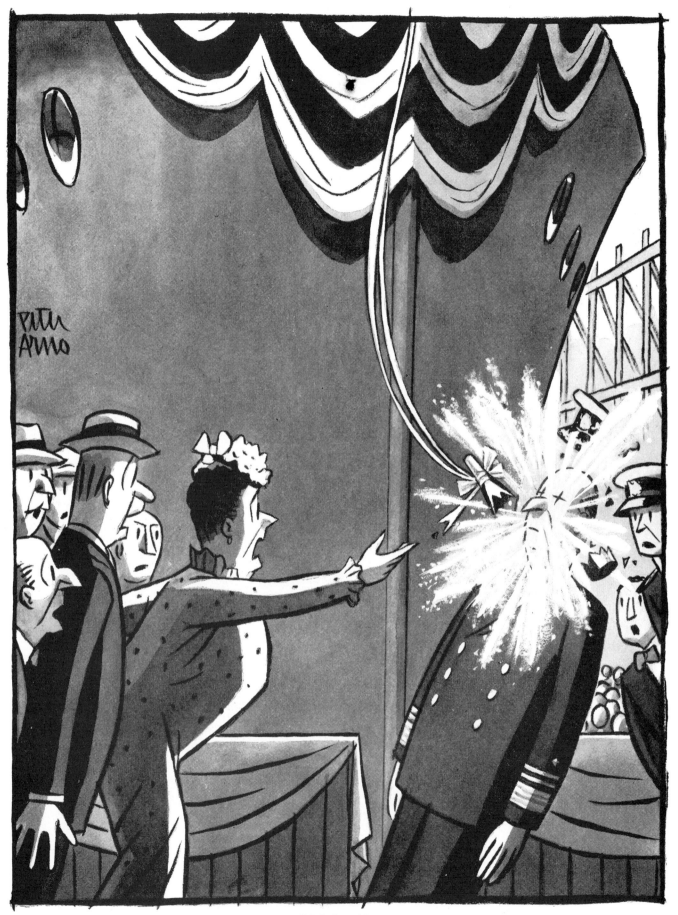

"Oh dear!"

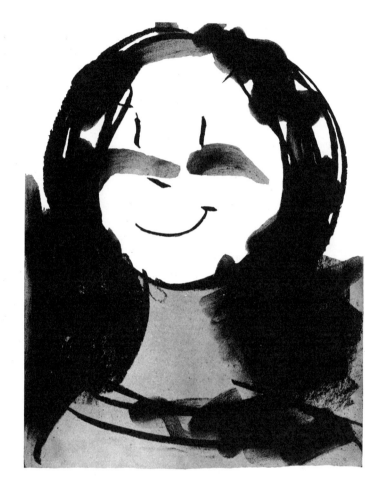

Happy Child

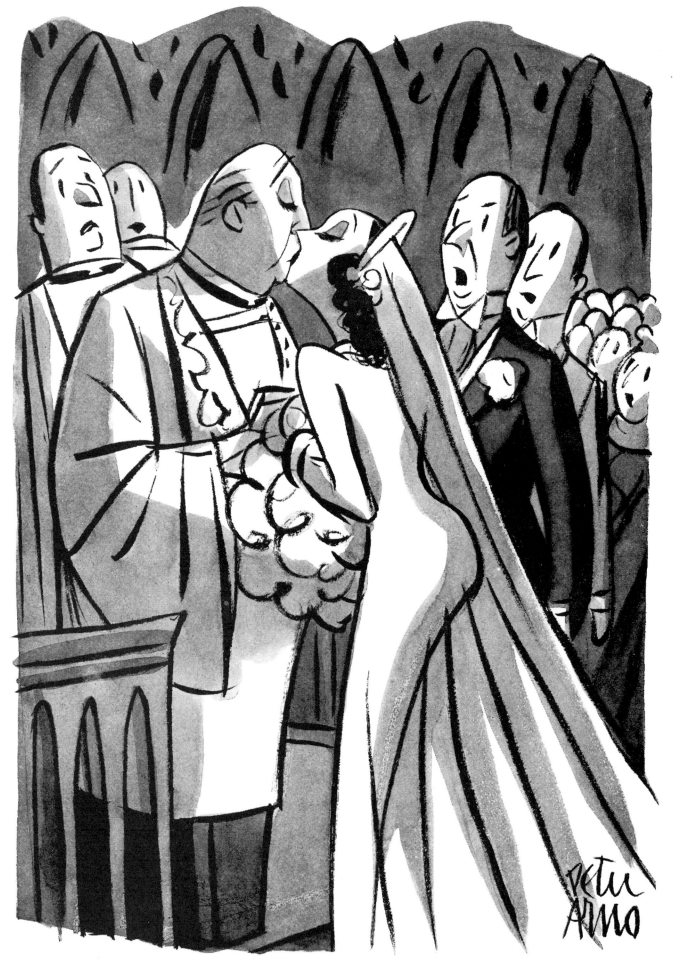

"Dr. Emerson! Please!"

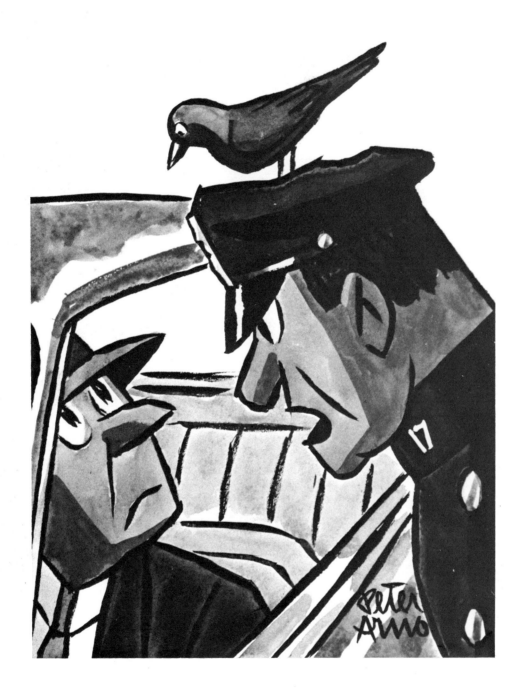

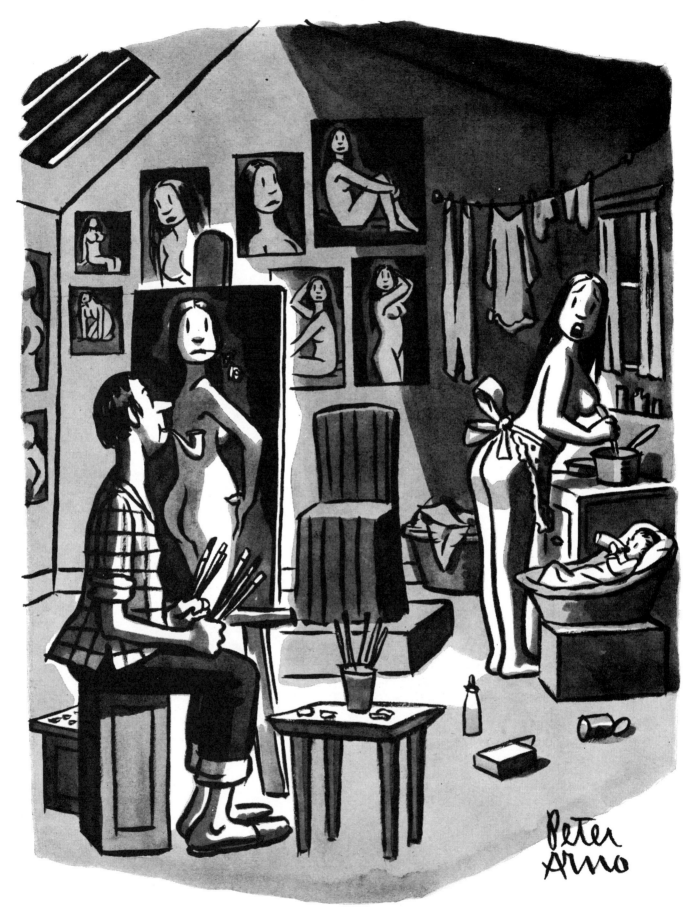

"In a minute! In a minute!"

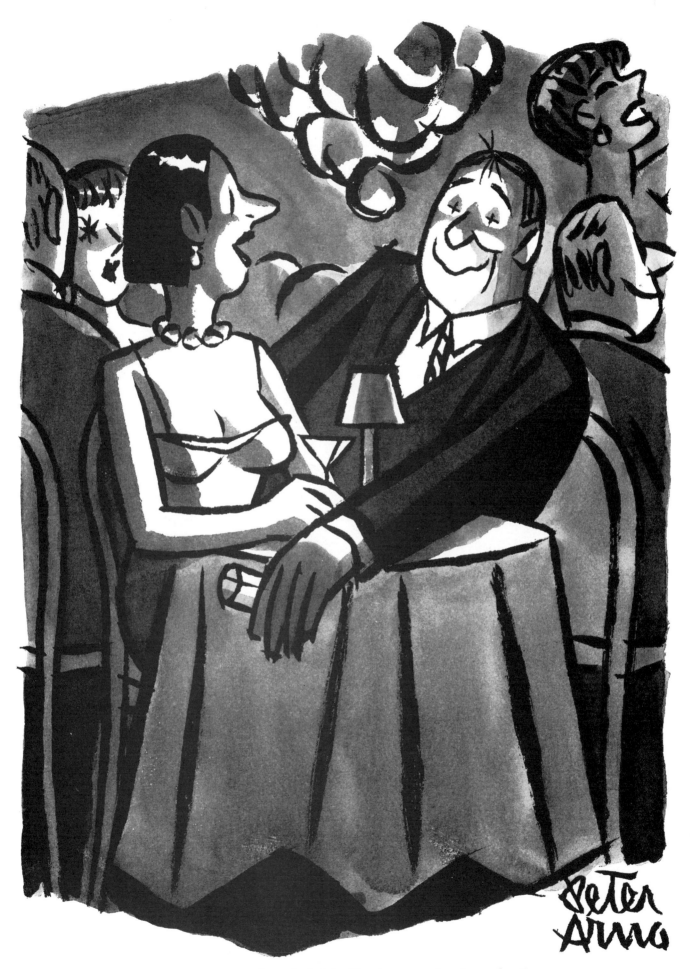

"You have a very penetrating mind, Mr. Harrington—drunk or sober."

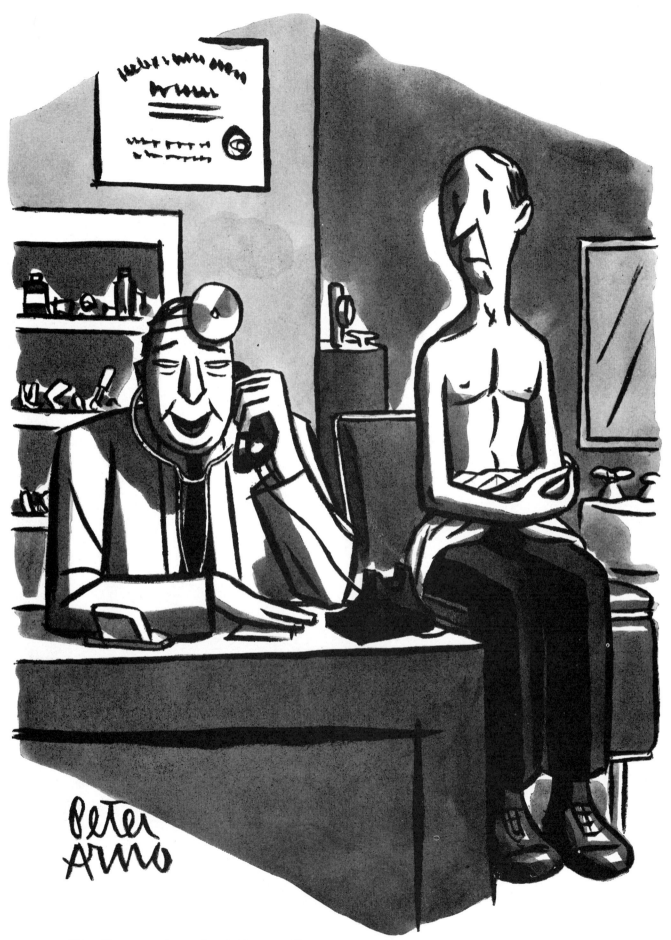

"By all means, dear—buy it if you really want it. We'll find the money for it somehow."

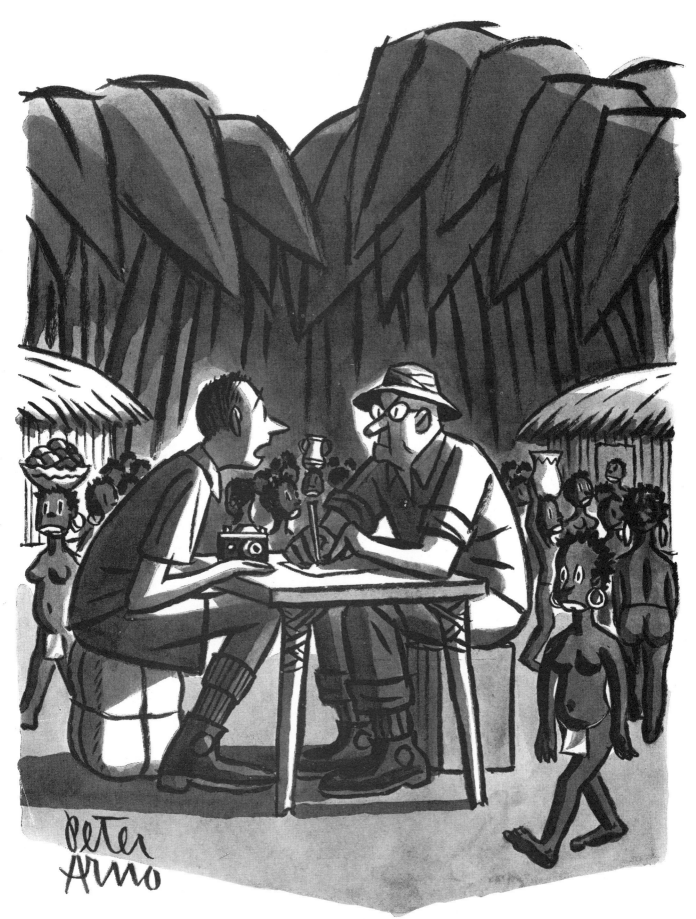

"There's something I ought to tell you, Dr. Gordon. I think I've fallen in love."

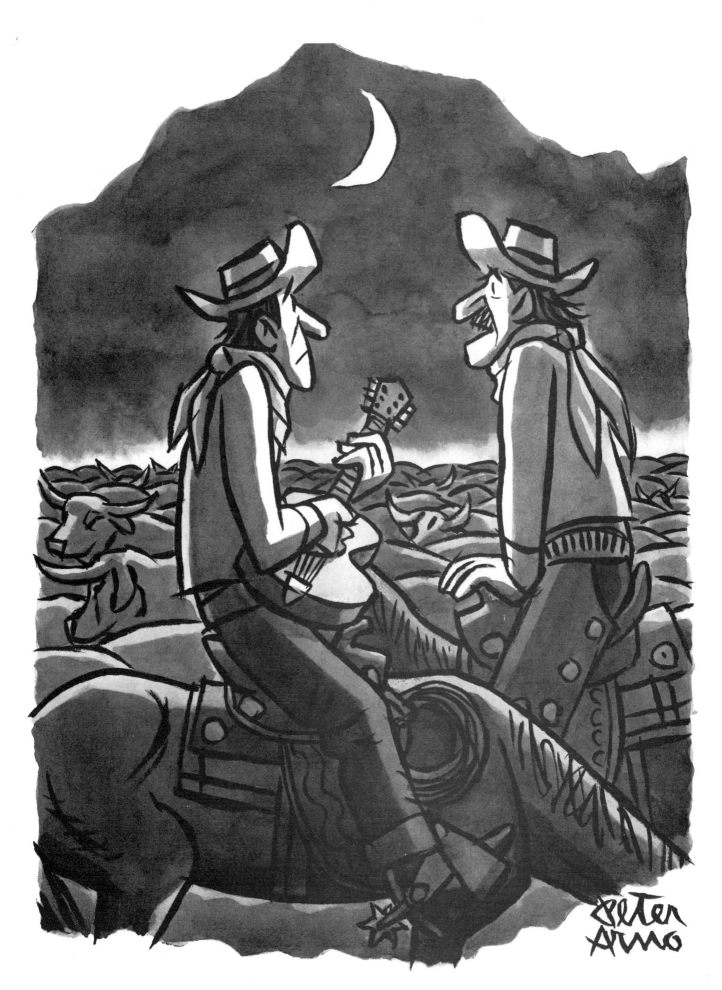

"I got nothin' personal against yore singin', Tex, but the cows need their sleep."

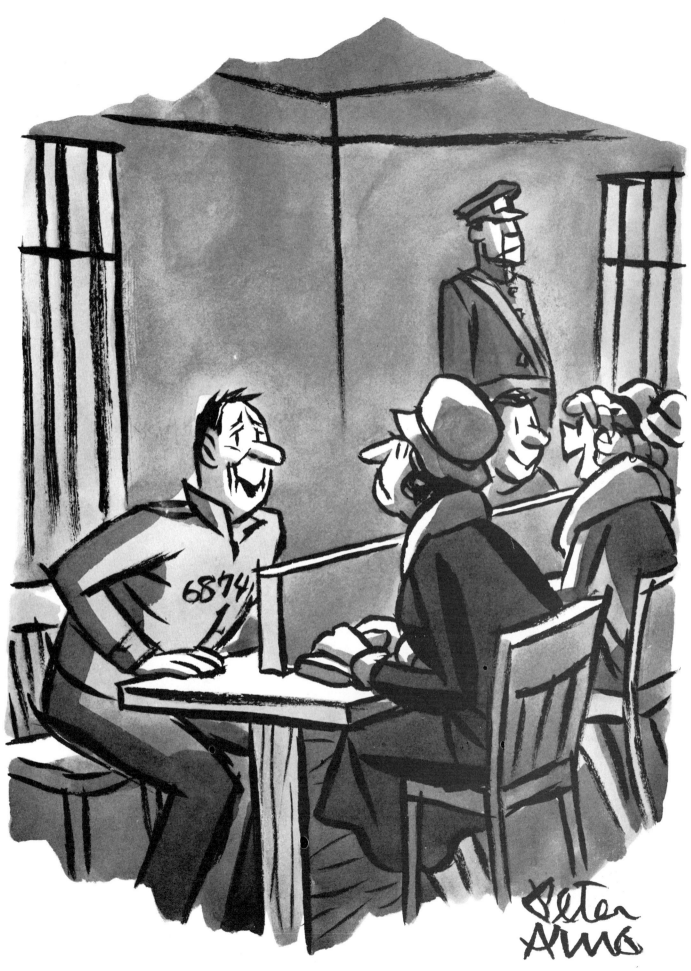

"I hate to interrupt, dear, but you're running over into our recreation hour."

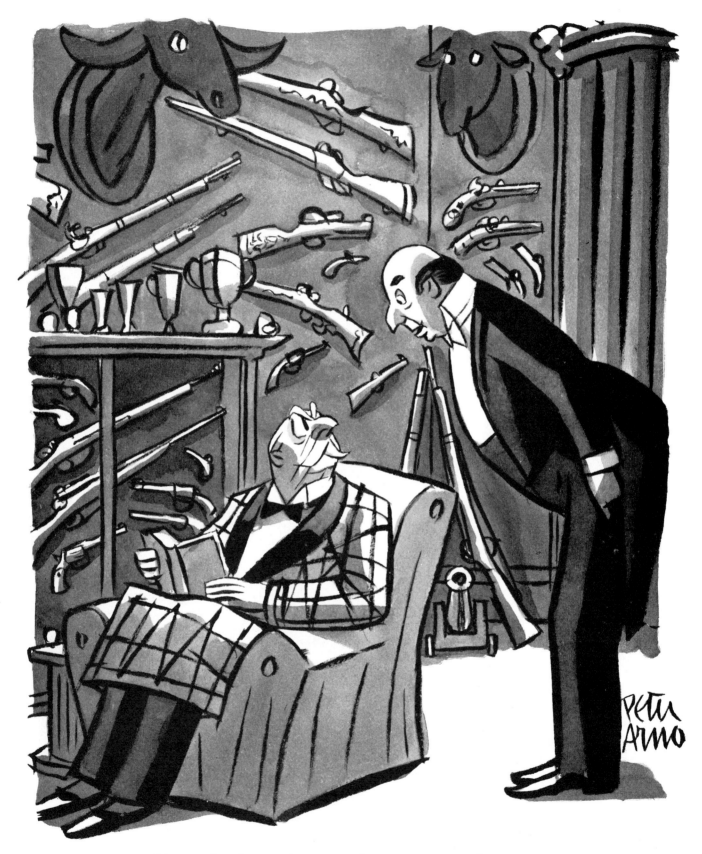

"There's a burglar prowling in the Blue Room, sir. Would you care to have
a crack at him before I notify the police?"

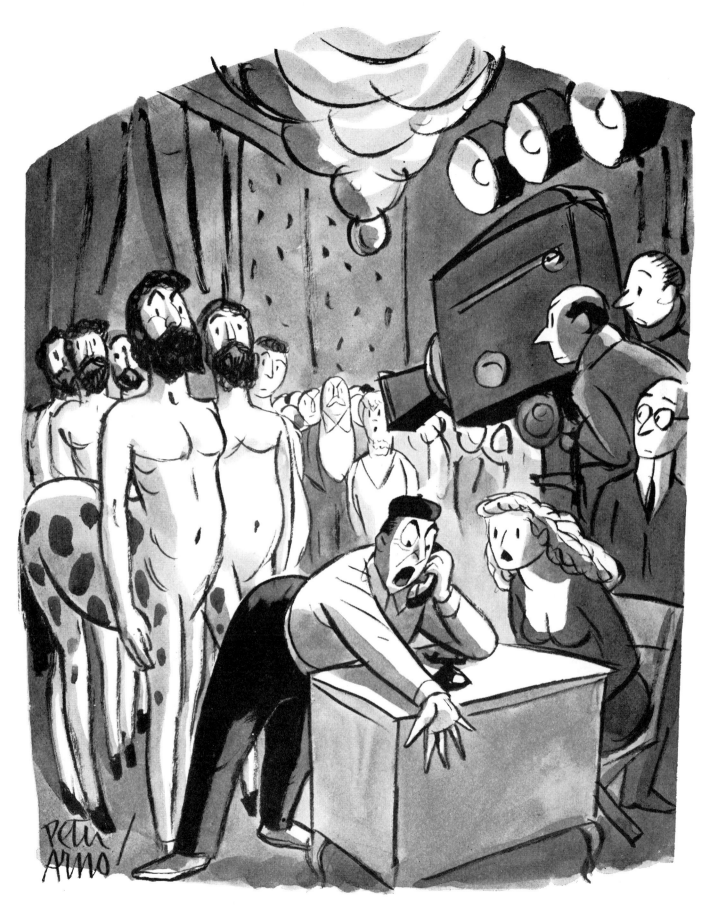

"My God, Plotz, I asked for Senators! SEN-A-TORS! Like in Washington!"

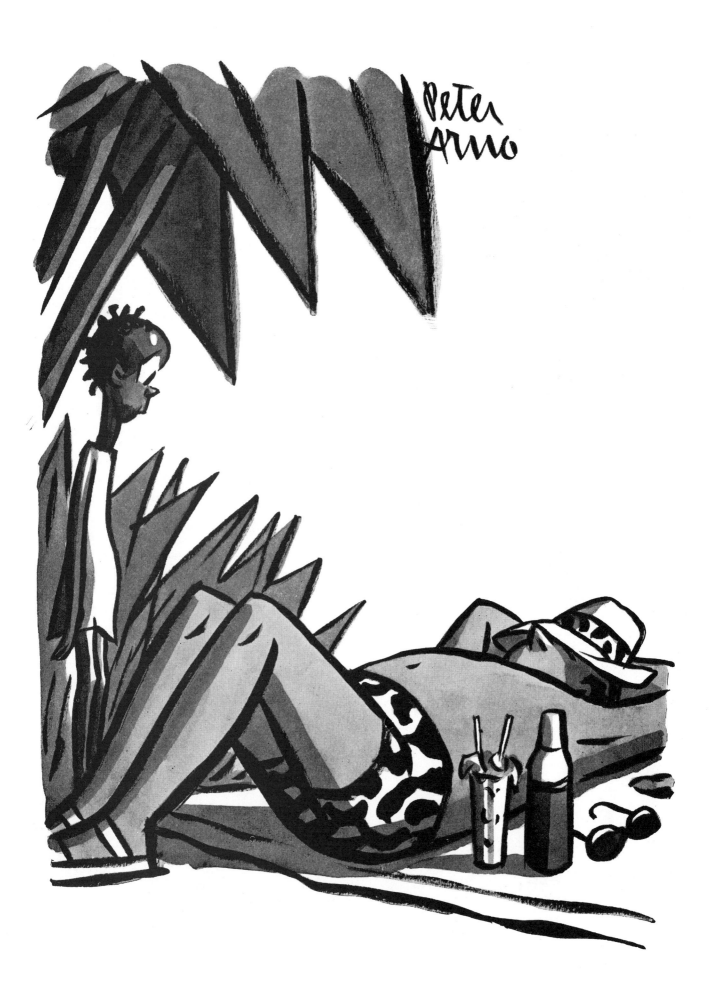

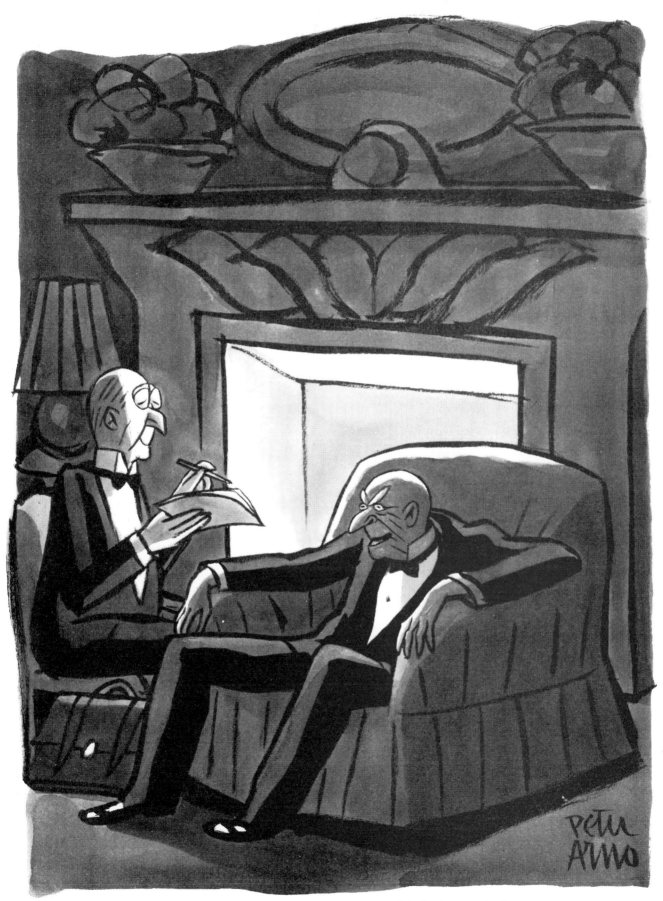

"*Now read me the part again where I disinherit everybody.*"

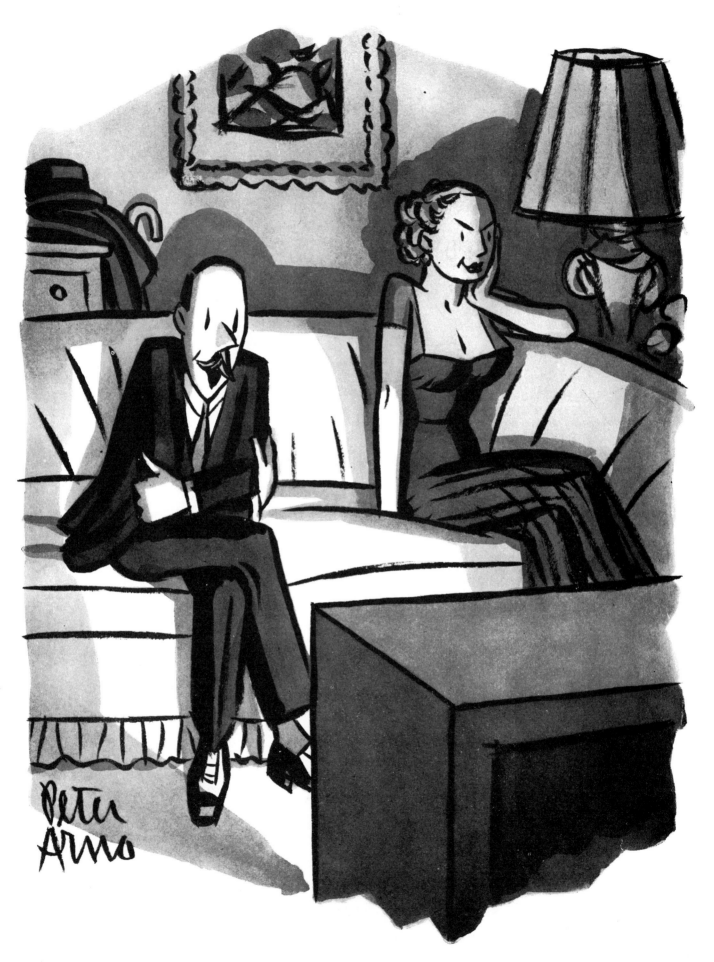

"It's hard to imagine what people used to do before television, isn't it?"

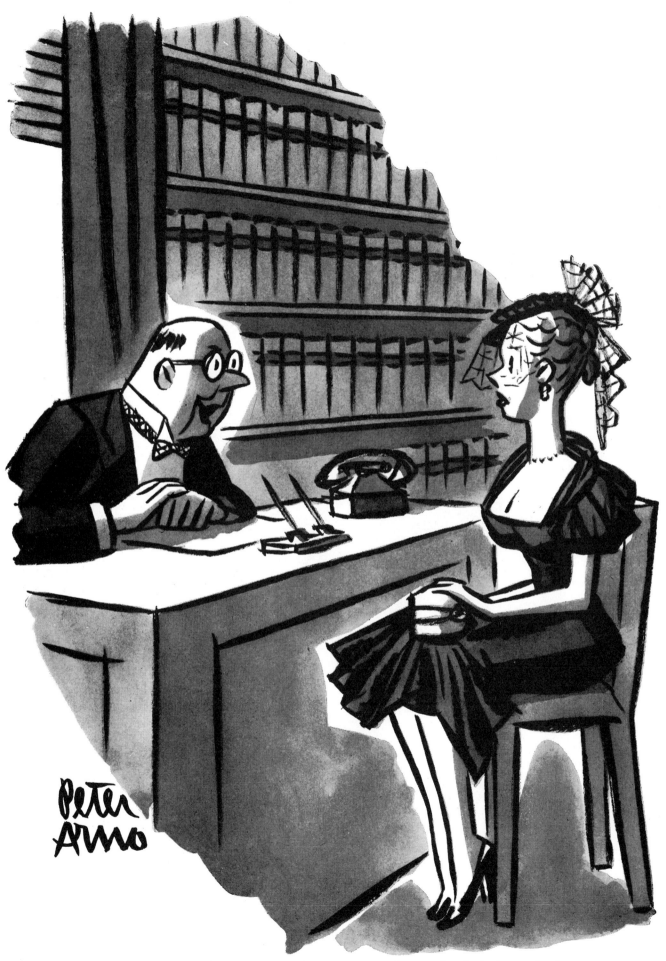

"Your husband agrees to the property settlement, but he insists on having custody of you for three months of the year."

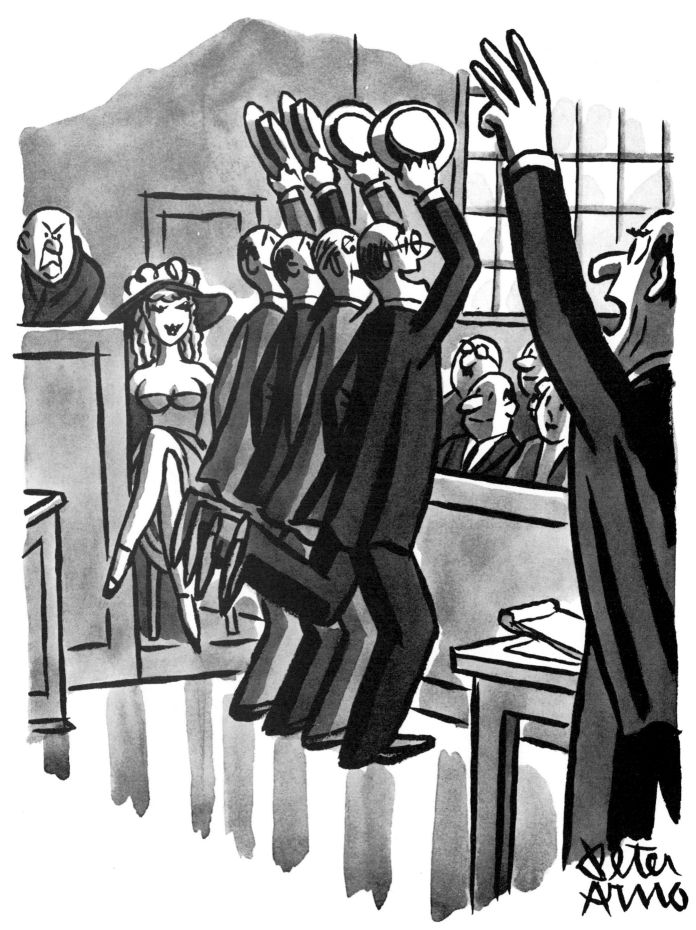

"*Your Honor, I object to the tactics of Lattimore, Finchley, Wilburn & Hatch!*"

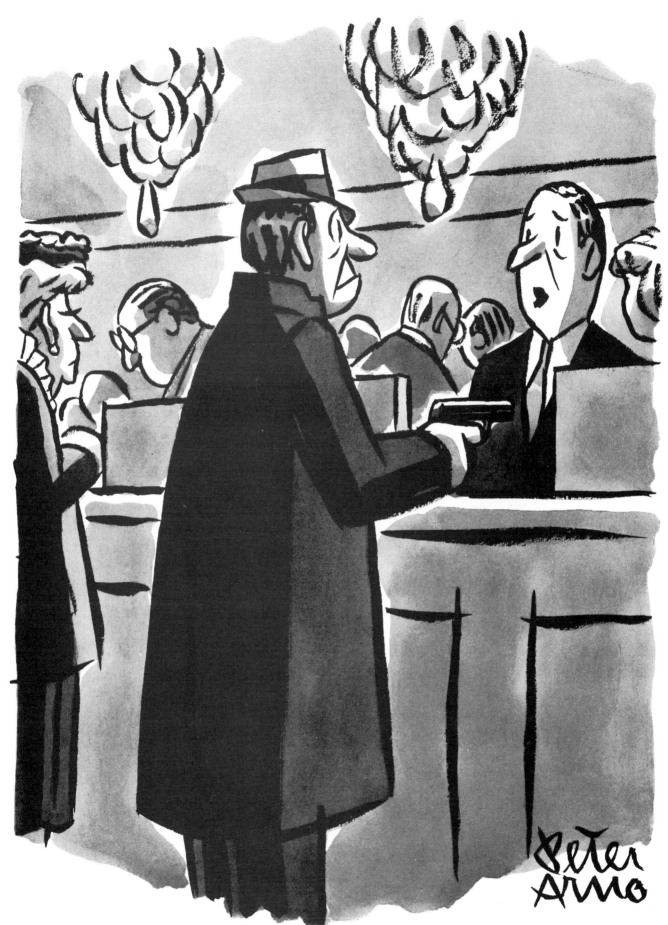

"I'll see what I can find, but aren't you supposed to provide the brown paper bag?"

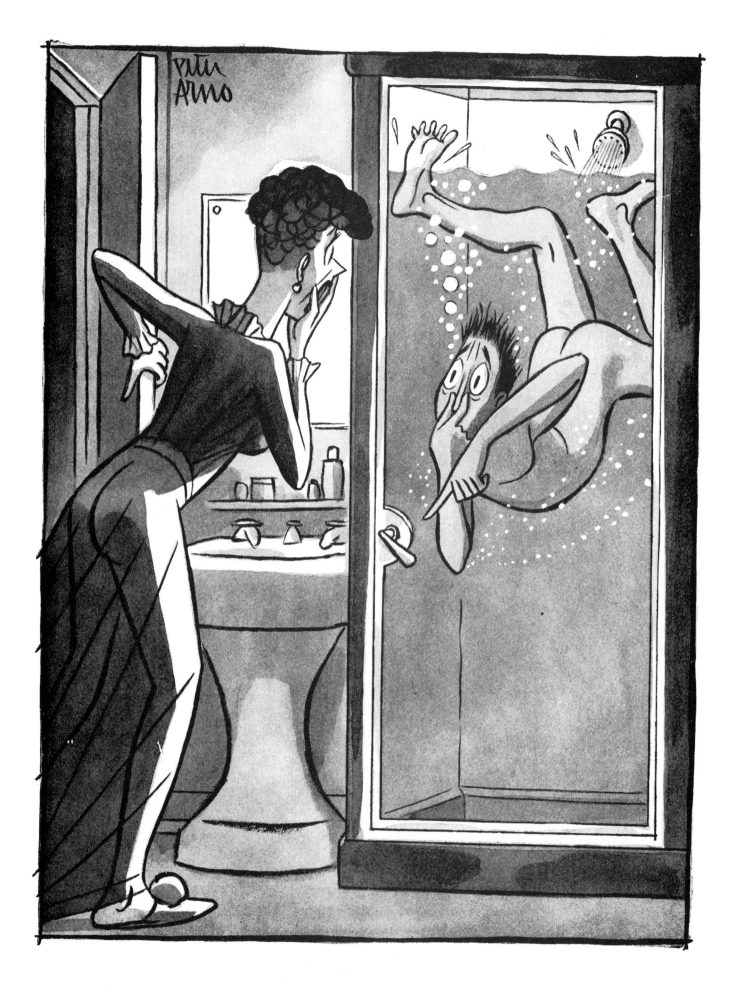

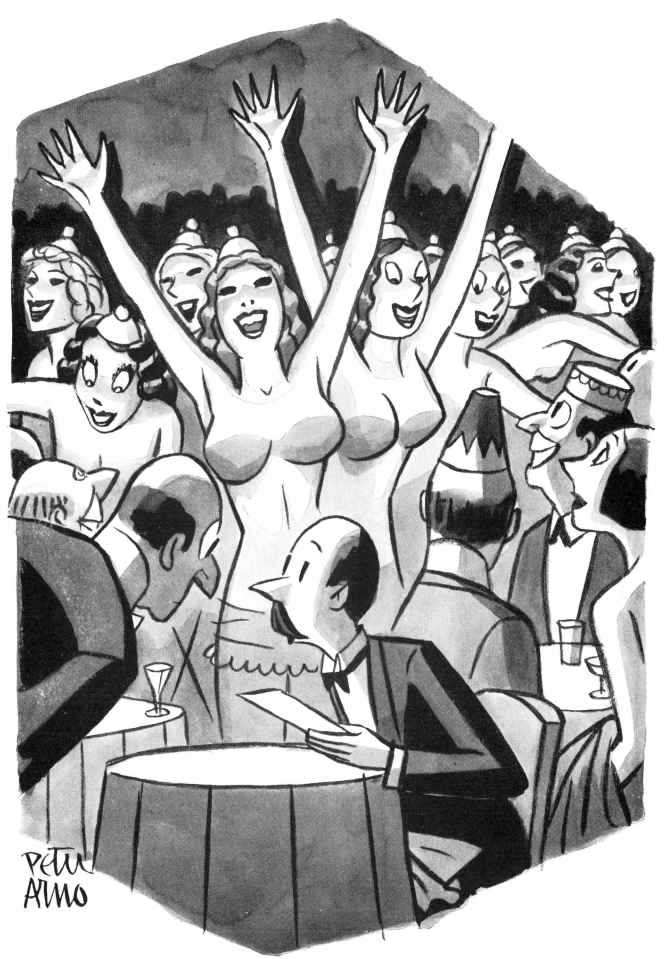

"What is the specialty here?"

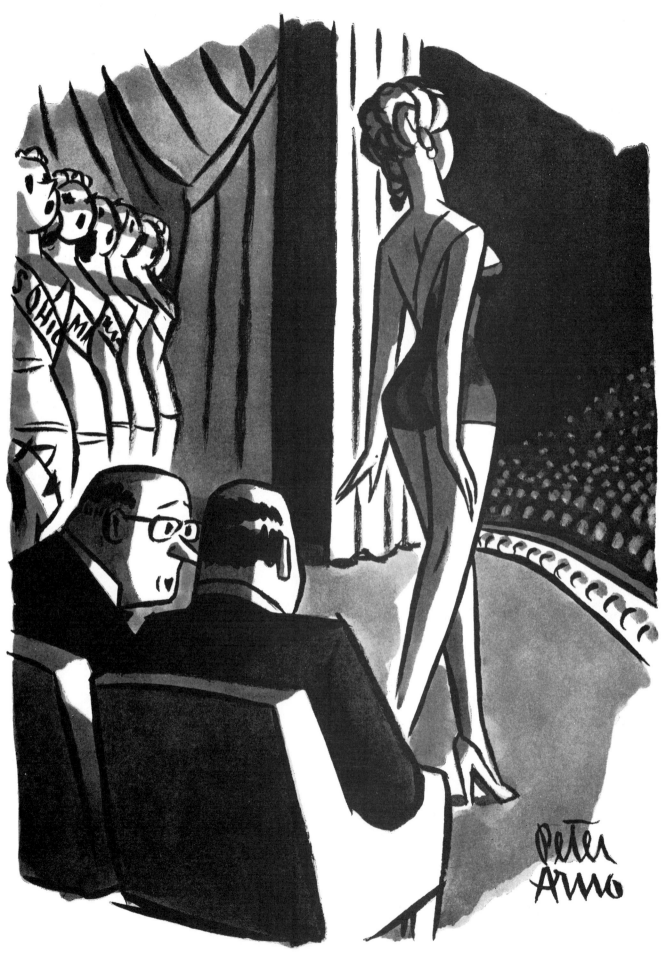

"*She seems to have all the earmarks of a winner.*"

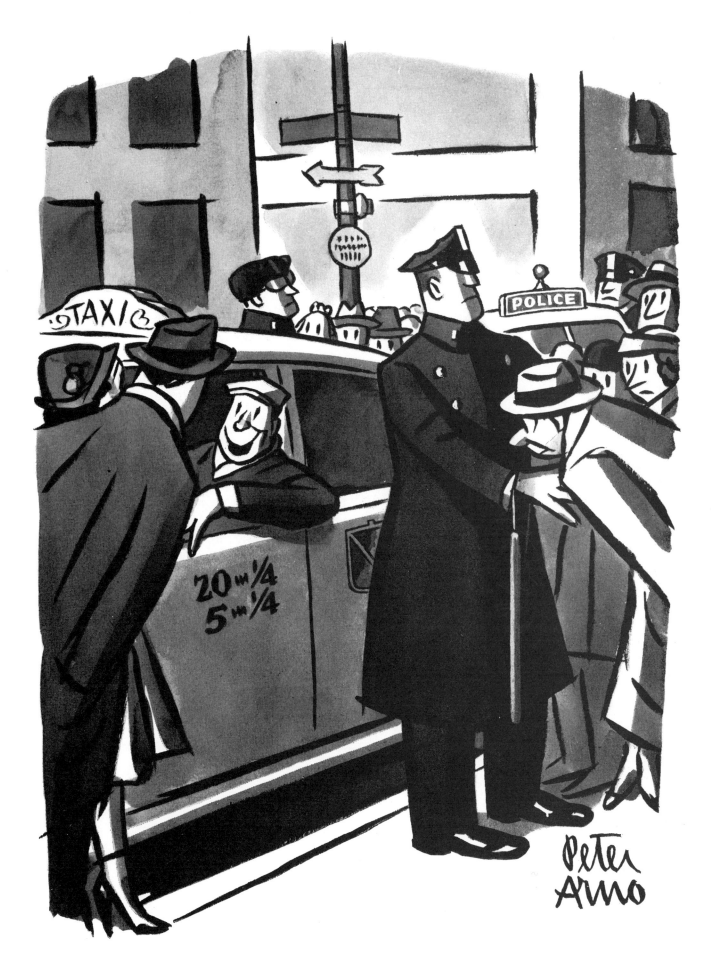

"It's a boy!"

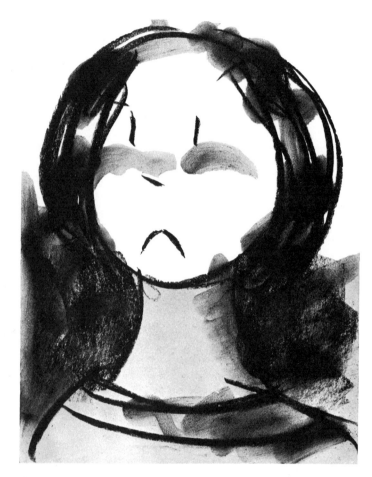

Unhappy Child

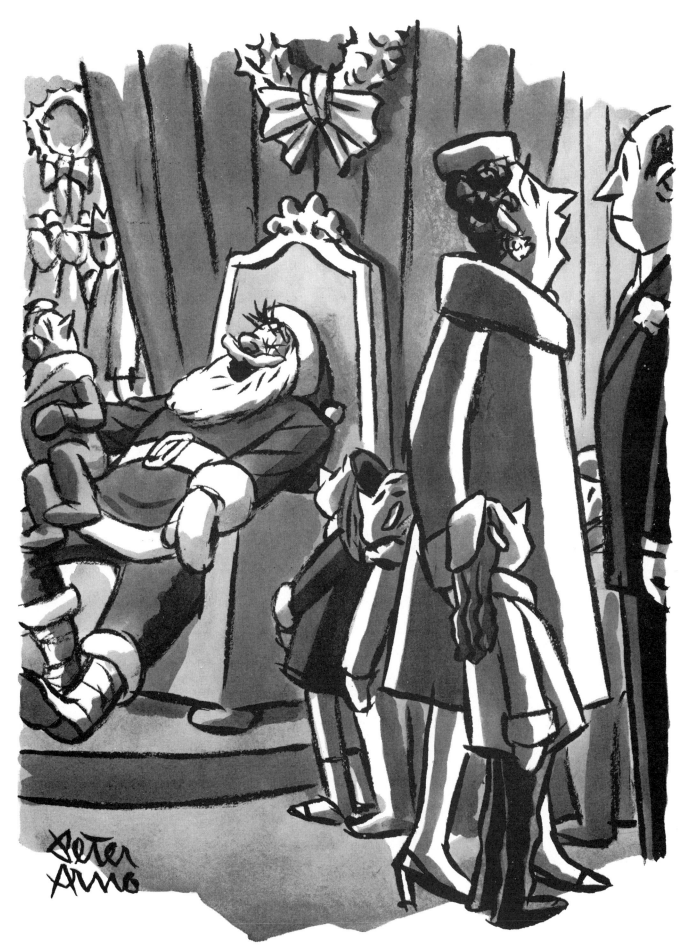

"I think your Anta-say is unk-dray."

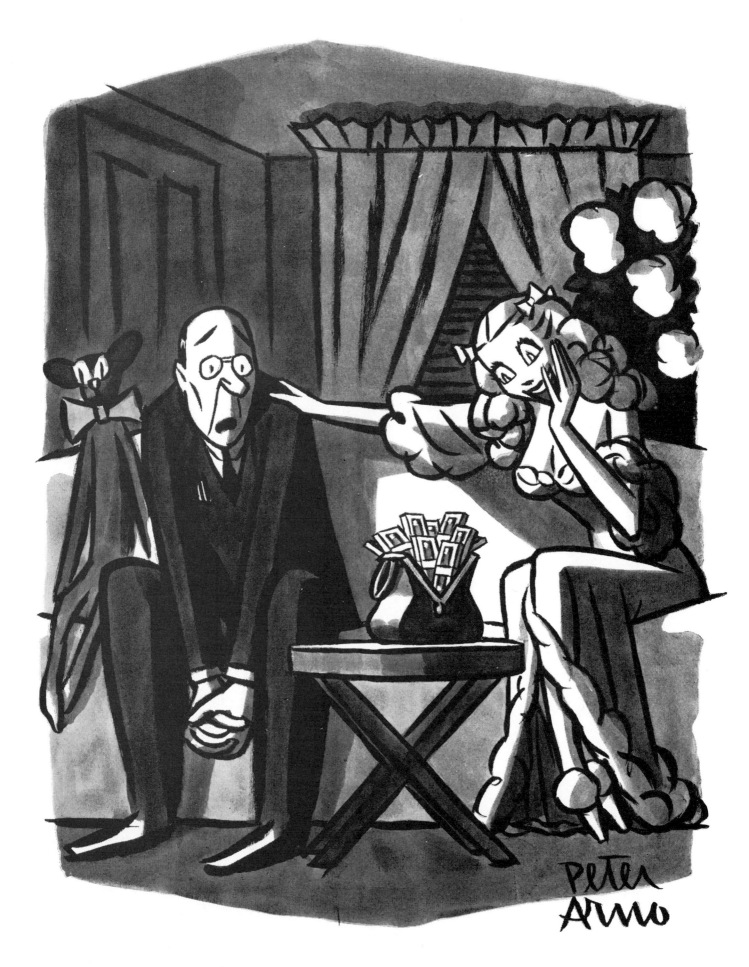

"*Of course you realize this washes me up at the bank.*"

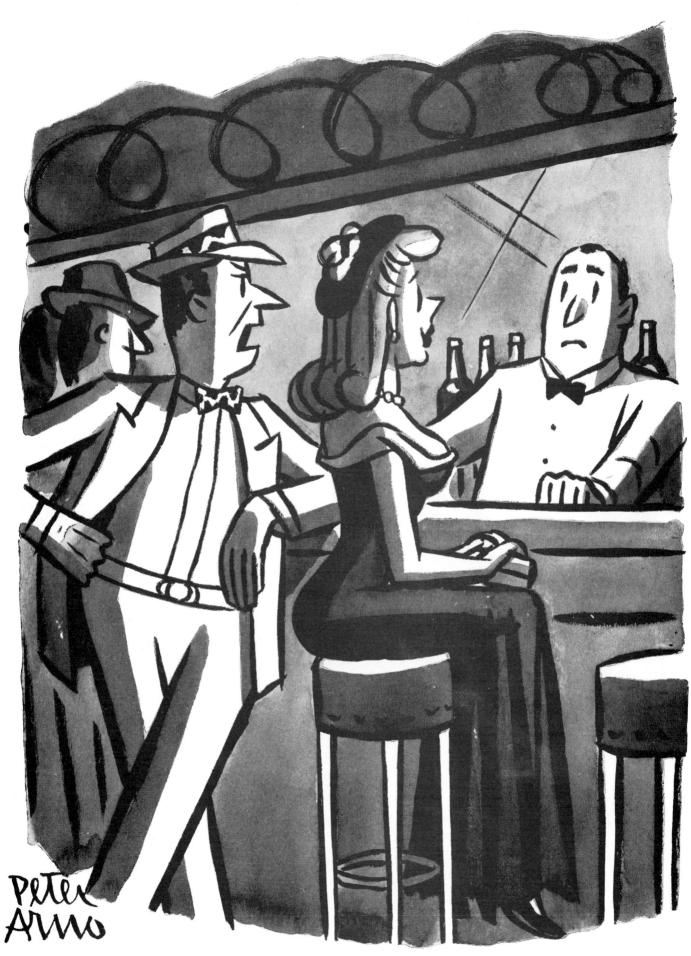

"Fill 'er up."

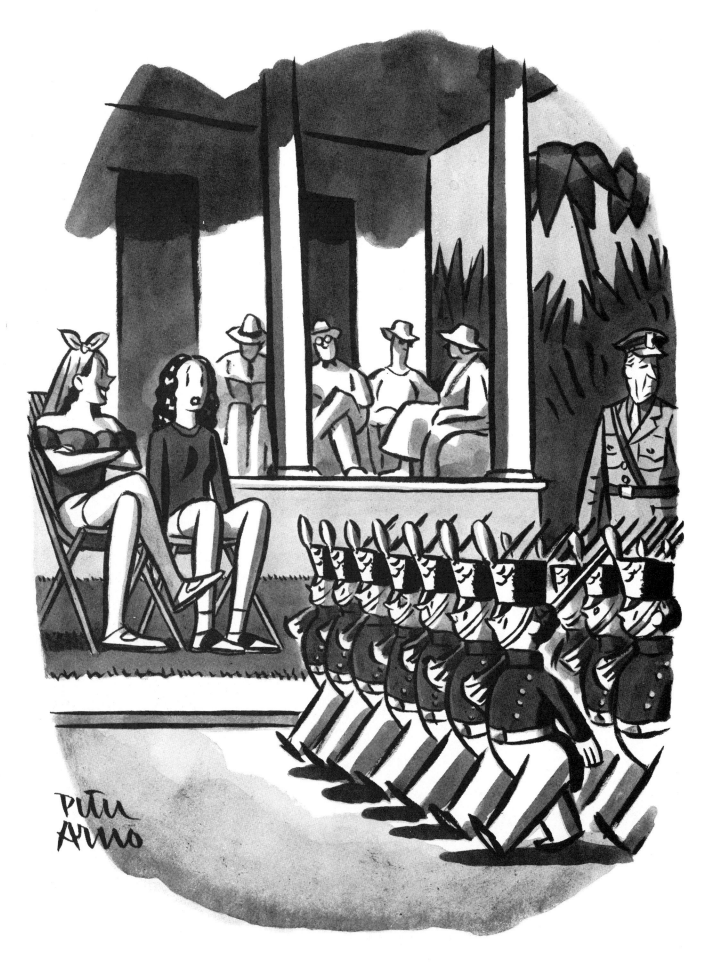

"Well, there's your 'nearby military academy.'"

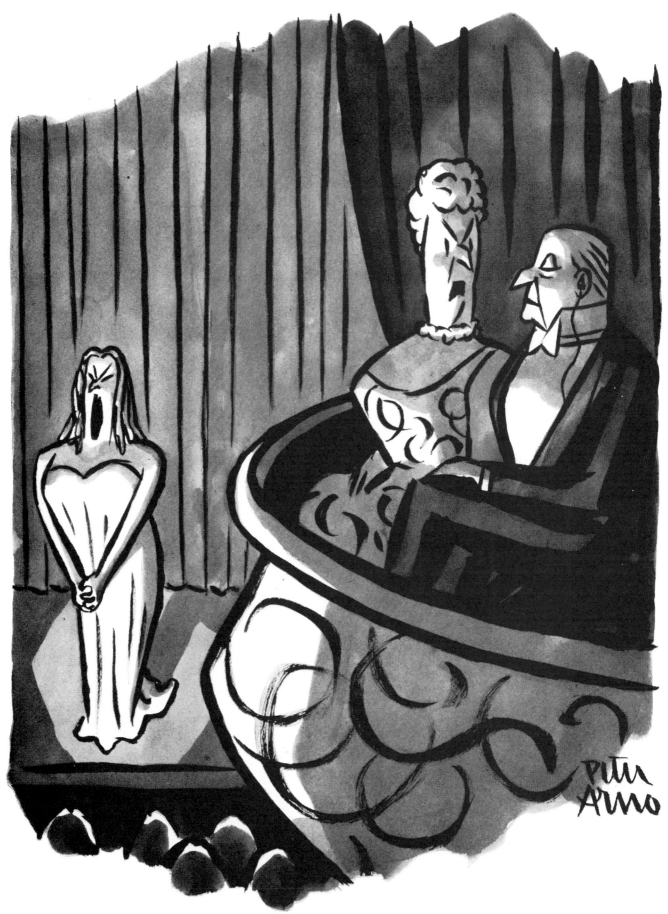

"You have <u>so</u> got it turned off!"

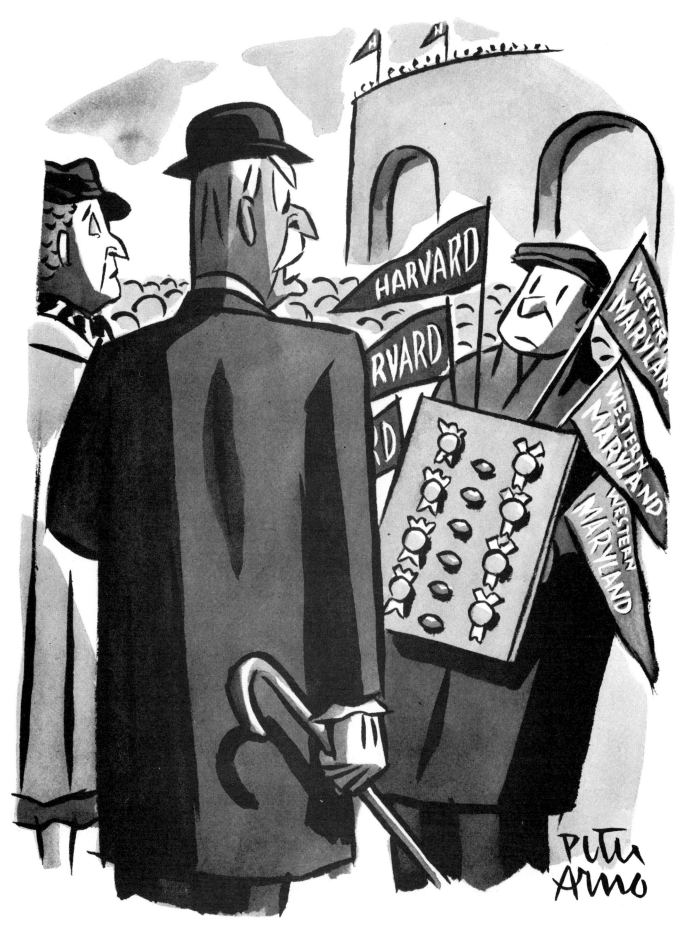

"Which one? Great heavens, are you mad?"

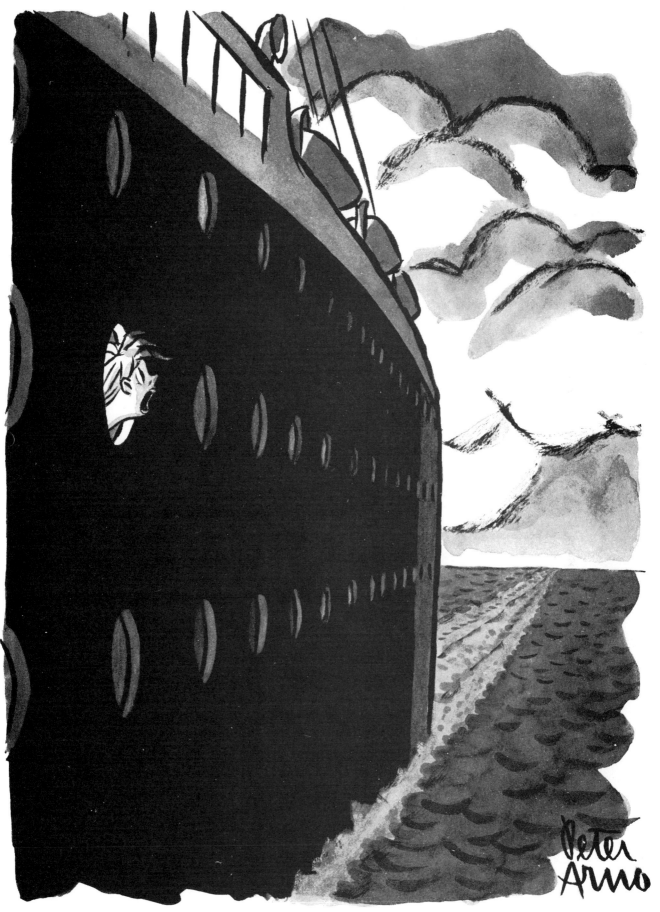

"HELP!"

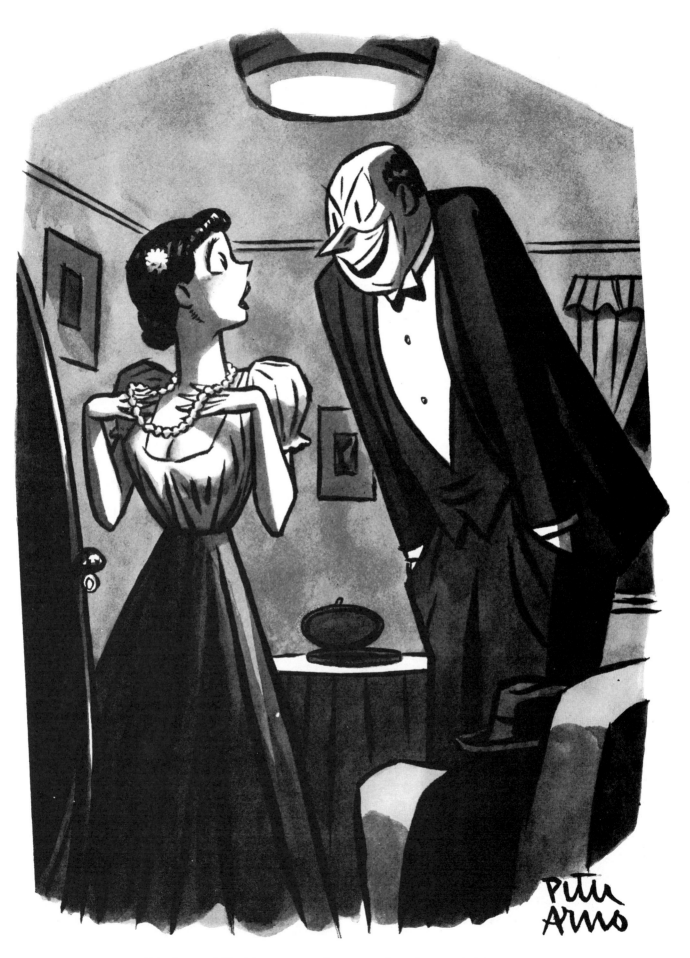

"*And now, Miss Evans, I wonder if I could take a small liberty?*"

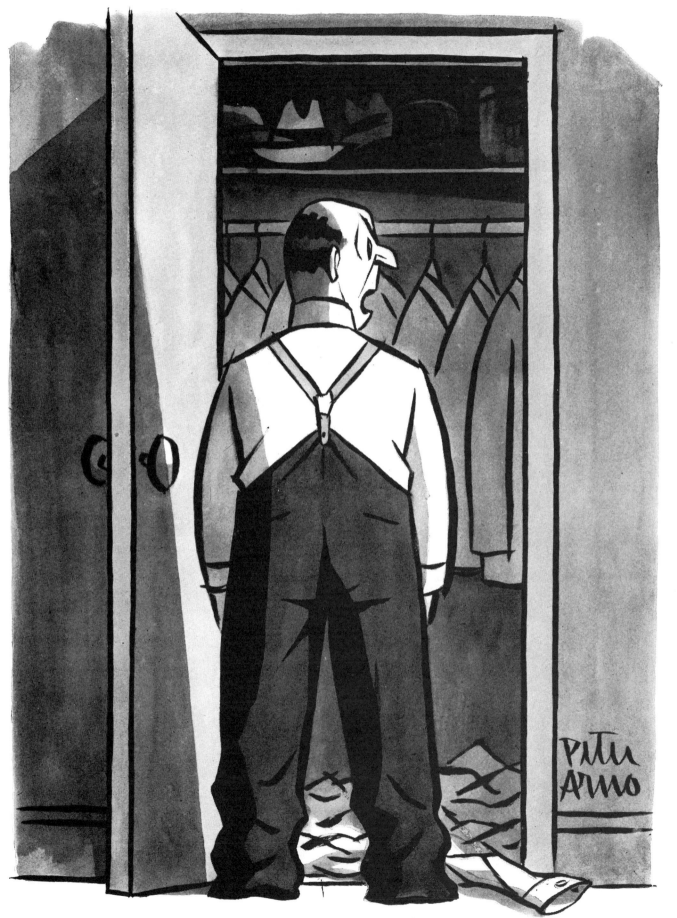

"For God's sake, Hortense, where are my elevator shoes?"

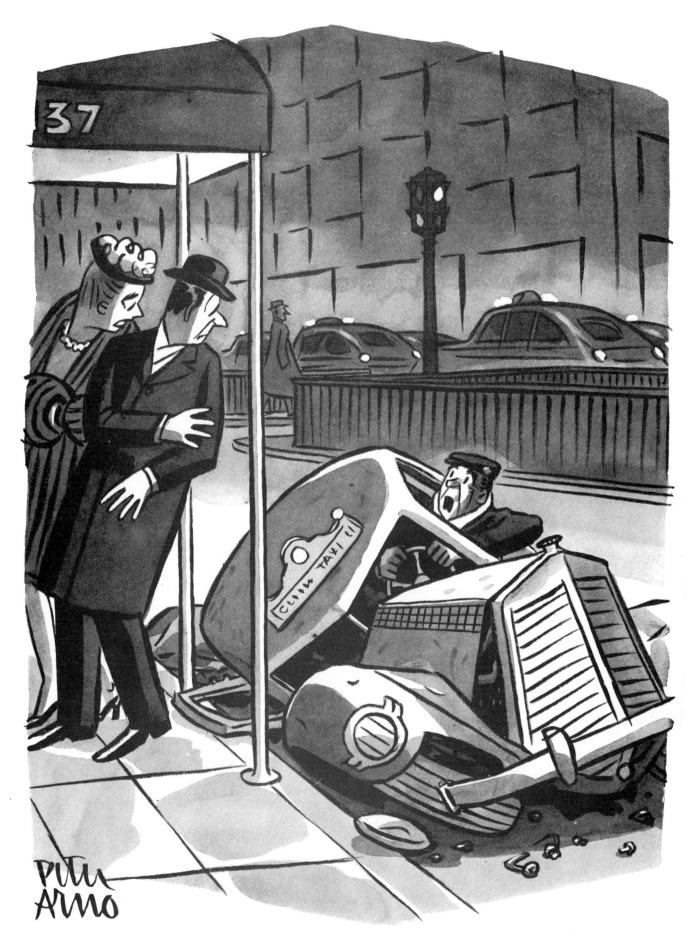

"I ast you not to slam the door!"

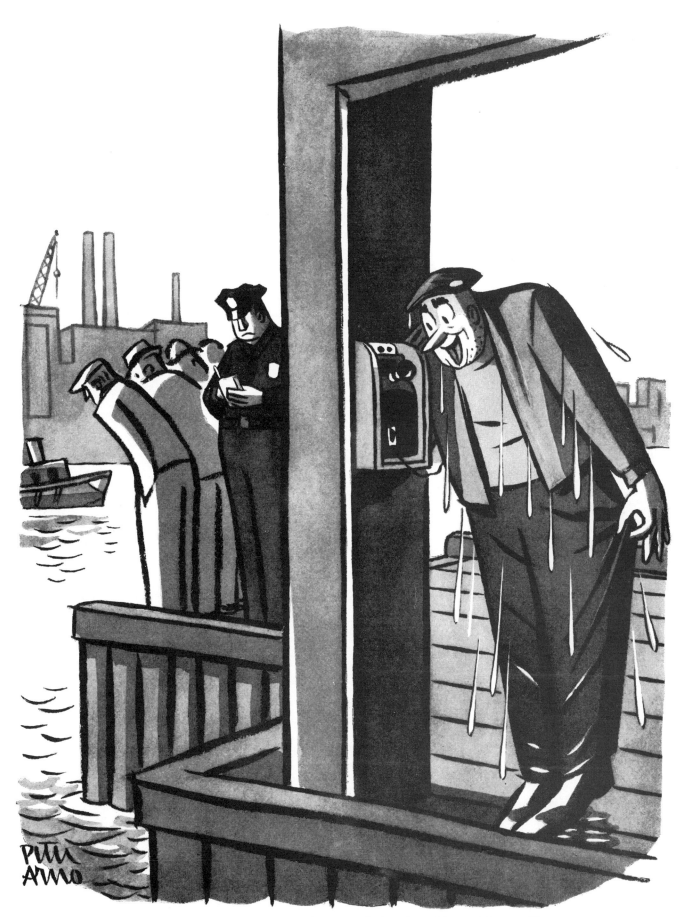

"Guess what happened to me and the truck, boss! . . . No . . . No . . . . No . . . , guess again."

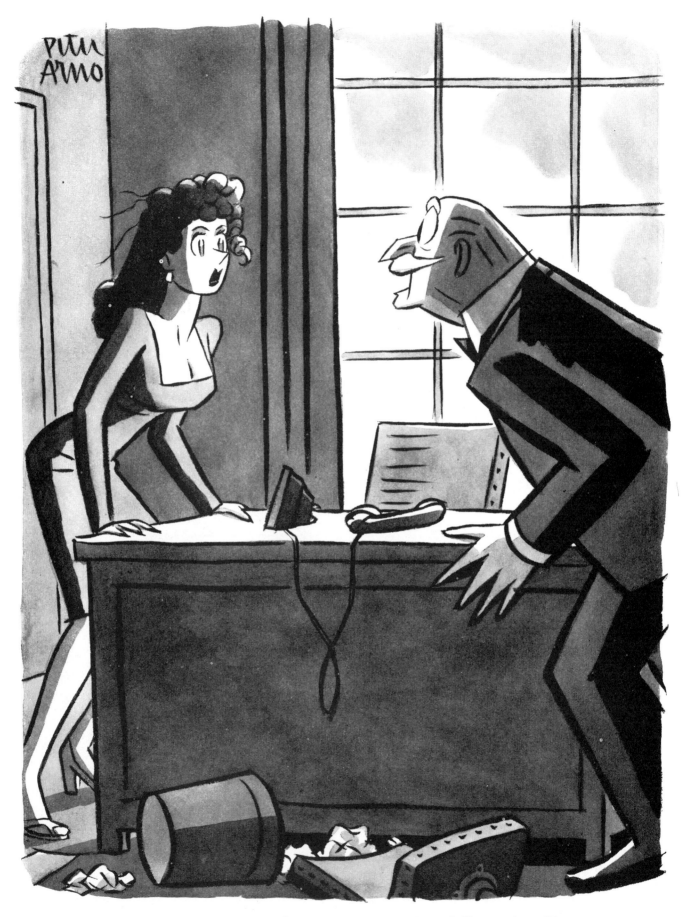

"*Young woman, do you realize my time is worth thirty dollars a minute?*"

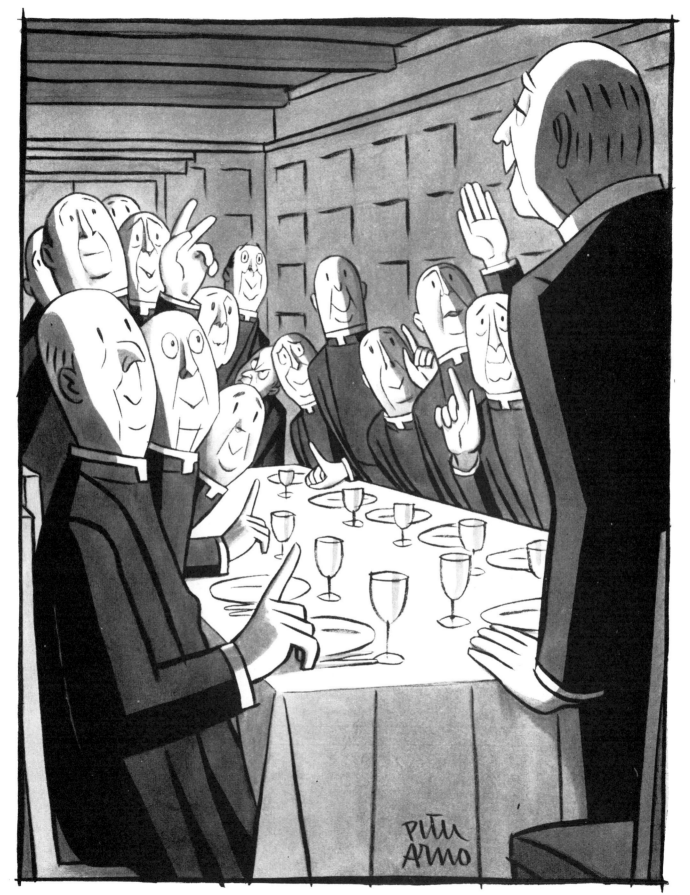

"Now who shall say grace?"

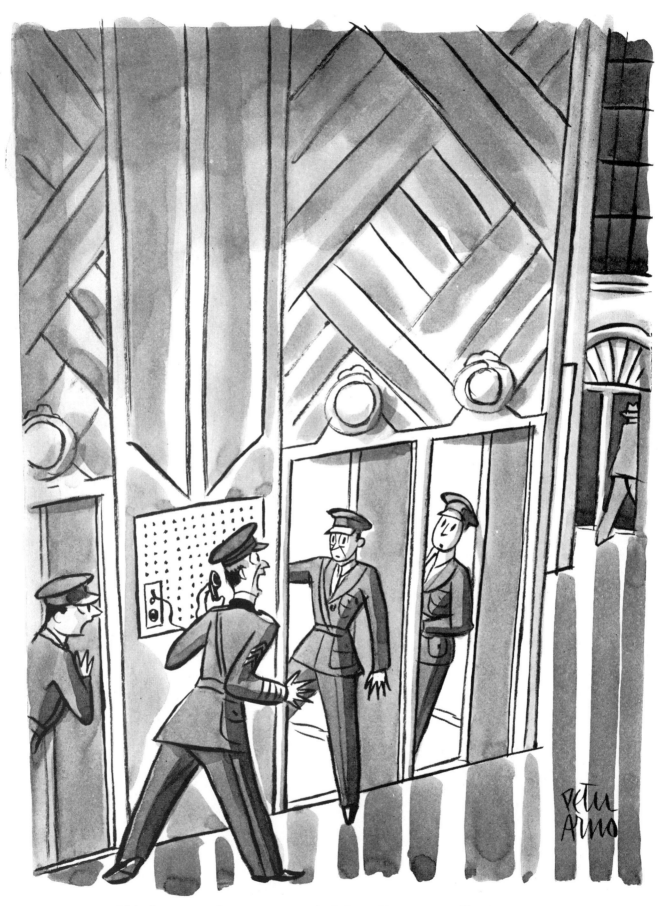

"It's Conover—Car 4—seventy-sixth floor. He's running blind in a fog!"

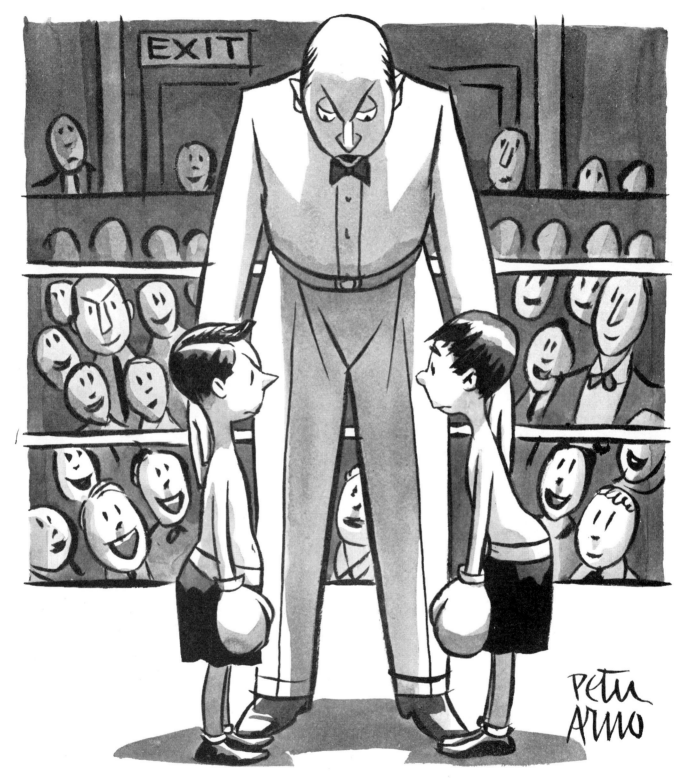

"*You boys know the rules. No low blows, no hitting in the clinches, break clean, and at all times keep your pants up.*"

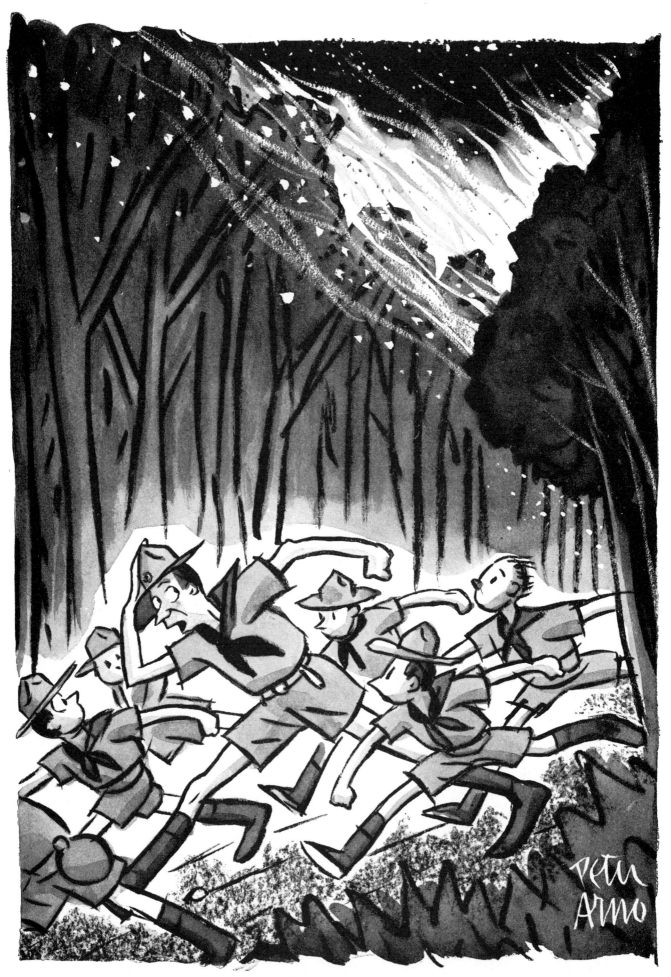

"Well, that's how it is, men. You just rub two dry sticks together."

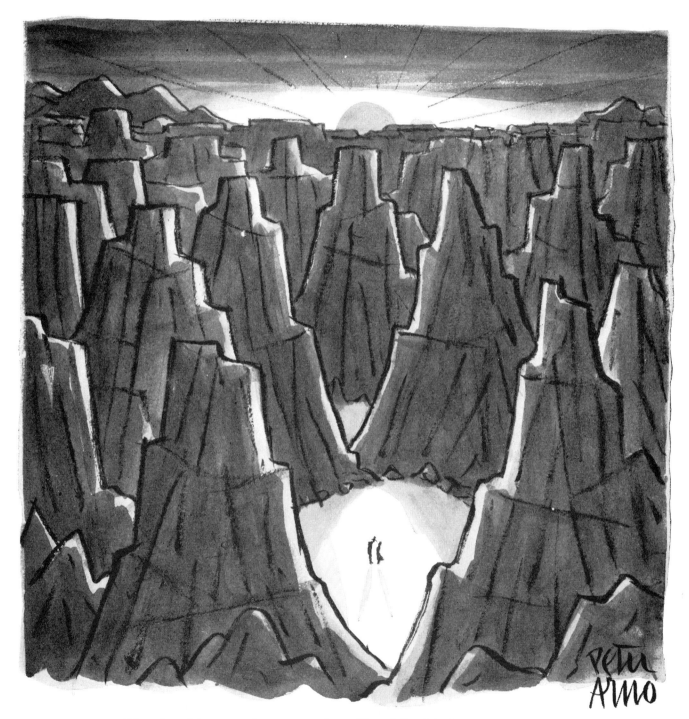

*"Out here Nature makes her own laws. You, Miss Marlowe, are a woman
and I am a man."*

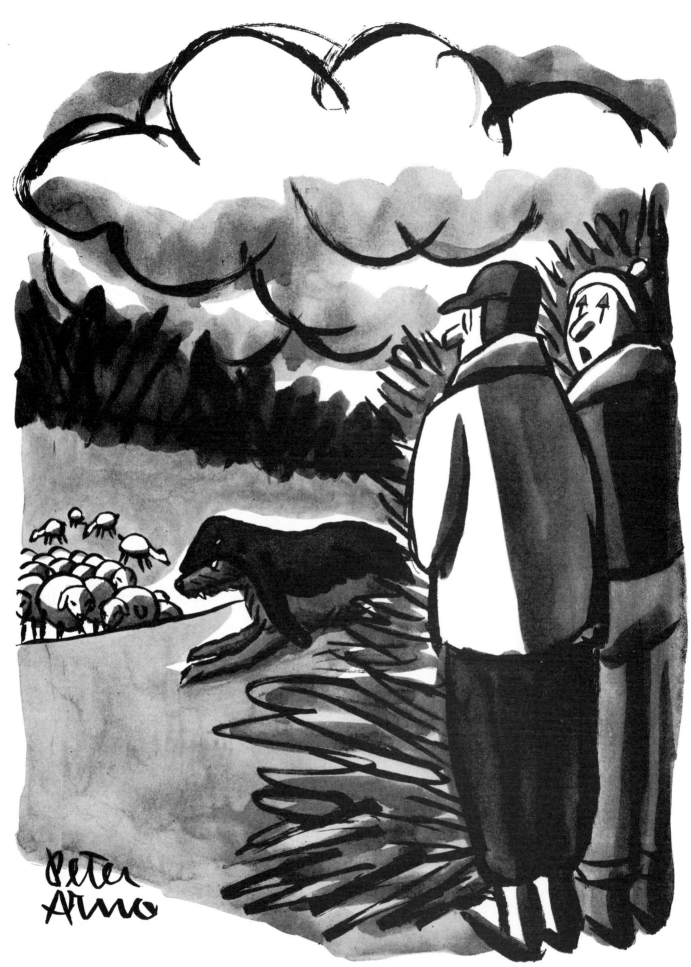

"*Now there's a complicated wolf.*"

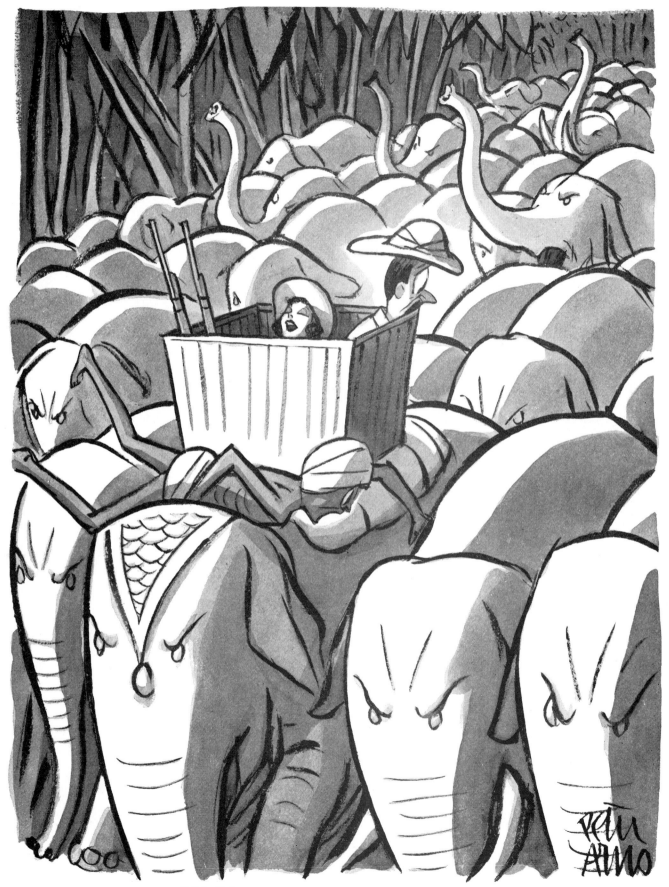

"*Oh, Edgar—I never <u>dreamed</u> it would be like this!*"

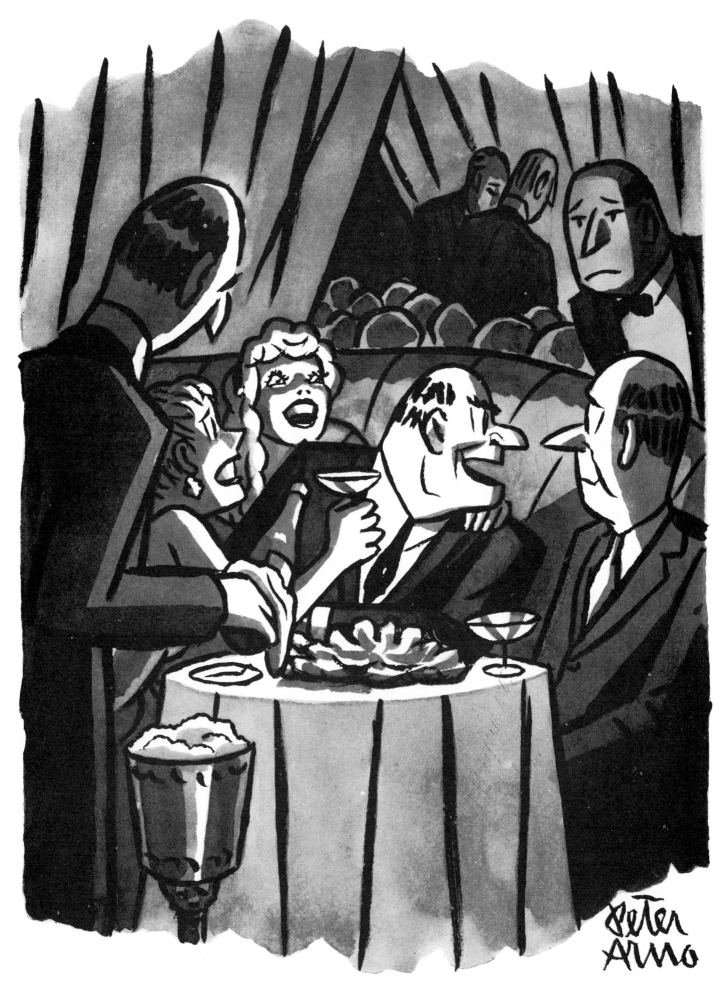

"*I love this country of ours, Summers. It's been good to me.*"

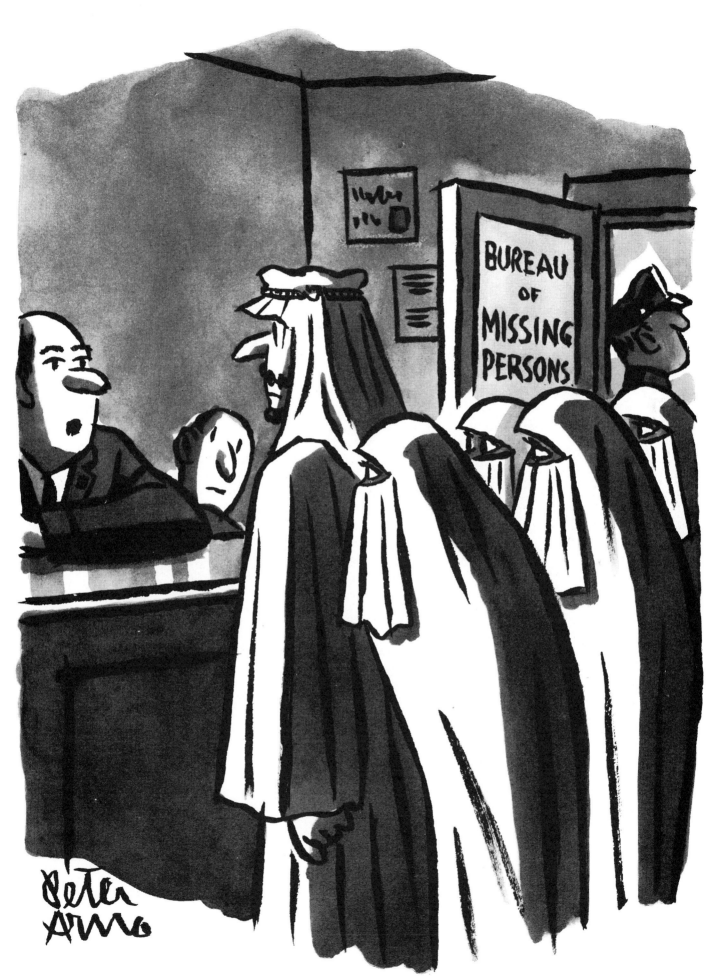

"*Are you positive you had five when you started out this morning?*"

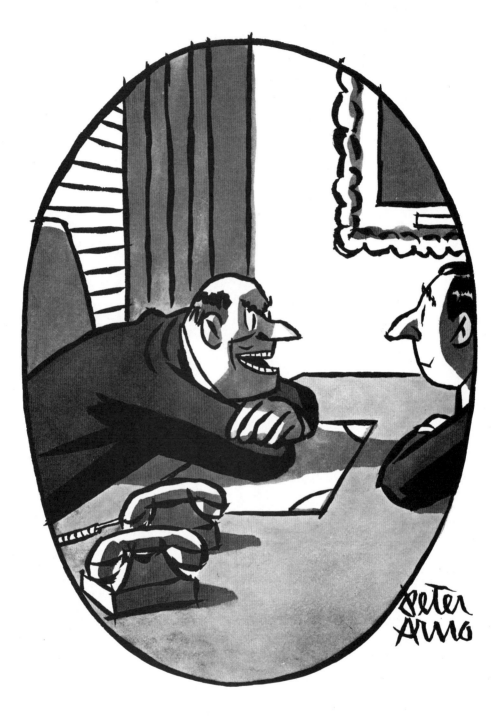

"*I think you'll be happier here, Dilworth, now that we've had a meeting of minds.*"

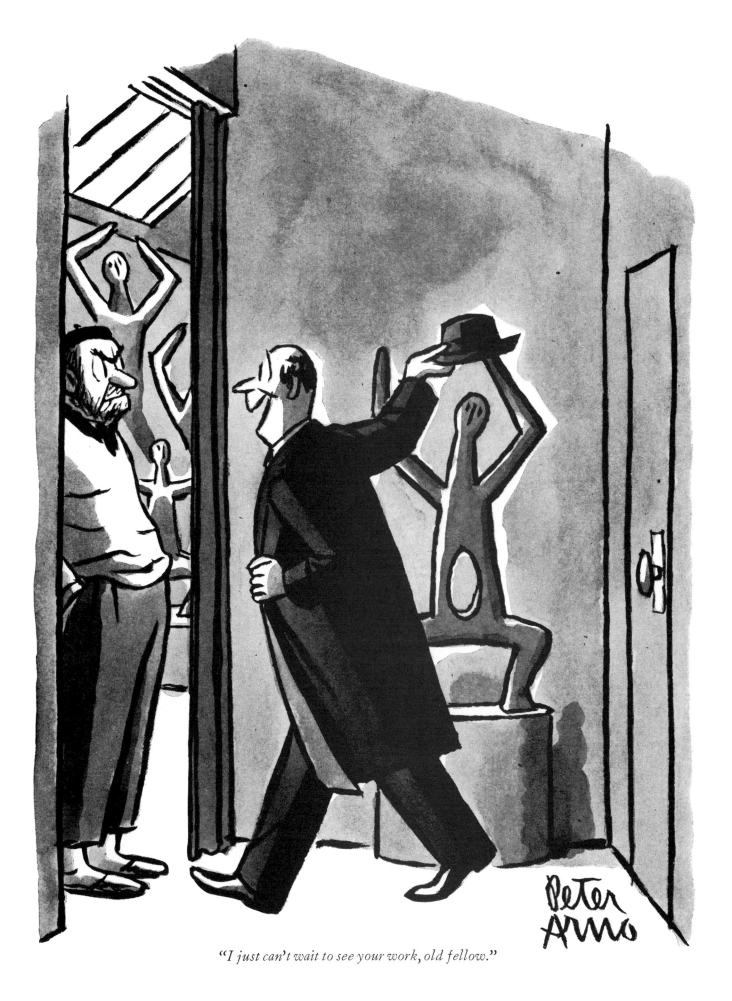

"I just can't wait to see your work, old fellow."

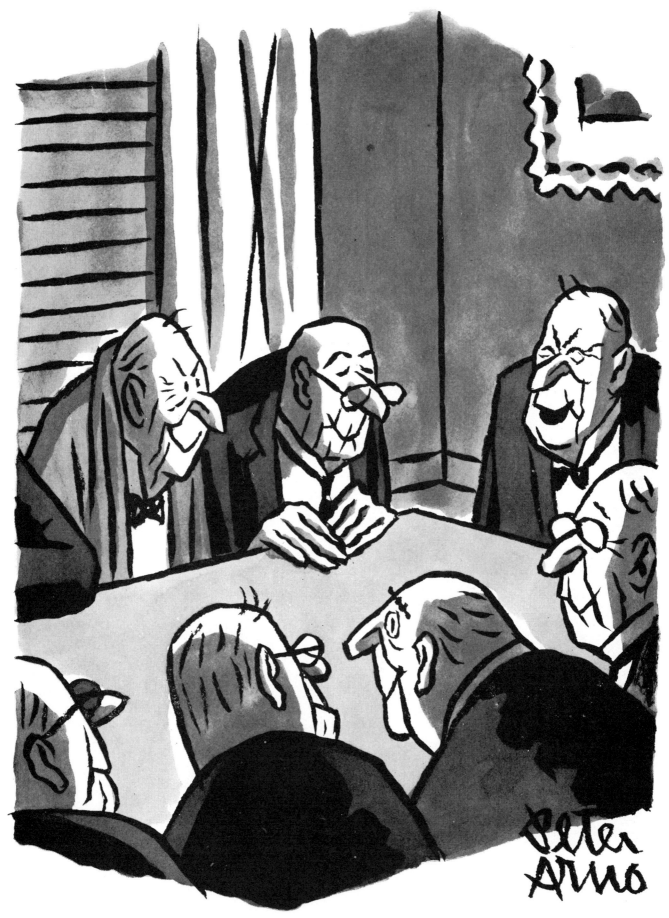

*"Then it's moved and seconded that
the compulsory retirement age be advanced to ninety-five."*

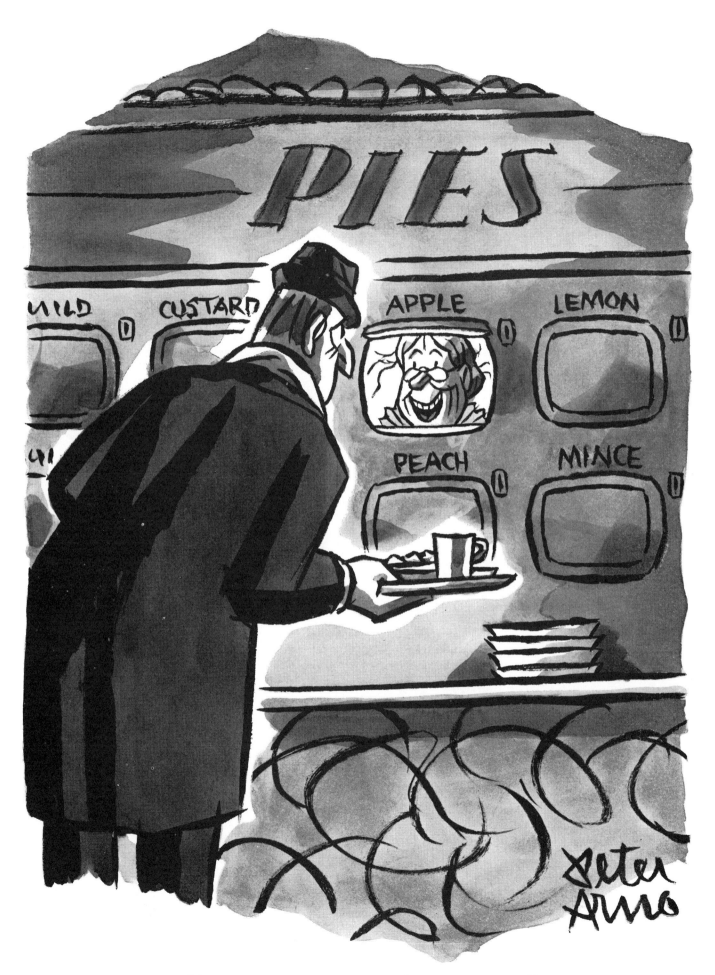

"Can you wait a minute? I have it cooling on the window sill."

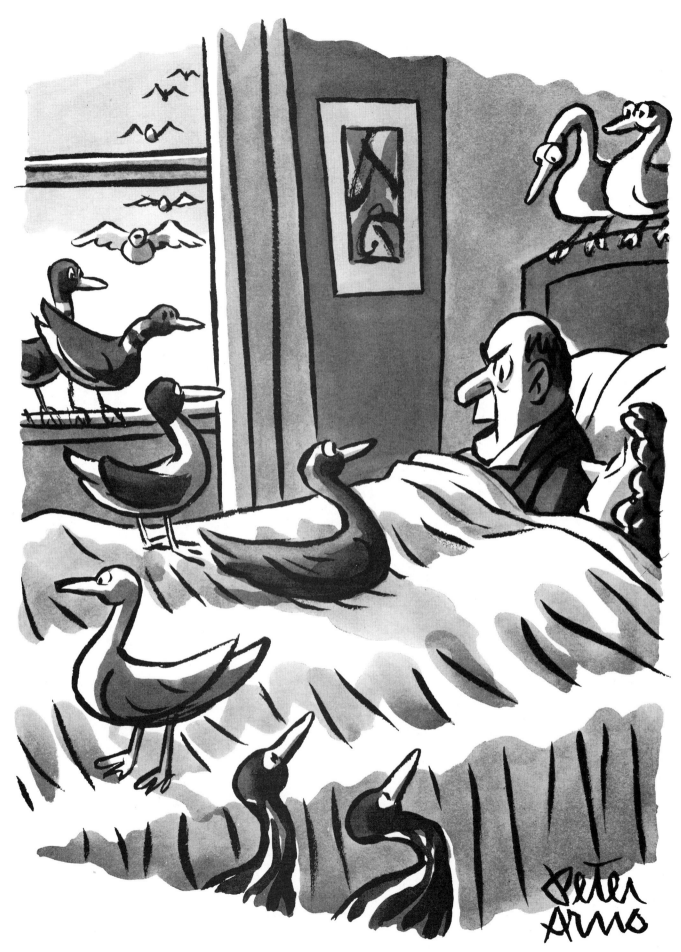

"*This does it! I've had enough of living in a migratory channel!*"

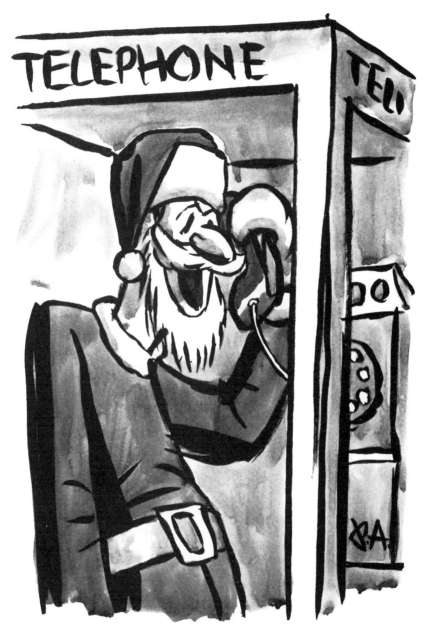

"Hi, Kitten. This is Oogie."

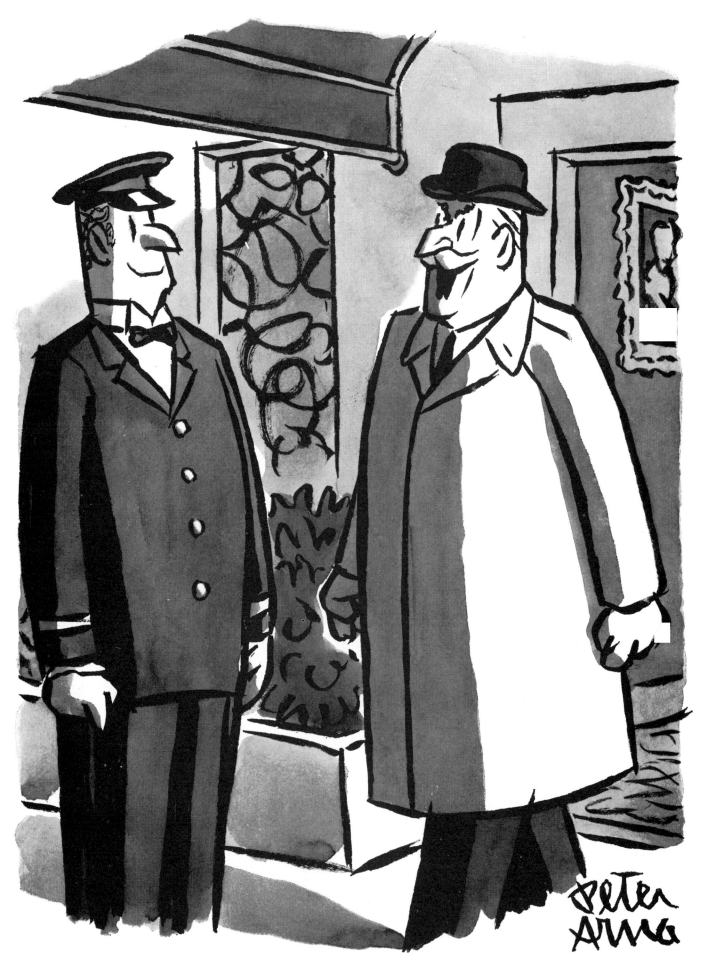

"What a magnificent day, Andrews! I've a good mind to zip out my lining!"

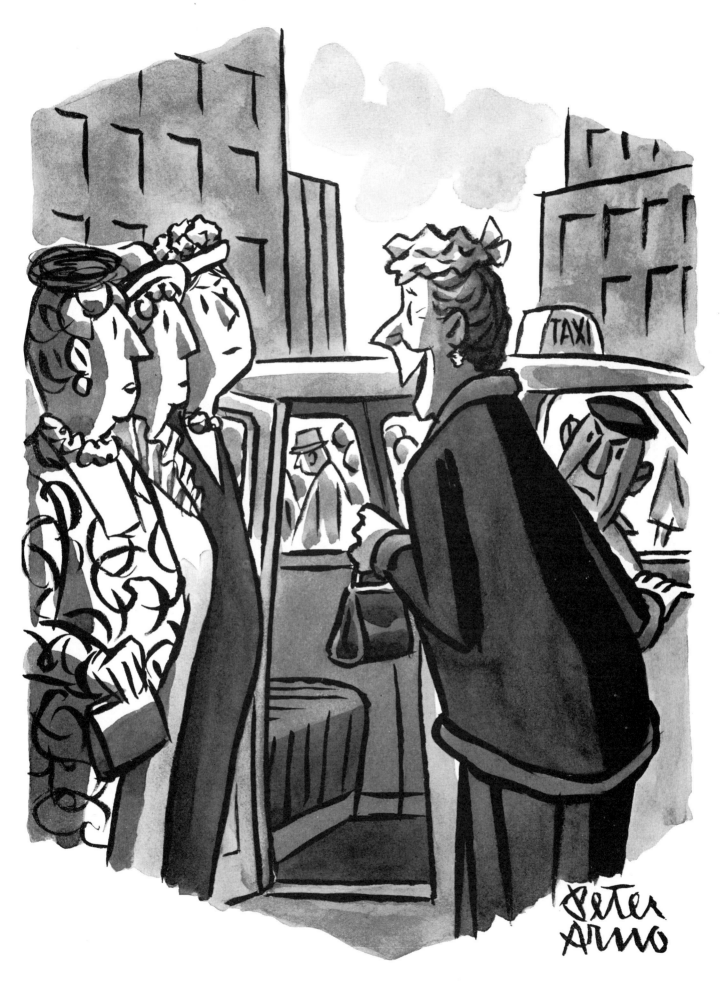

"You three sit in back. I'll ride shotgun."

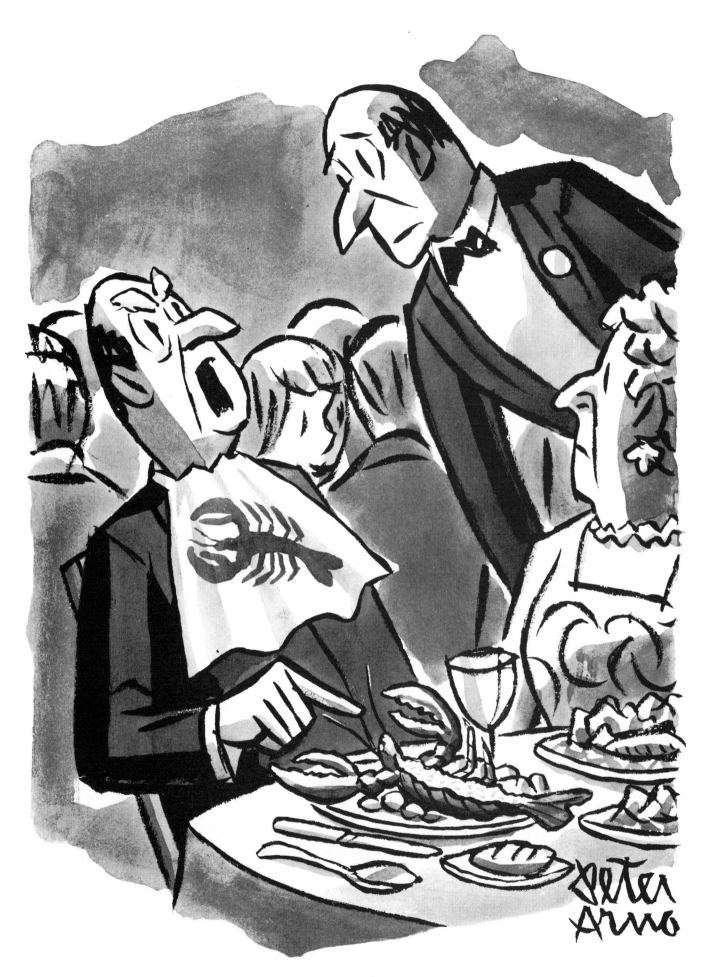

"This is __not__ the one I selected! I never forget a face!"

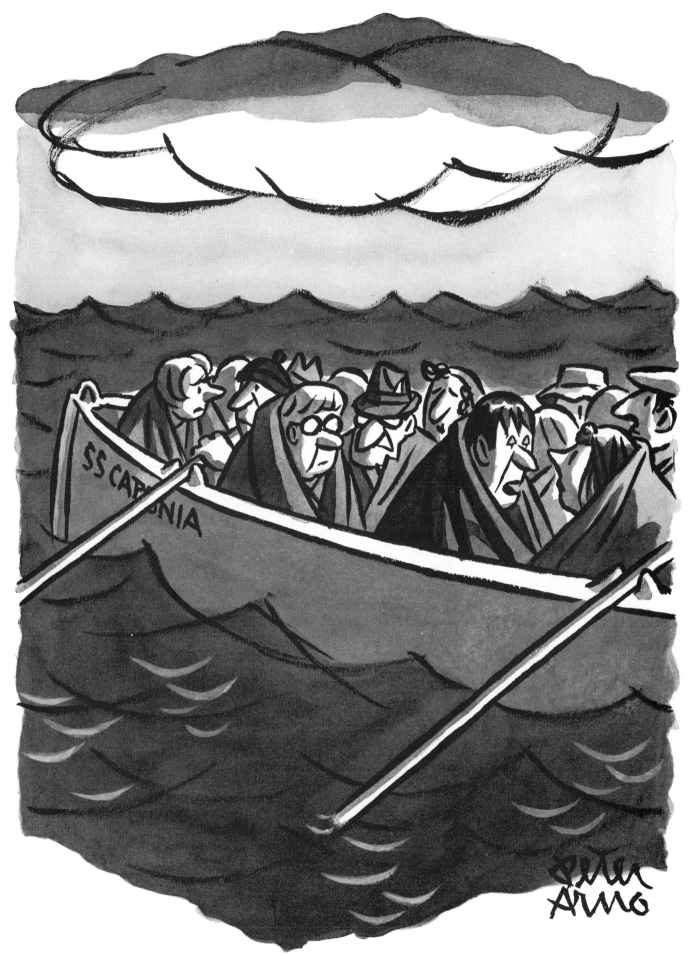

*"Now I suppose we can look forward to a reunion with this crowd every year
for the rest of our lives."*

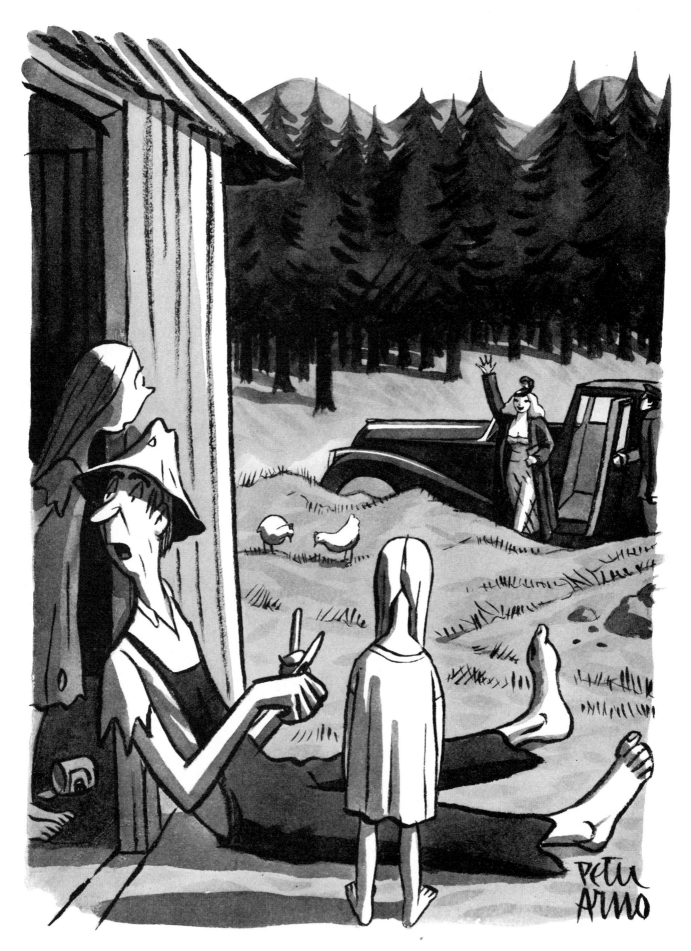

"*Maw! Myrtle's back. Looks like she made good.*"

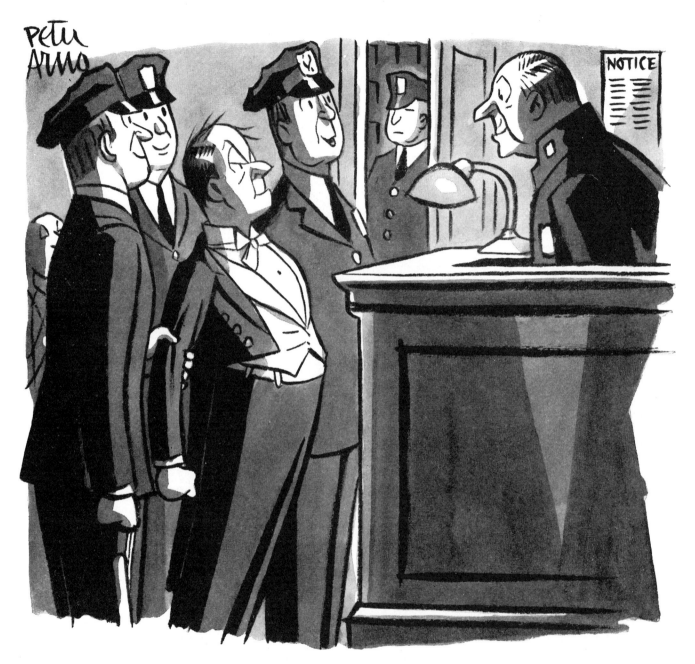

"Sergeant, this is Mr. J. Stanhope Alderson. He has money, position, many
influential friends, and we can't do this to him."

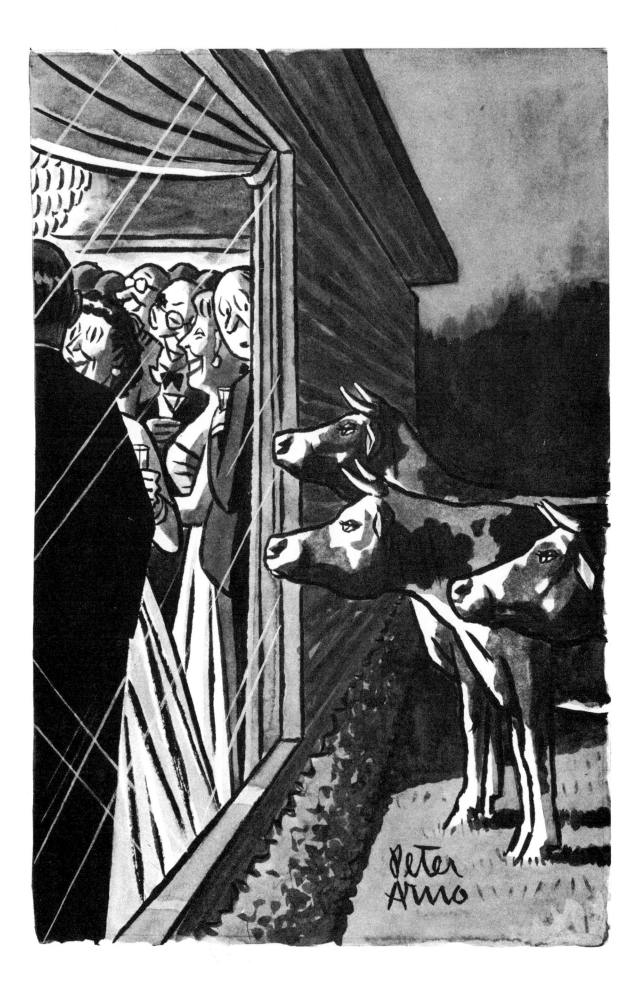

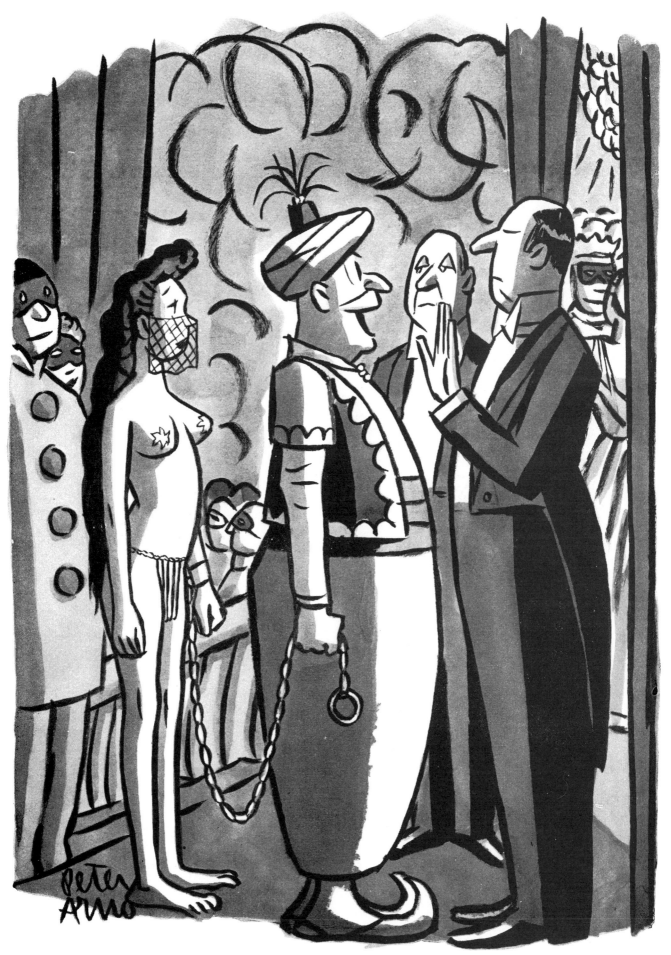

"But you've <u>got</u> to let her in! She's part of my costume."

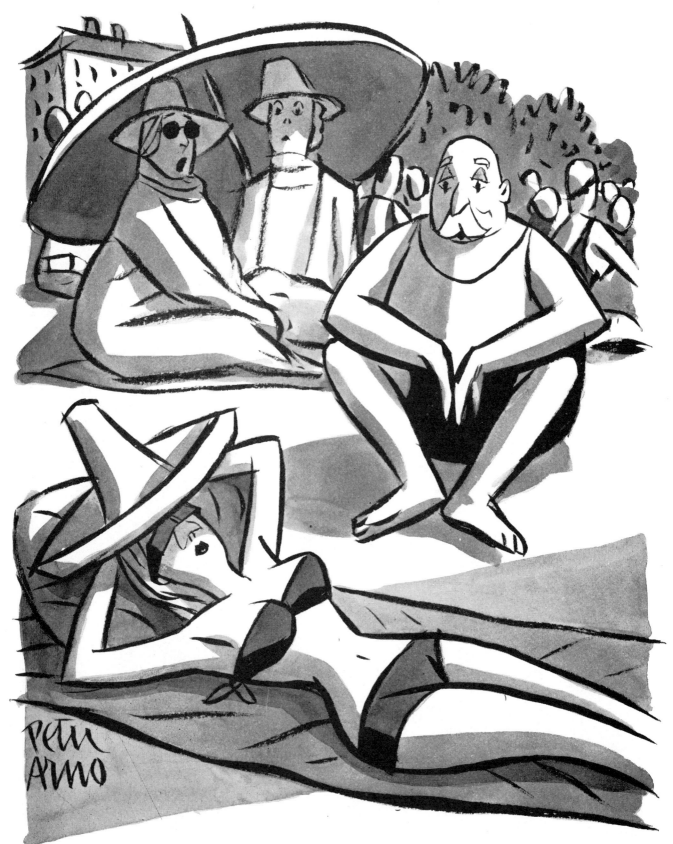

"He always was a fool for a pretty face."

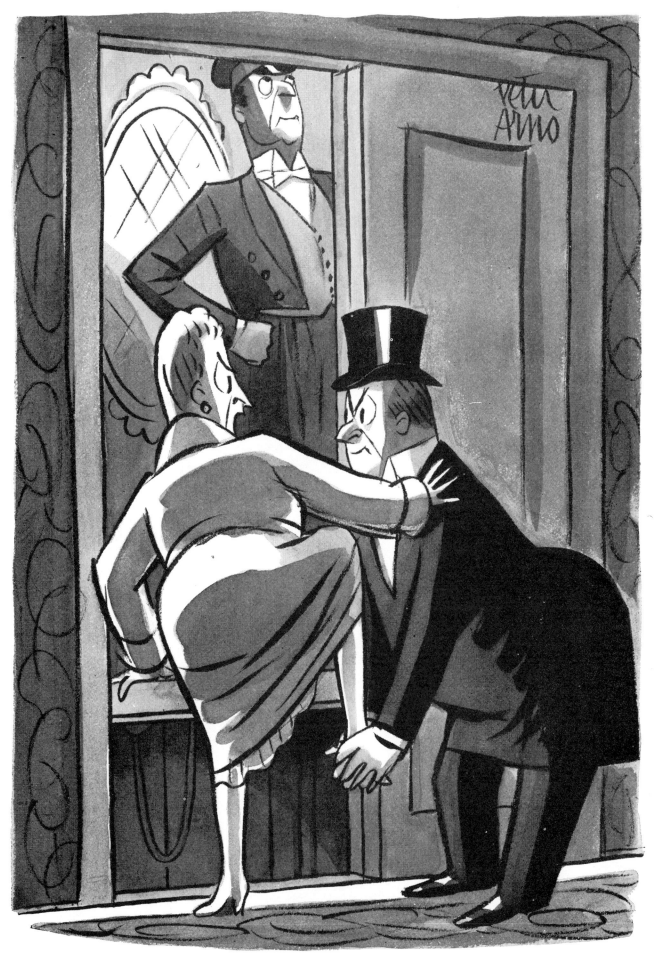

"*I told you we should have given them something for Christmas.*"

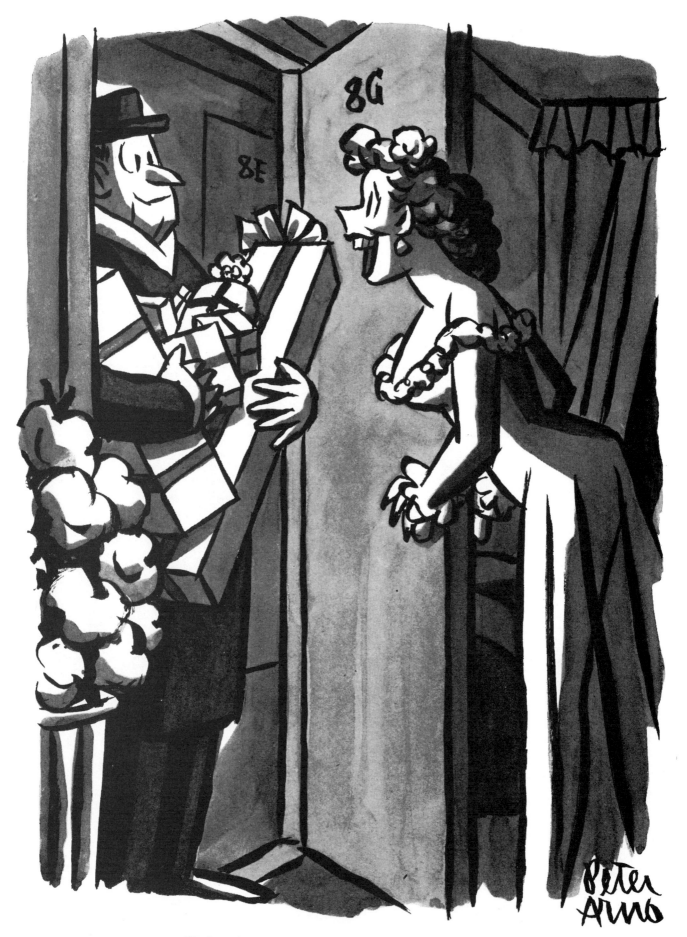

"I thought I heard the jingle of sleigh bells, Mr. Patterson!"

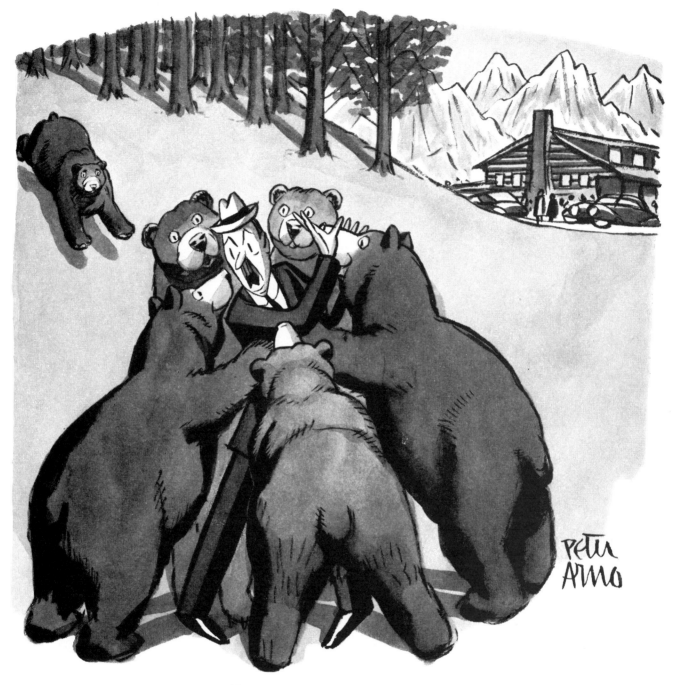

"But I don't <u>have</u> a lump of sugar!"

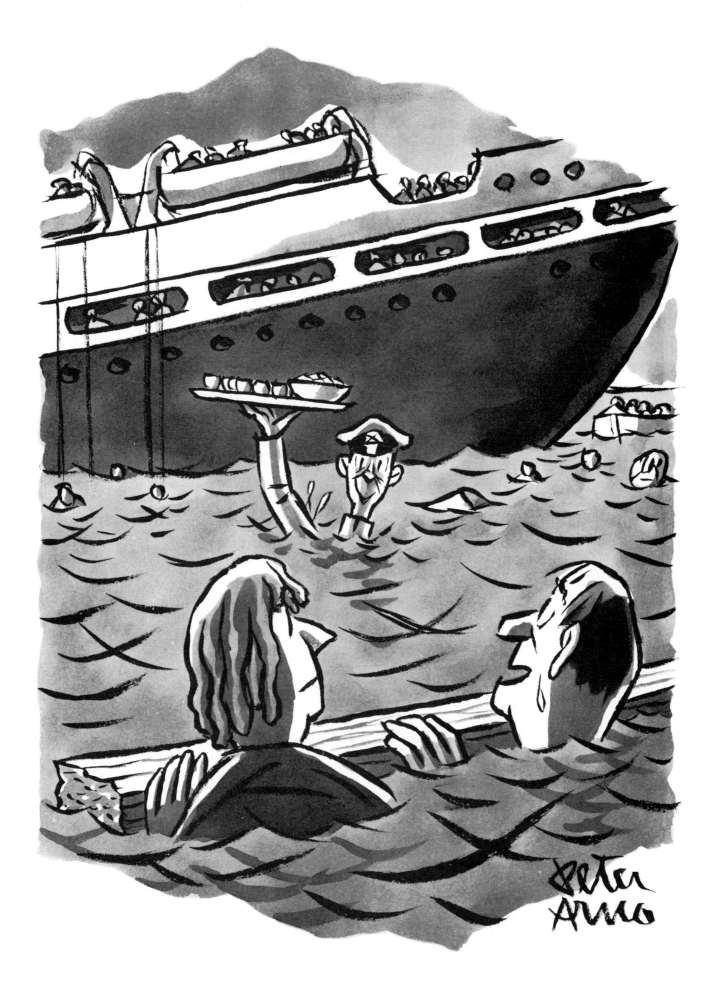

"Well, here's the 11 A.M. bouillon—right on the dot."

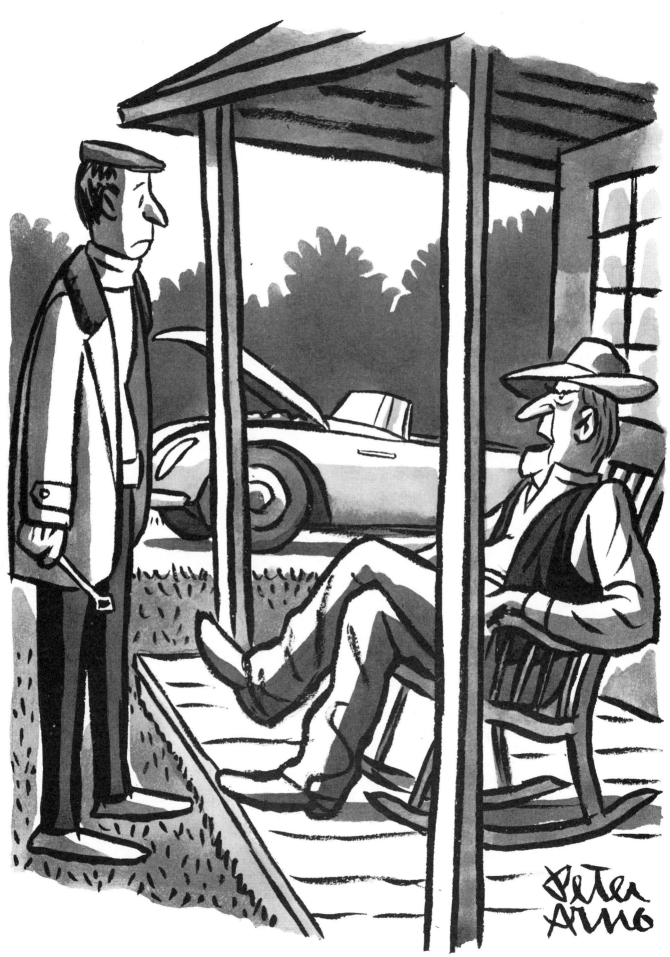

"*The fact that I live in a house by the side of the road, Mister, doesn't mean
I'm a friend of man.*"

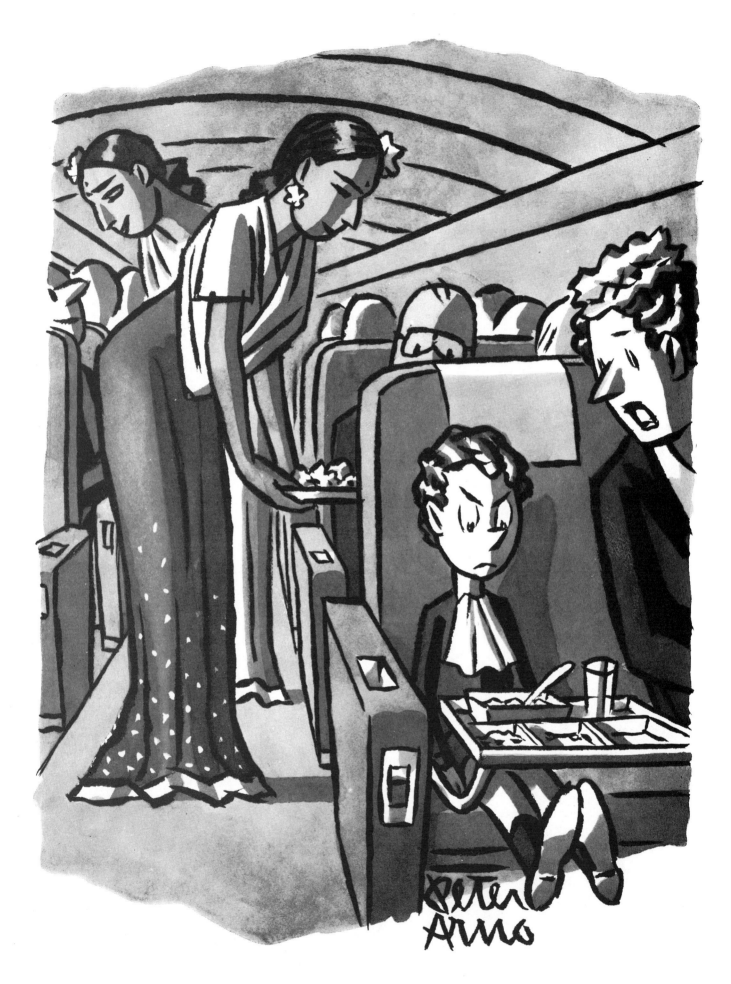

"Come, dear. Finish your doodh pak!"

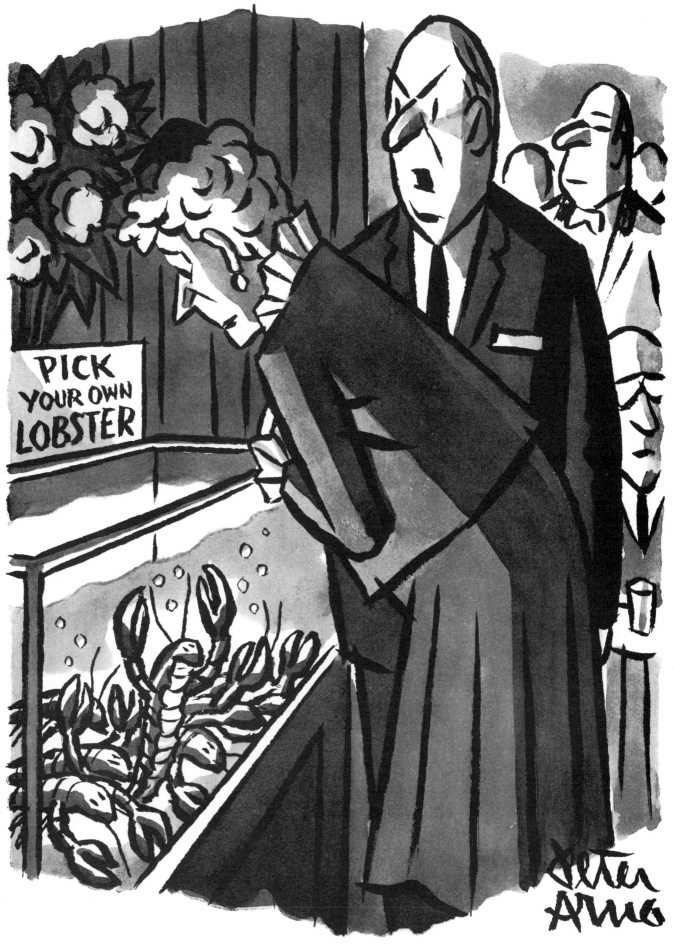

"For God's sake, Emma! They wouldn't think twice about eating you!"

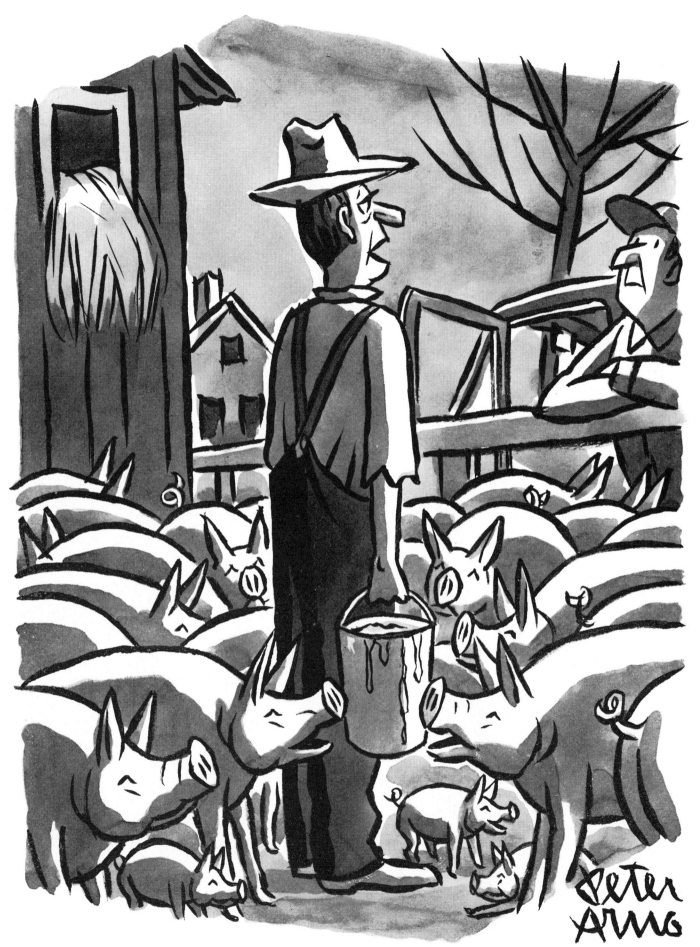

"It's an oink-oink here, an oink-oink there, here an oink, there an oink, everywhere an oink-oink."

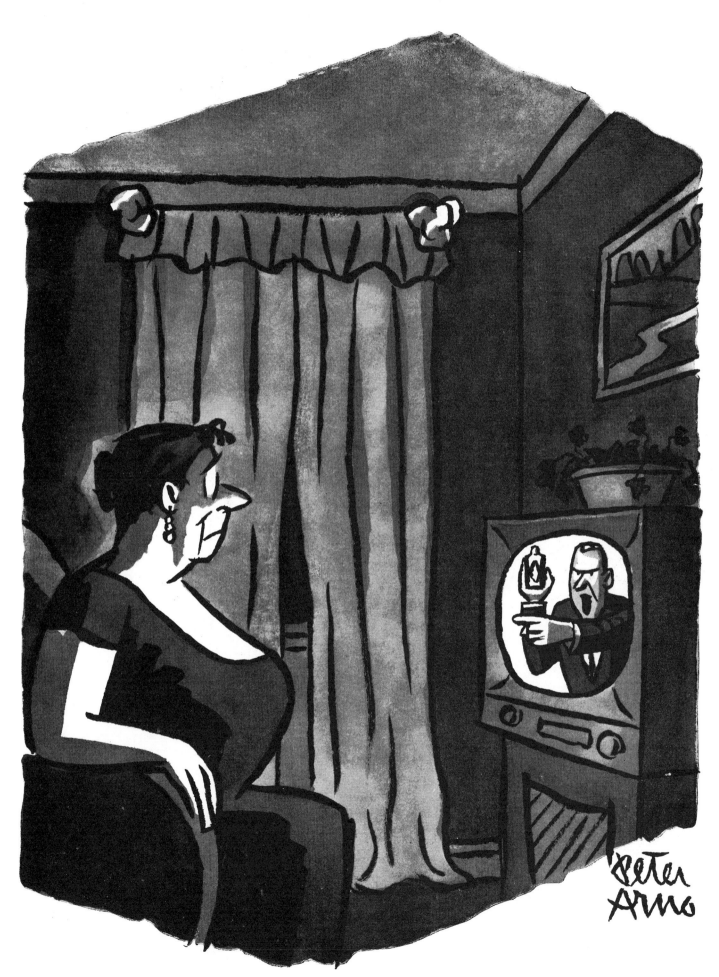

"*Are you the girl your husband married?*"

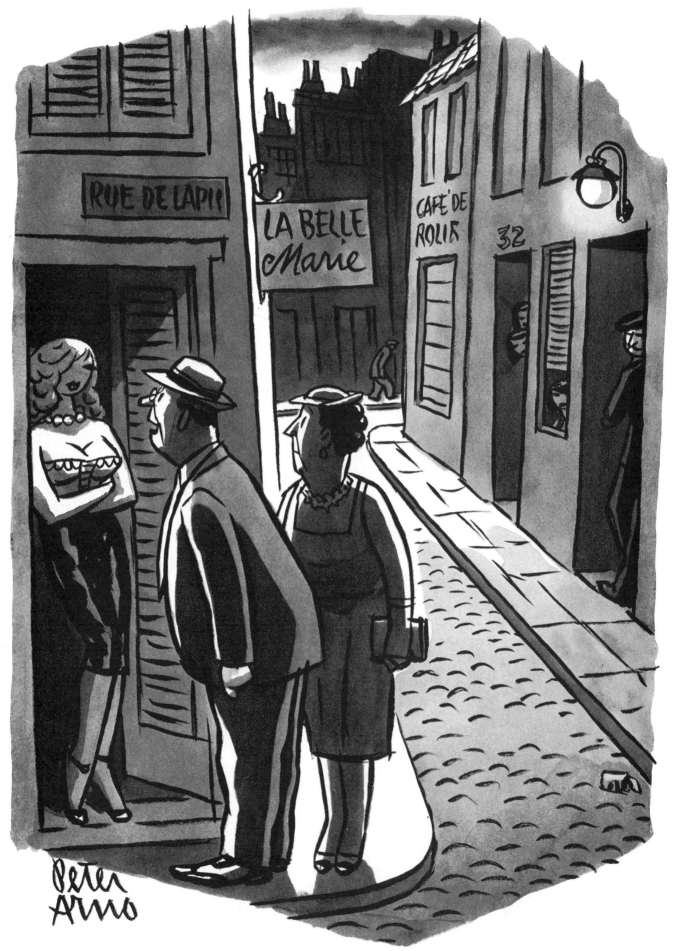

"We've lost our tour."

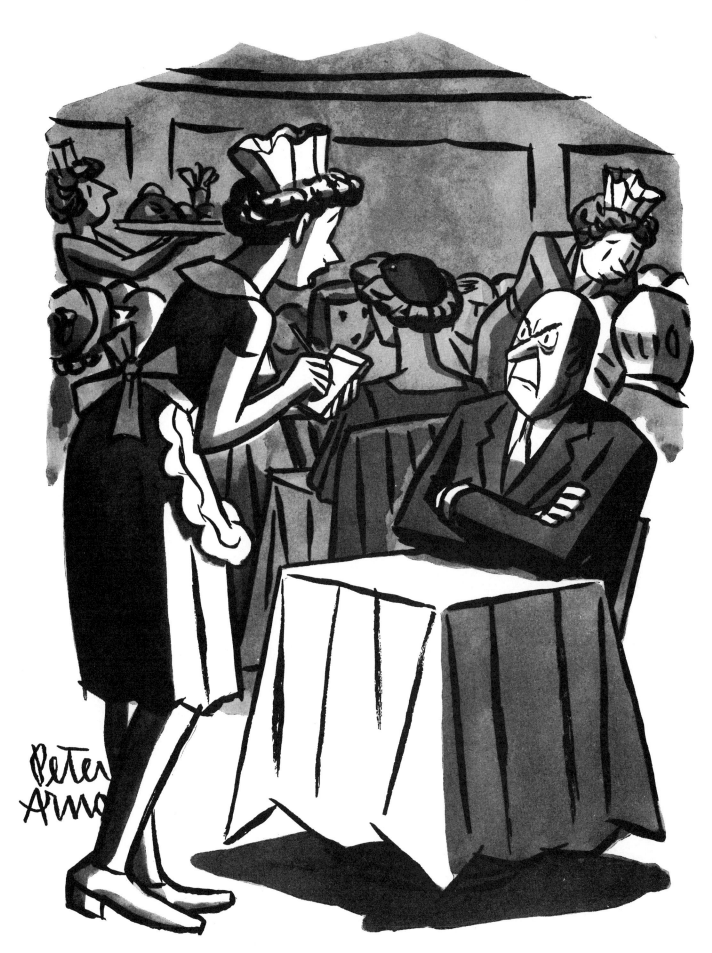

"Are you the gentleman who's fit to be tied?"

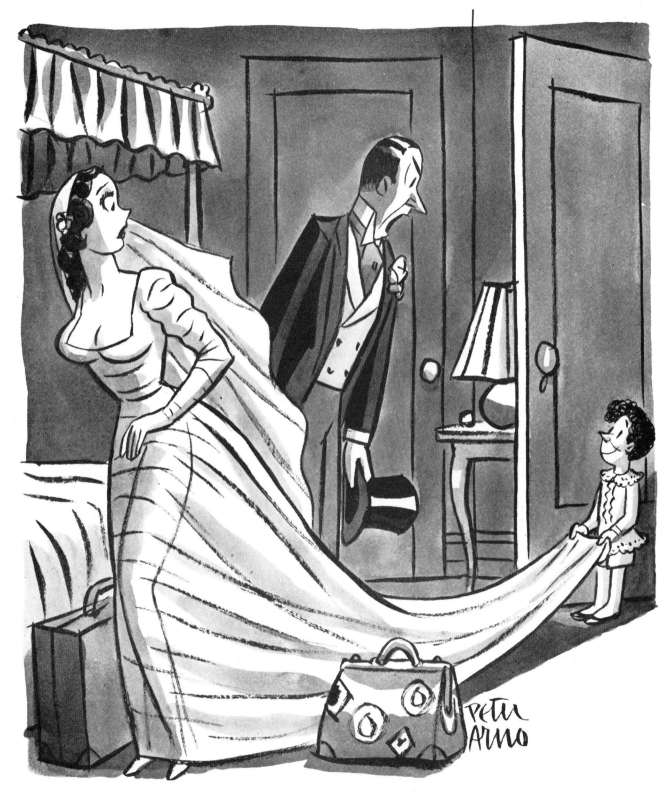

"Now that's enough! Run along!"

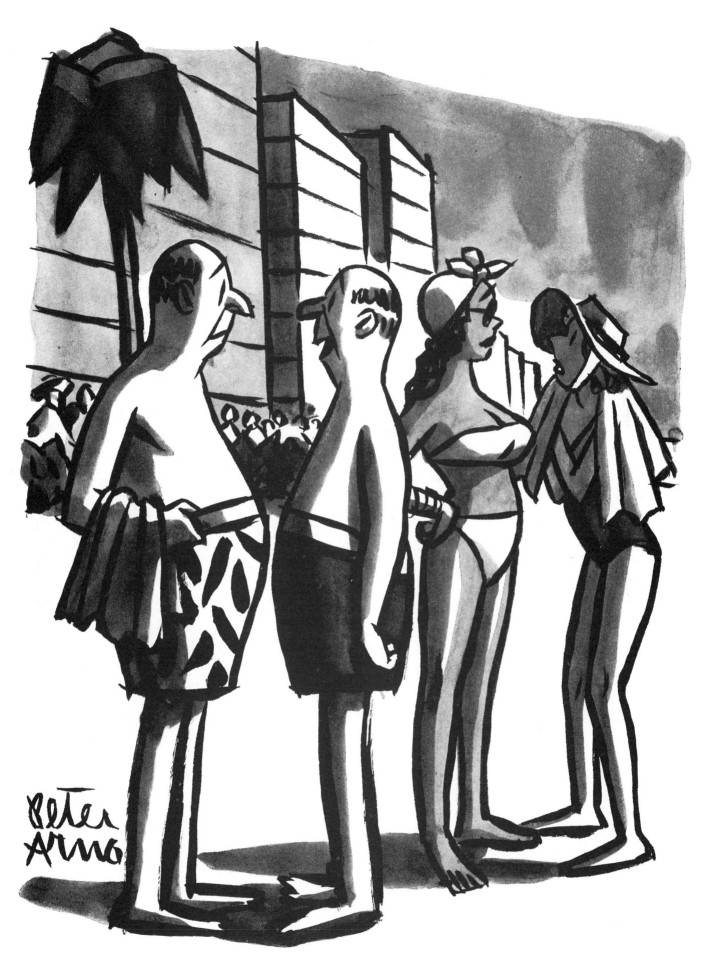

"*You sure know how to pick 'em. Mine keeps peeling all over the place.*"

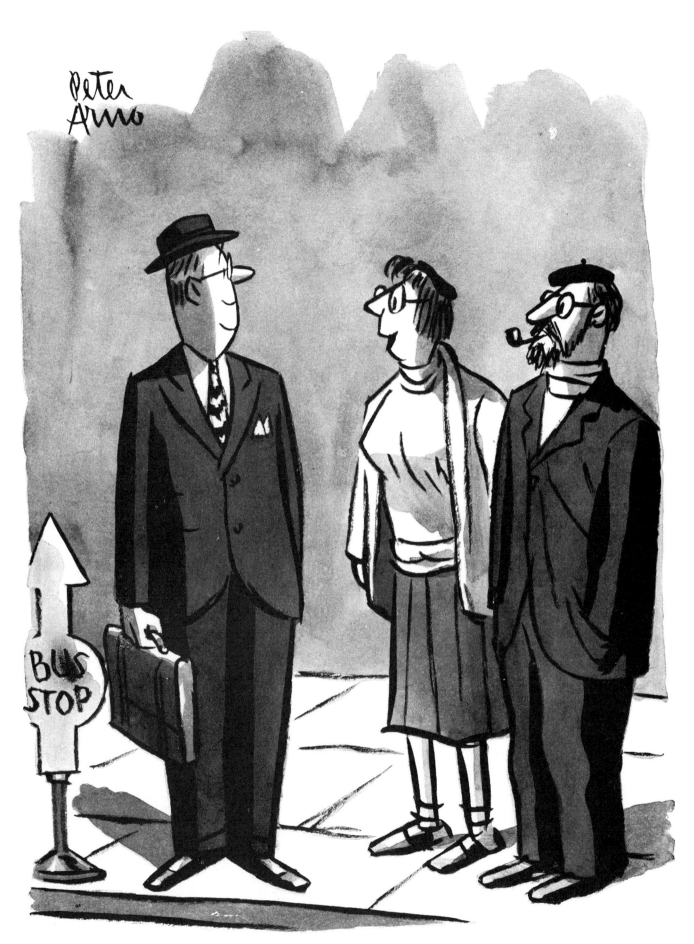

"Why, Howard! When did you go underground?"

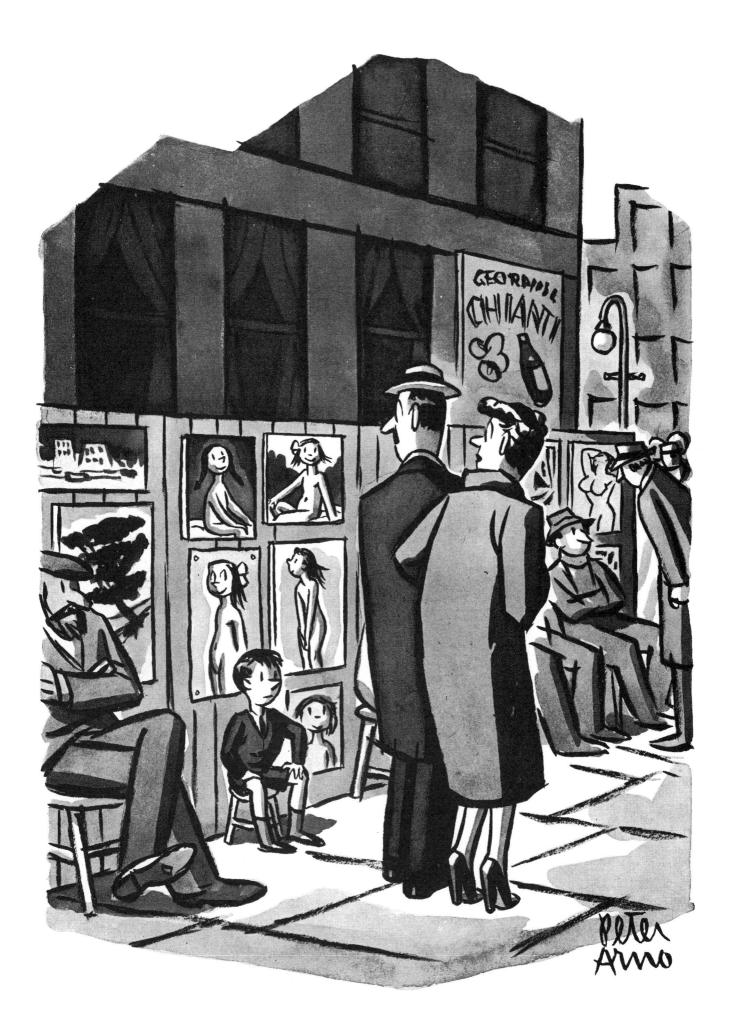

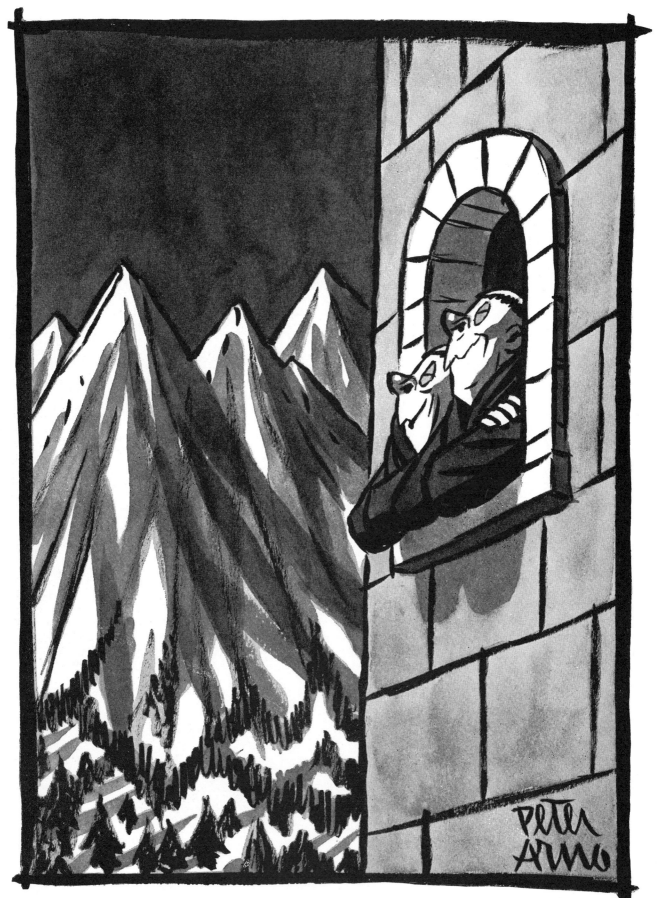

"Intoxicating, isn't it?"

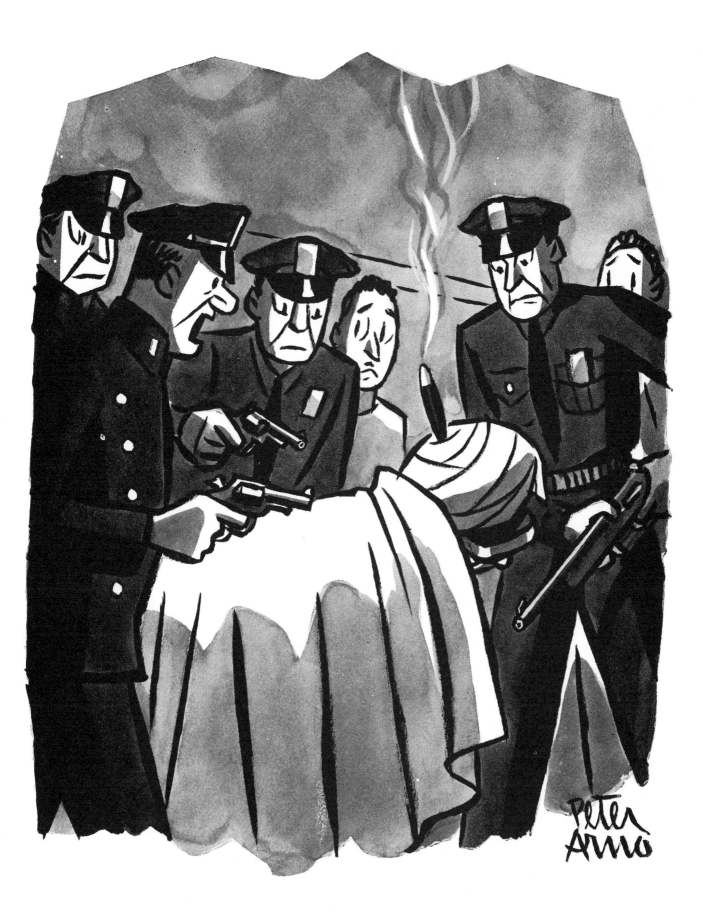

"All right, McGrath—we know you're in there!"

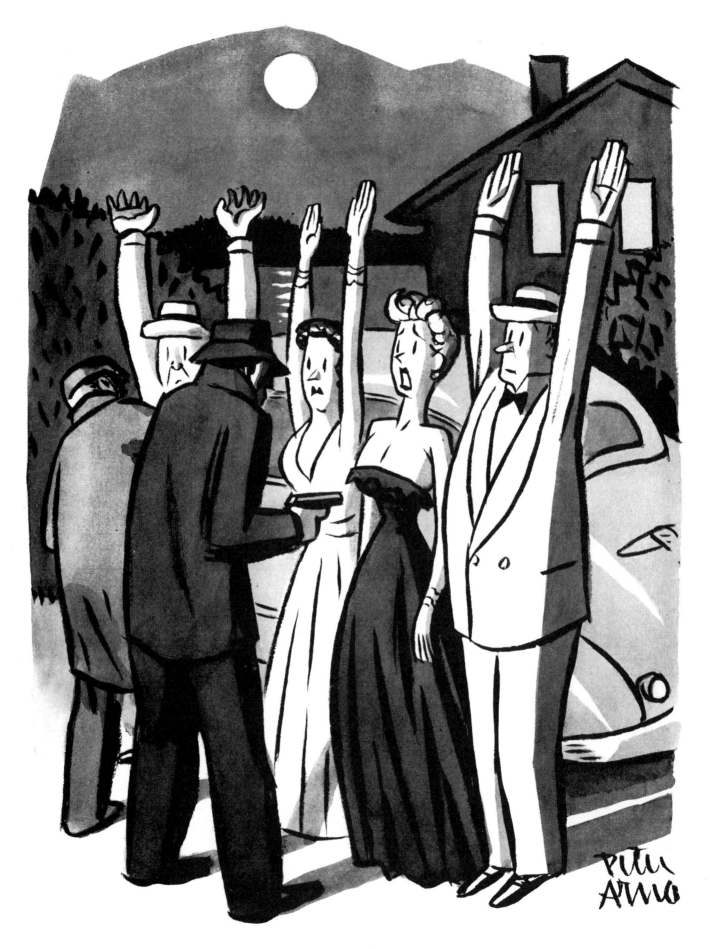

"But I can't!"

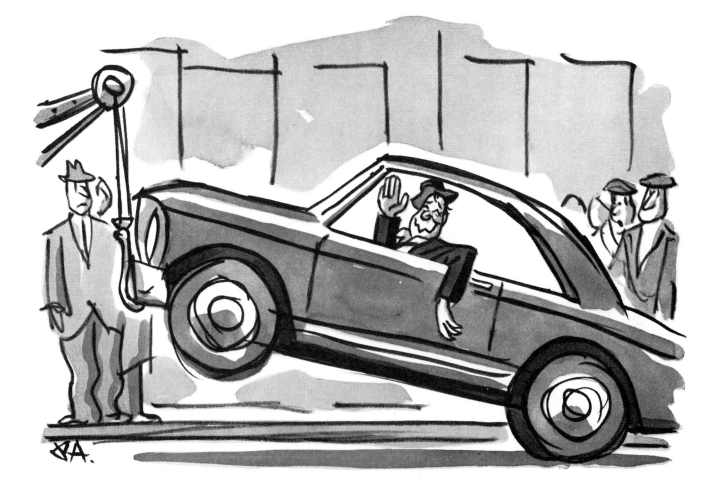

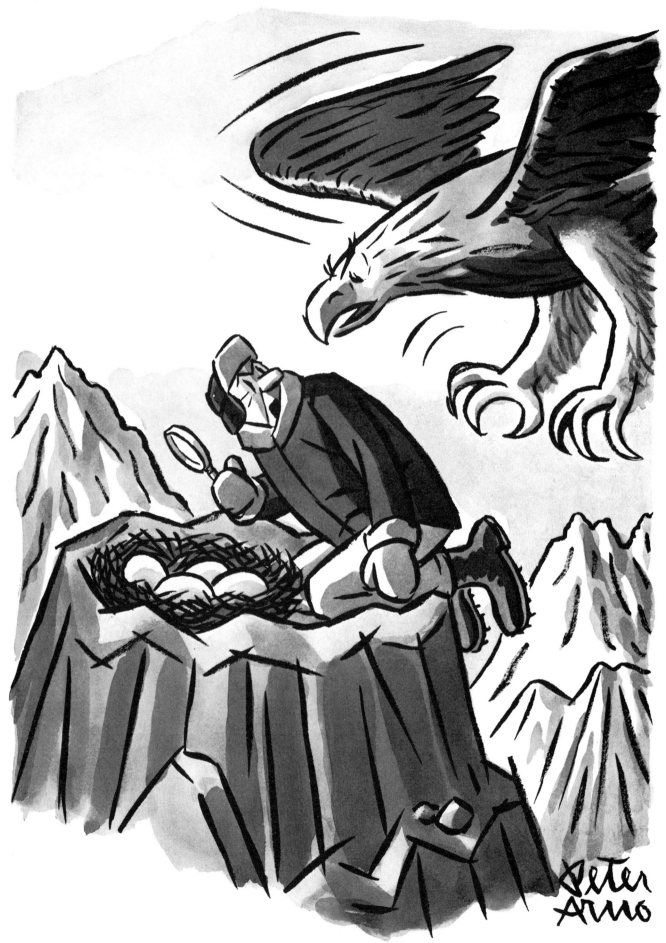

"I'm an American citizen!"

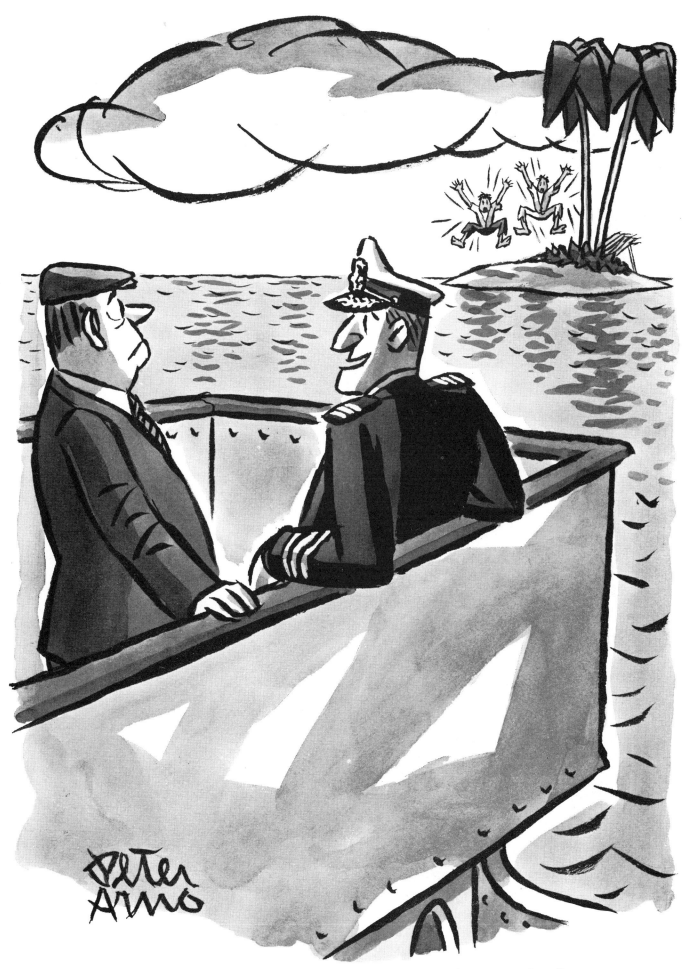

"*Couple of kooks, I guess. They carry on like that every time we pass here.*"

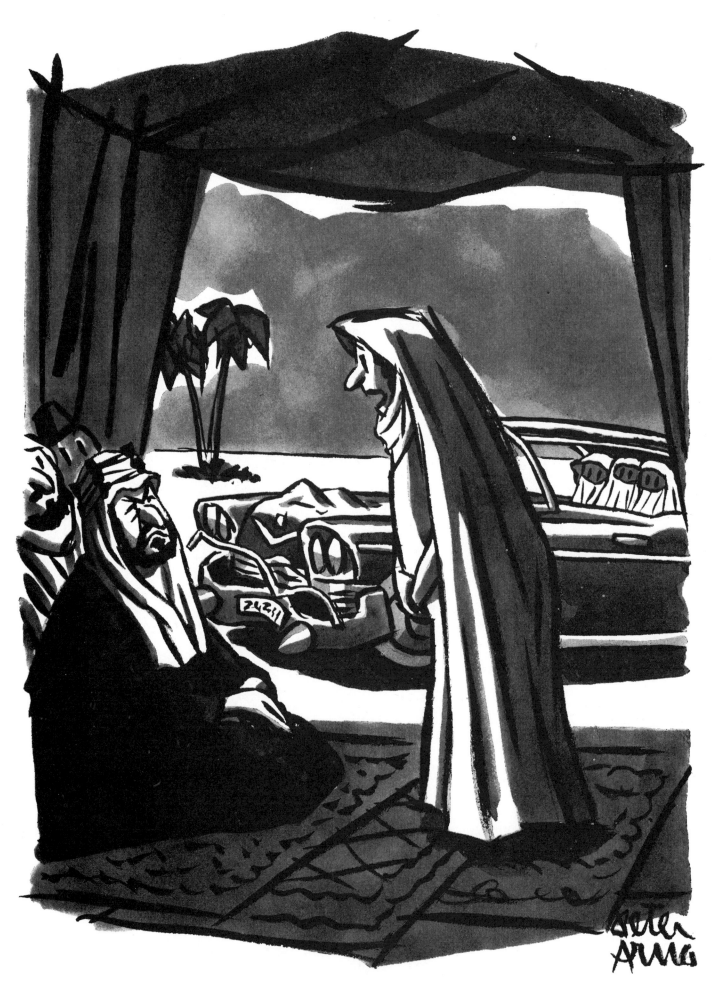

"I ran into the pipeline."

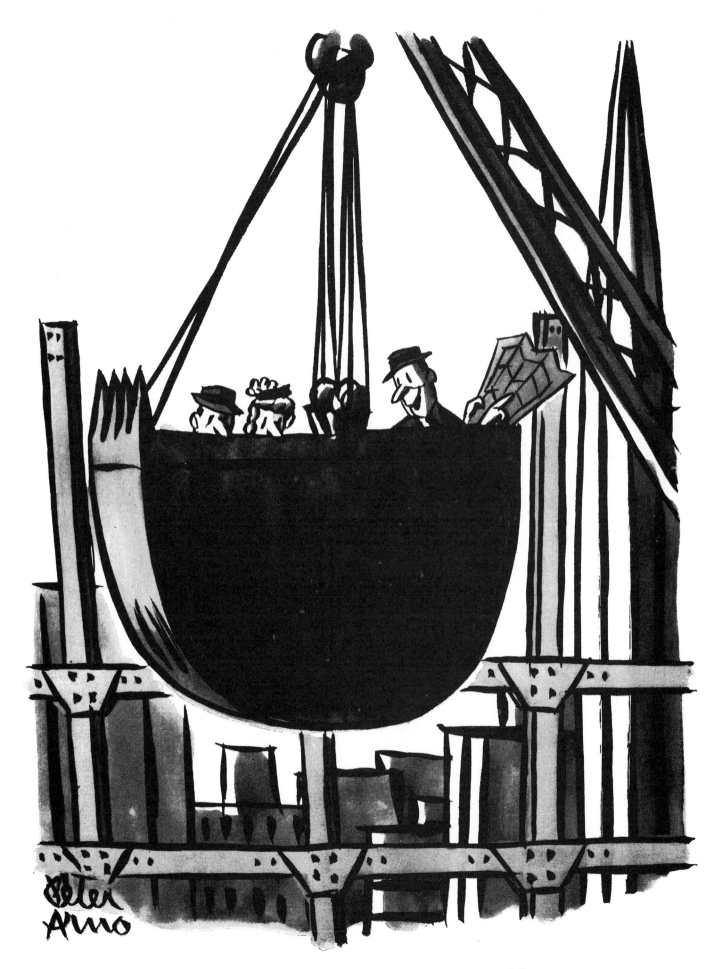

"Right now you're standing just about in the dining-nook."

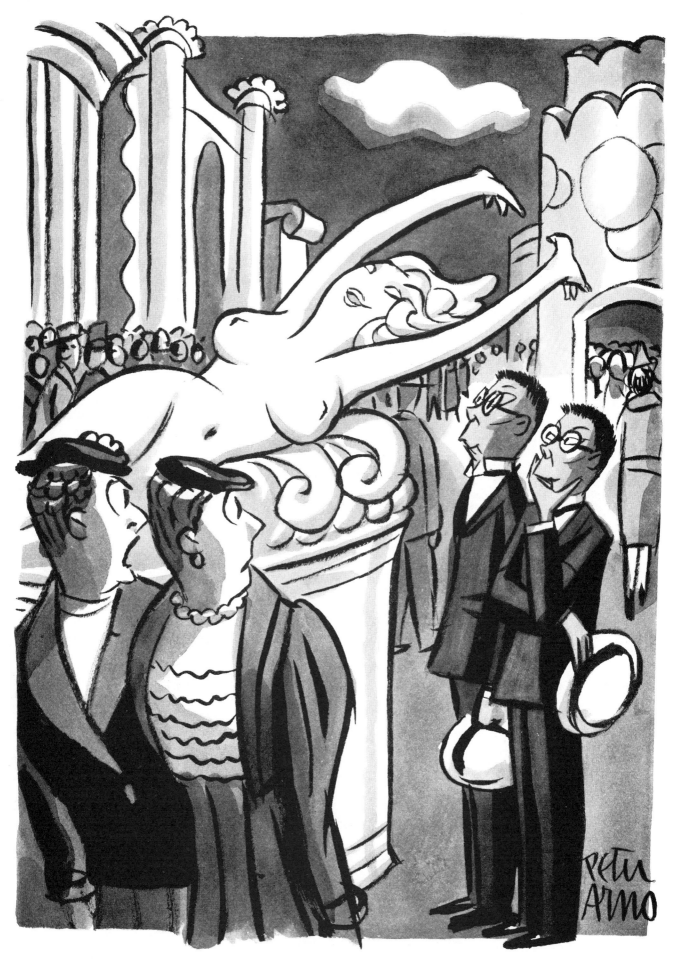

"You never can tell what they're thinking, can you?"

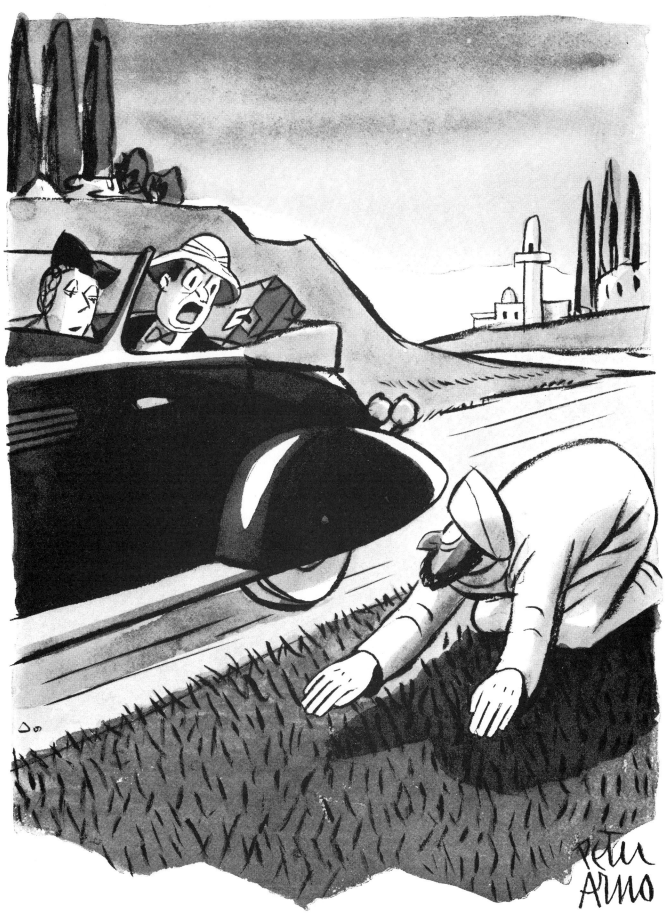

"Hey, Jack, which way to Mecca?"

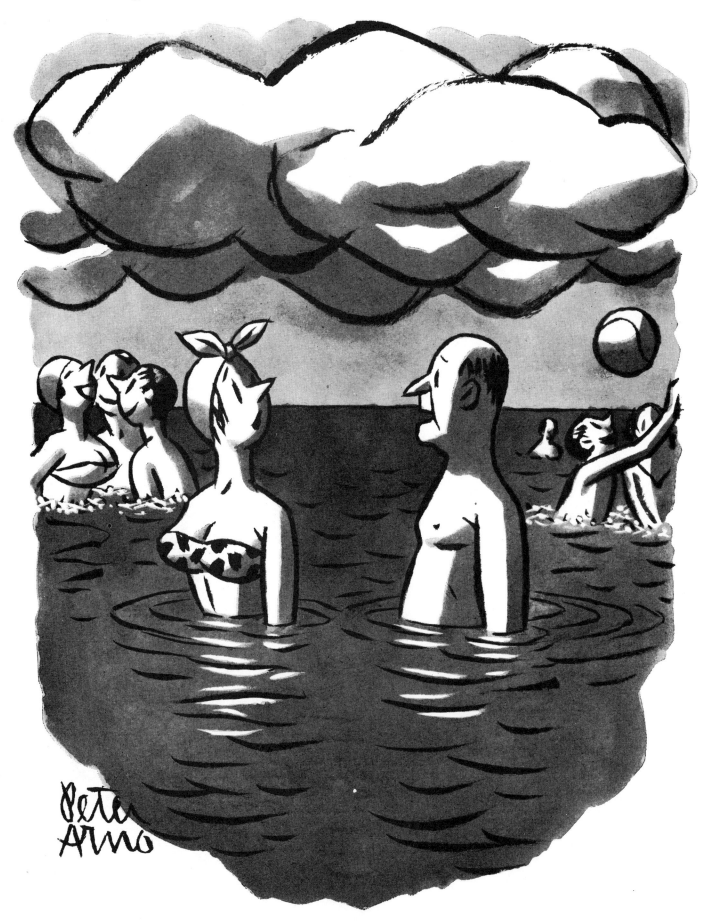

"*Pardon me, Miss. You're standing on my flippers.*"

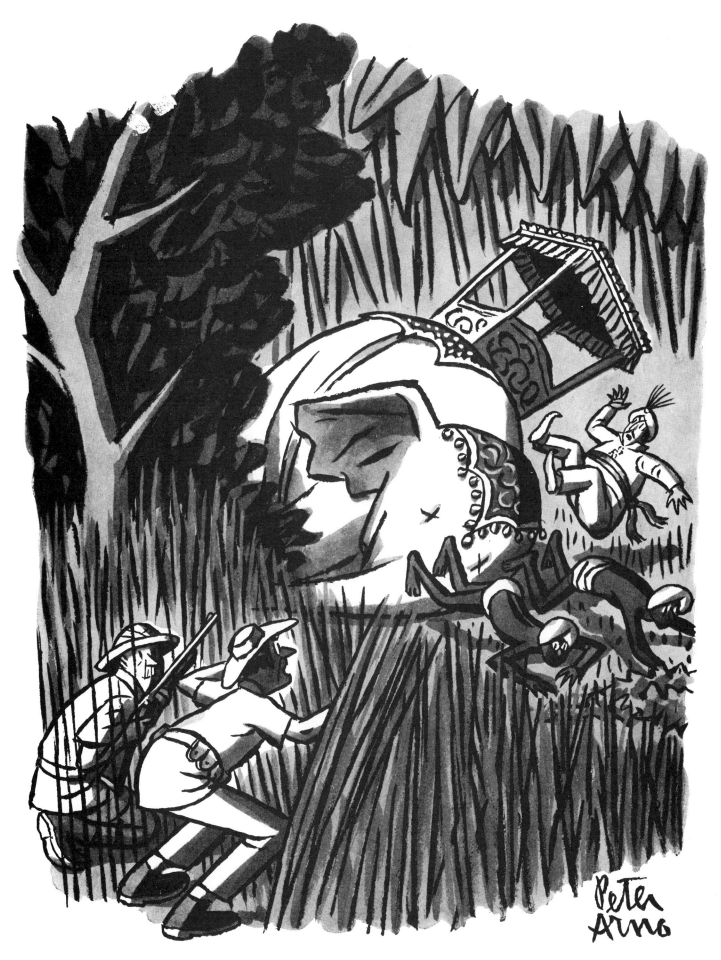

"Oh-oh!"

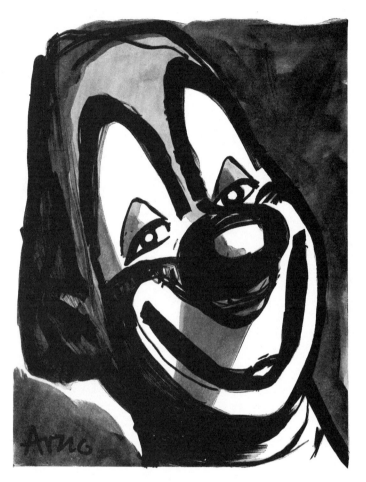

Laughing Clown

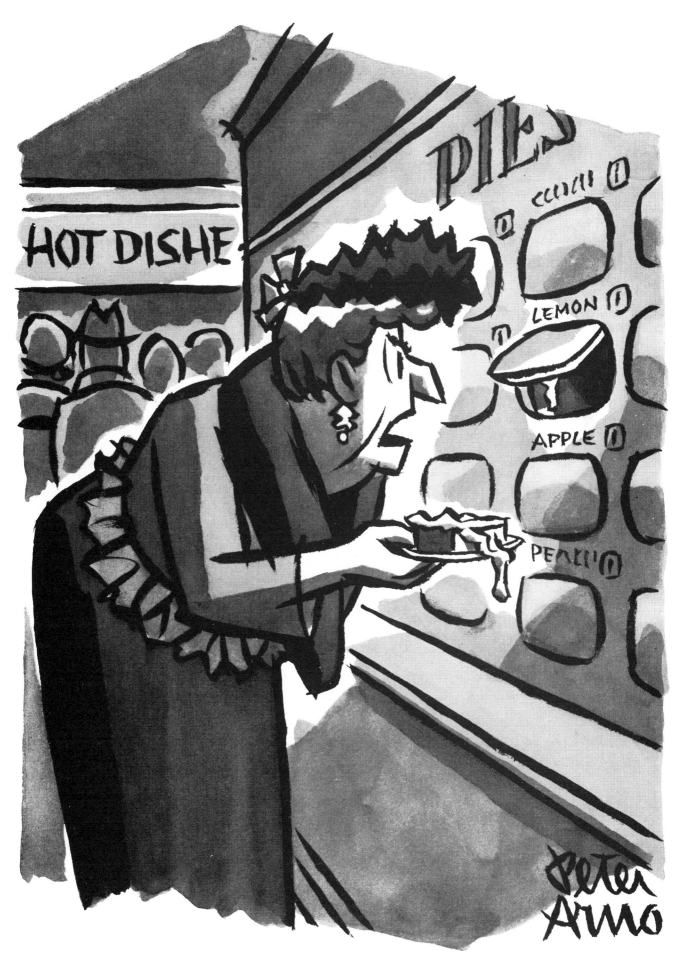

"I said the lid snapped my meringue off!"

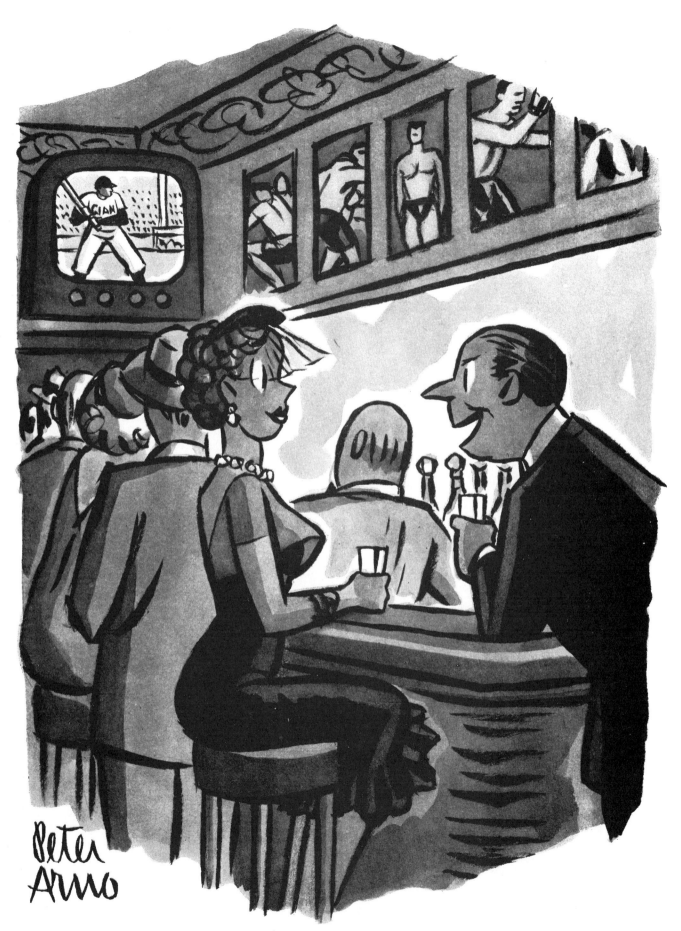

"It's certainly refreshing to find someone who's interested in something besides sports."

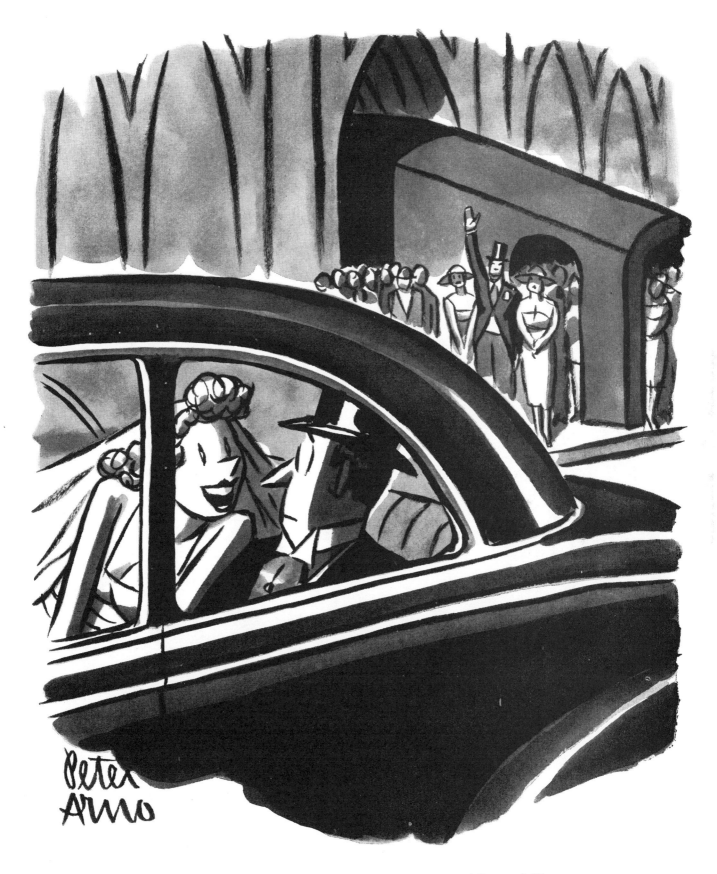

"*Just when do I get endowed with all thy worldly goods?*"

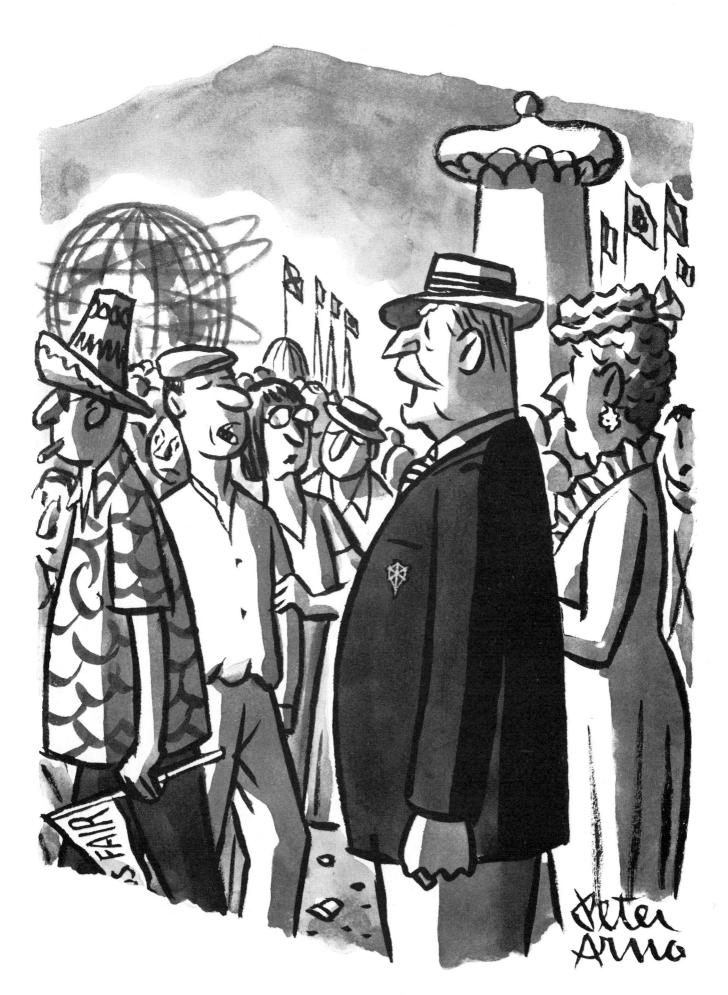

"Who <u>are</u> these people?"

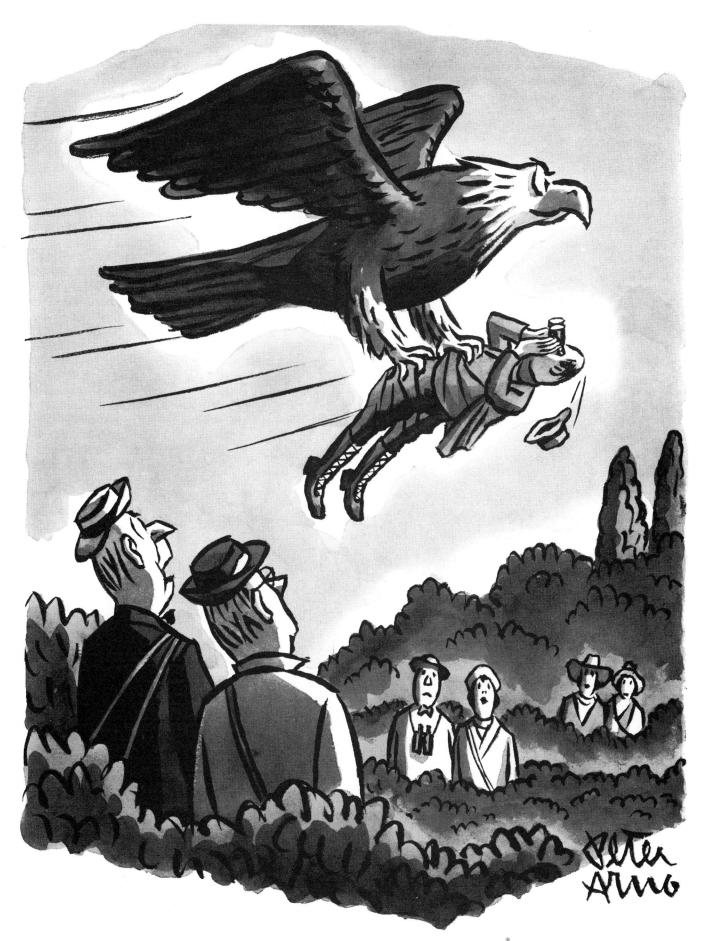

"By George! Most dedicated bird watcher I've ever known!"

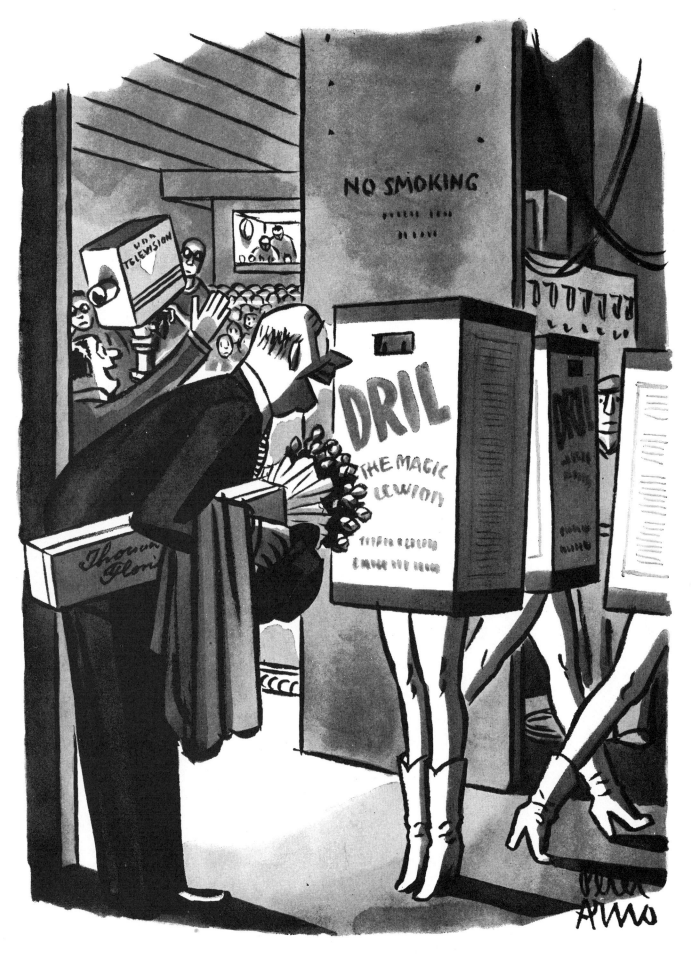

"My dear, you were superb!"

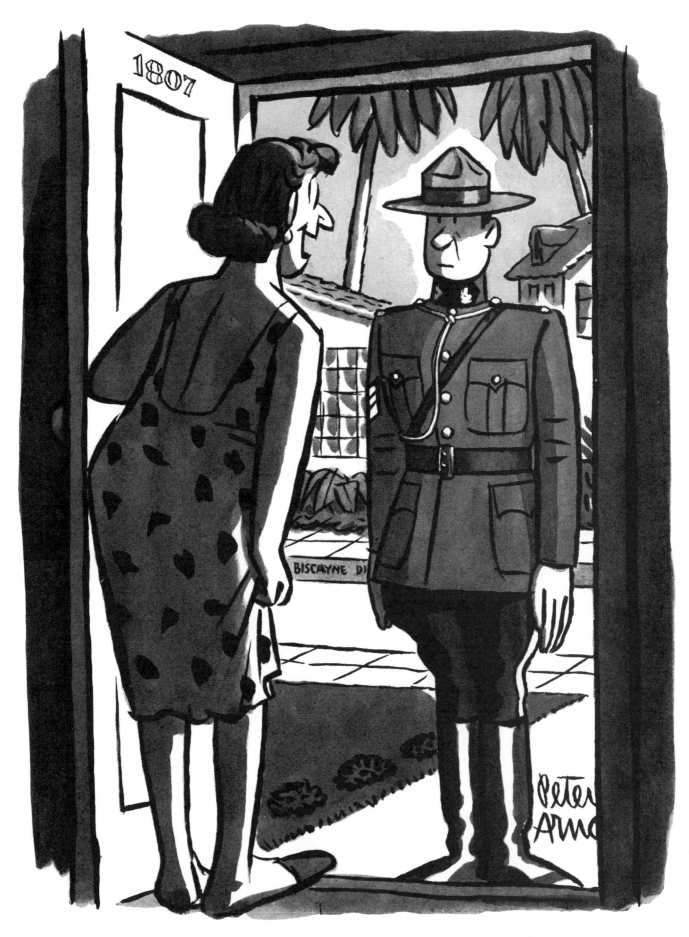

"*Why, the last I heard from him he was up in Saskatchewan someplace.*"

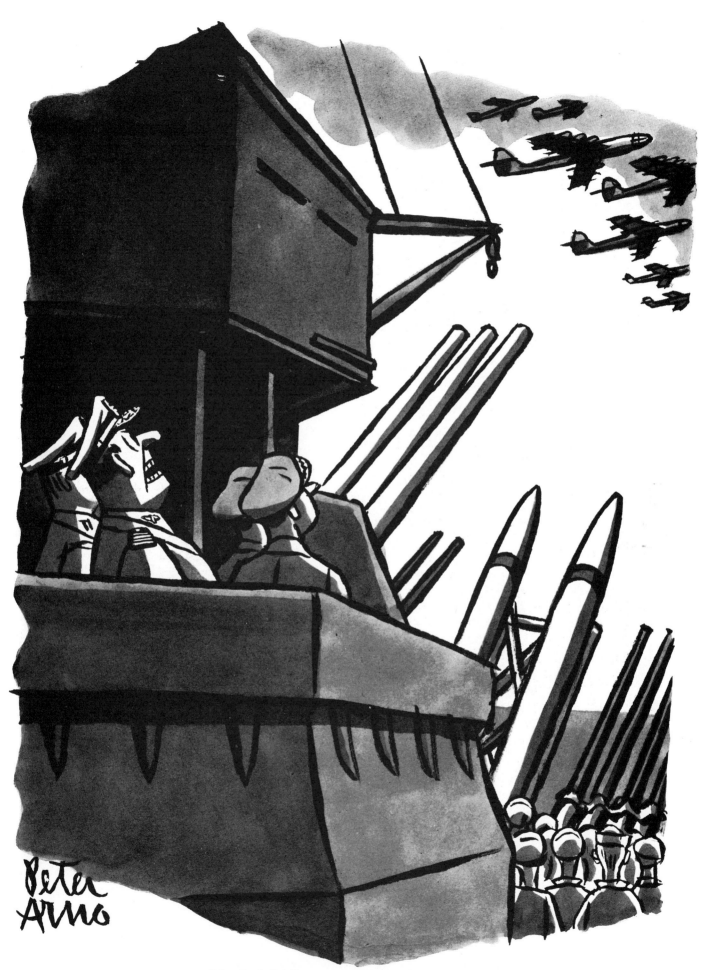

"By God, I'd like to show them who's obsolete!"

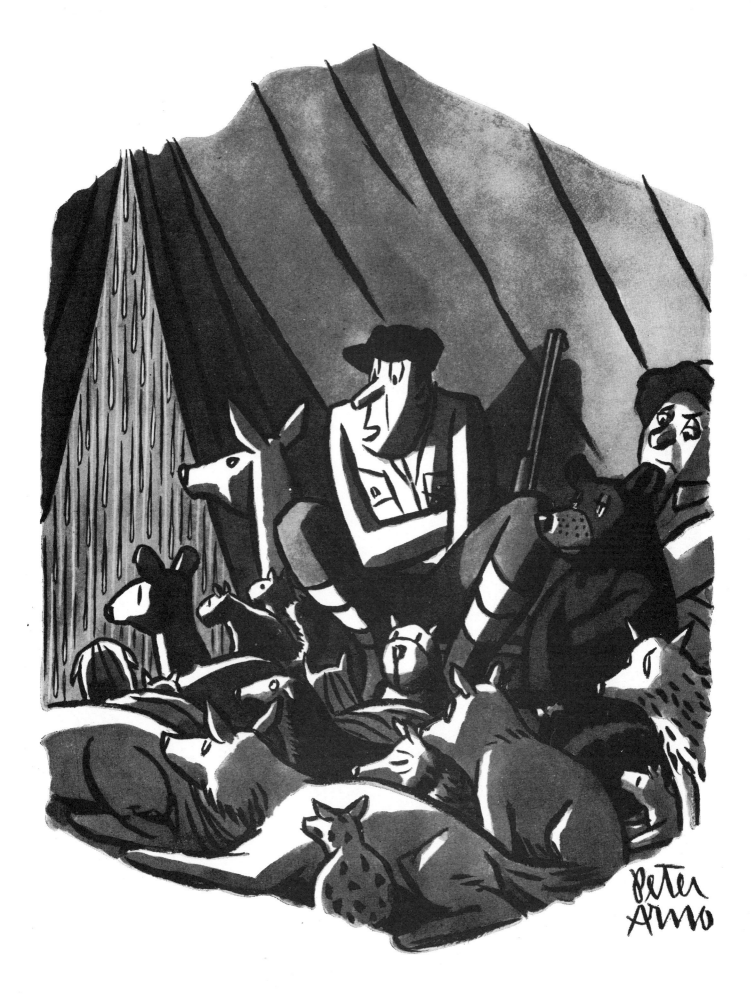

"I wonder what they did before we got here."

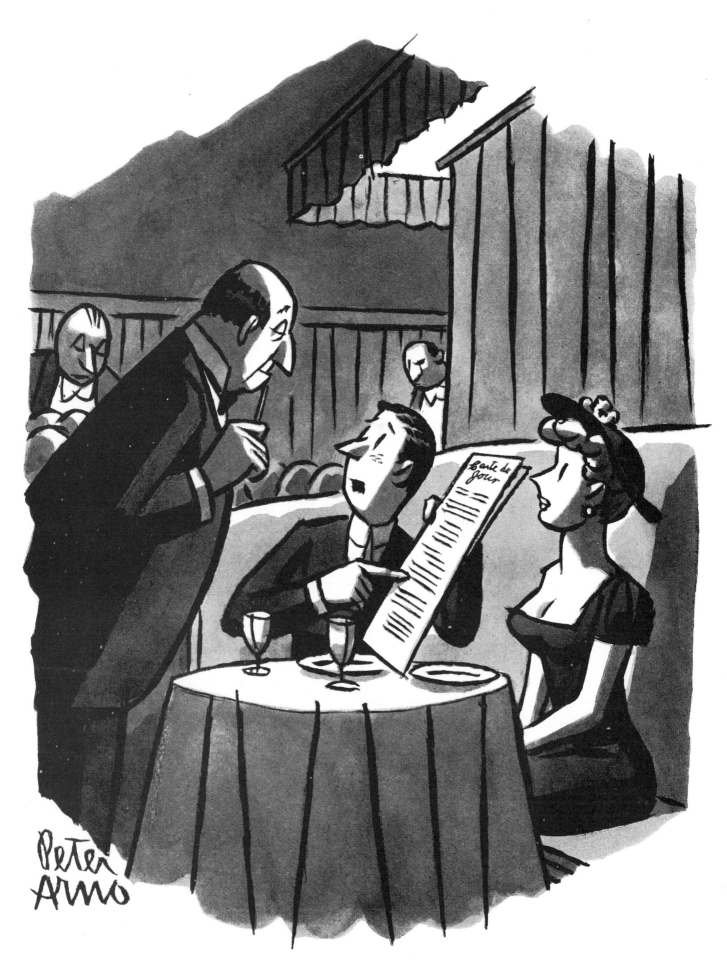

"Cette . . . and cette . . . and cette . . . and cette."

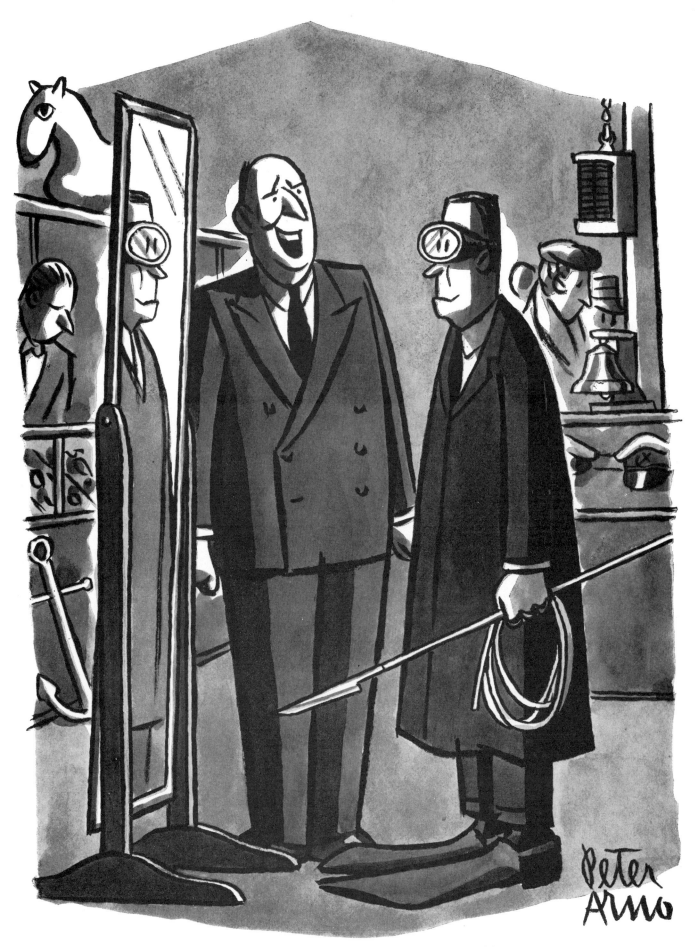

"Bermuda, here we come, eh, Mr. Stanton?"

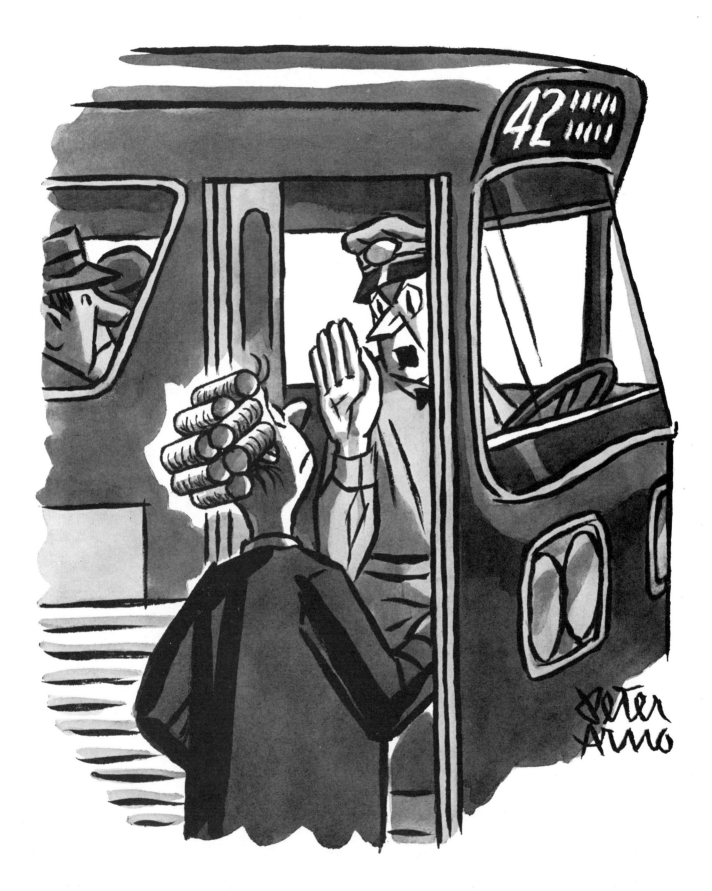

"Not on my bus, lady!"

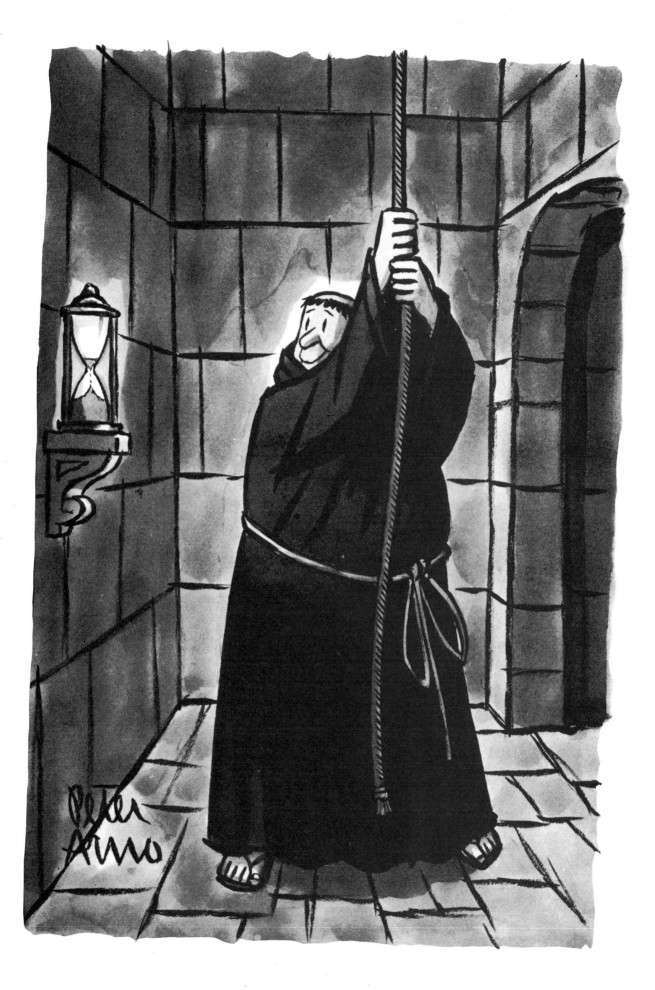

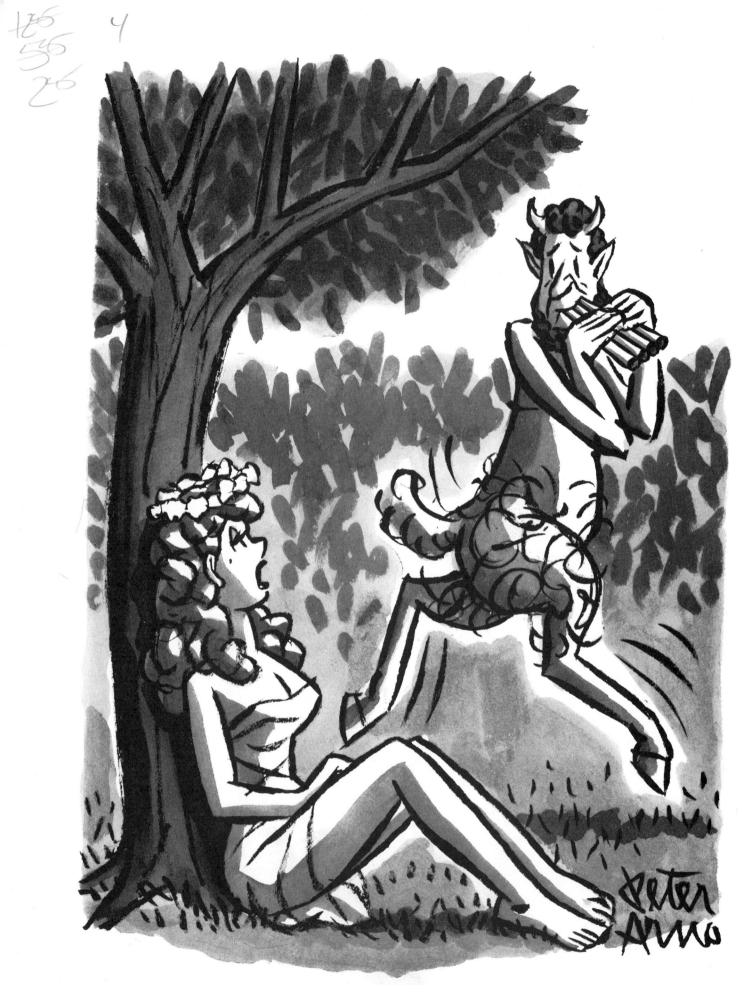

"Oh, grow up!"